AN ARCHAEOLOGICAL HISTORY OF MONTANA

Six Hundred Generations

Carl M. Davis

Illustrations by Eric S. Carlson

RIVERBEND PUBLISHING

About the title: ***Six Hundred Generations***

Native Americans have likely inhabited Montana for some 15,000 years, as inferred from Monte Verde, Meadowcroft Rockshelter, Buttermilk Creek and other pre-Clovis archaeological sites in the Americas. Using a mean female generational interval of 25 years, which is commonly used in biological and genealogical research, this time span calculates to 600 generations. Of course, female generational intervals (the average time period when children are born and raised) actually vary (between approximately 20 to 30 years) among different human societies. Further, the baseline date for first arrival of humans in the Americas might tentatively be pushed back another thousand years or more. So, it is certainly possible that the generational number is larger than this estimate. Regardless, the generational number shows that American Indian people have lived and thrived in Montana far longer than anyone else.

Six Hundred Generations

Published by Riverbend Publishing, Helena, Montana

ISBN 13: 978-1-60639-111-2

Printed in the United States of America.

2 3 4 5 6 7 8 9 0 VP 25 24 23 22 21 20

Front cover illustration by Eric S. Carlson.

Cover and text design by Sarah Cauble, www.sarahcauble.com

Riverbend Publishing
P.O. Box 5833
Helena, MT 59604
406-449-0200
www.riverbendpublishing.com

Dedicated to the Memory of Dr. Floyd W. Sharrock

CONTENTS

PREFACE

FIRST THINGS

Montana is Indian Country. It has been so since the arrival of the first hunter-gatherers from northeast Asia near the end of the last great Ice Age, some 15,000 years ago. This fact is widely known today, but many aspects of the state's rich archaeological history are not. Not long ago Montana schools mostly taught Western expansion and settlement. In that version, "history" began with late eighteenth and nineteenth century European and American explorers and fur trappers, not Siberian hunter-gatherers of millennia ago. In all fairness, before the 1960s, archaeologists had limited knowledge of Montana's ancient history, and what archaeologists did know was not widely available to the public.

Things are very different today, for several reasons. First, passage of the National Historic Preservation Act (NHPA) in 1966 made the preservation of antiquities a national priority.[1] This act created federal cultural resource management (CRM) programs to identify, evaluate, and protect archaeological and historical resources on public lands. Second, Article 9, Section 4 of Montana's progressive 1972 Constitution required the legislature to provide for the "identification, acquisition, restoration, enhancement, preservation, and administration" of cultural resources and to provide "for their use and enjoyment by the people." Third, the state legislature passed the Montana Human Skeletal Remains and Burial Site Protection Act in 1991 (amended with the Montana Repatriation Act of 2001) and the Montana Antiquities Act (MAA) in 1995. The NHPA and the MAA, combined with environmental laws requiring that federal and state agencies take cultural resources into account in their planning, created a sustained commitment to historic preservation in Montana, surpassing past efforts by the Works Progress Administration, Smithsonian Institution, state universities, and Montana Archaeological Society chapters.

During the late 1970s and 1980s, archaeology came of age in Montana and throughout the United States. Federal, state, and tribal cultural resource management (or heritage) programs gave birth to a bounty of new archaeology jobs when few to none had been available outside of academia and museums. Agency cultural resource management and university research programs generated a wealth of new archaeological data. Inquisitive students no longer needed to await college courses for their first exposure to Montana's rich archaeological and Indigenous past. American Indian cultures, past and present, are now part of primary and secondary school curricula.[2] Archaeology programs flourish at state universities and tribal colleges. Anyone can visit federal and state cultural resource interpretive facilities and even participate as a volunteer for archaeological projects.

My goal in writing this book is to acquaint readers with this newly accumulated archaeological knowledge and to explain its importance in a succinct and non-technical way. I choose to tell the story of Montana's first history through the lens of a dozen representative archaeological sites, focusing on different time periods and key themes. My approach has the virtue of simplicity but obviously omits important archaeological sites and overlooks the contributions of many people. A legion of anthropologists, archaeologists, historians, tribal elders and culture specialists, climatologists, geographers, geologists, ecologists, geneticists, and journalists have written in great detail about ancient and early Montana. Many of them are listed in the bibliography.

Carl M. Davis
Missoula, Montana

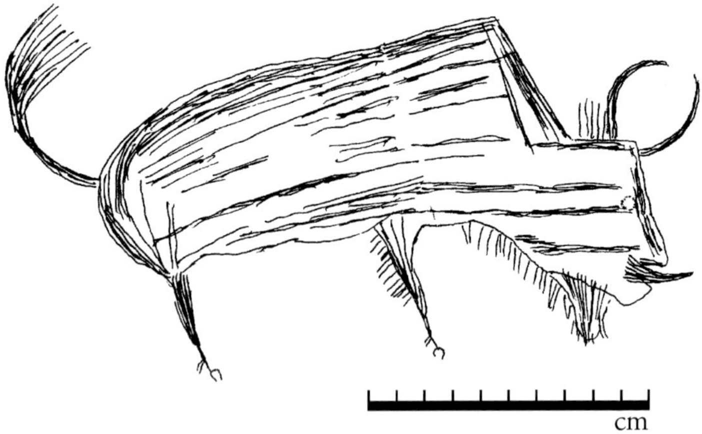

The First Peoples reached the plains and mountains of Montana millennia ago, at the close of the last great Ice Age. Since then, various American Indian bands, tribes, and nations have always been here. One reason Native peoples settled here and seasonally came here was to hunt bison, represented by this drawing of a bull bison in an aggressive posture (indicated by the upraised tail and protruding tongue) at the Bear Gulch rock art site, but there were many factors, both well-known and obscure, for Native peoples inhabiting this land. Illustration courtesy of Jim Keyser.

NOT ONE STORY BUT MANY

Under its famous big sky, Montana encompasses 147,164 square miles—the fourth largest state in the Union.[3] Built up by the deposit of ancient sea sediments, volcanic eruptions, and tectonic shifts in the earth's crust, and then worn down by Ice Age glaciers, floods, and other geological processes, the state is a land of physiographic contrasts. Its complex geological and paleontological records are exposed in a wide array of distinctive landforms readily visible from almost any Montana highway and attract university field schools from throughout the United States.

The western third of Montana is part of the Northern Rocky Mountains physiographic province.[4] The Rockies stretch from the stunning, rugged, snow-capped peaks of northwestern Montana and Glacier National Park to the more restrained but no less beautiful ranges of southwestern Montana and the Greater Yellowstone area. Separating the Columbia and Mississippi river drainage systems, the Continental Divide winds a circuitous route through the long chain of western Montana mountain ranges. Pine, spruce, and fir forests carpet the slopes below mountain peaks, and turquoise-blue alpine lakes fill old glacial scours. Bitterroot, lamb's quarters, and other species grow on drier slopes while willow, camas, sedges and other moisture-loving plants thrive in wet meadows. Mountain valleys vary widely in size and elevation; for example, the narrow Kootenai Valley

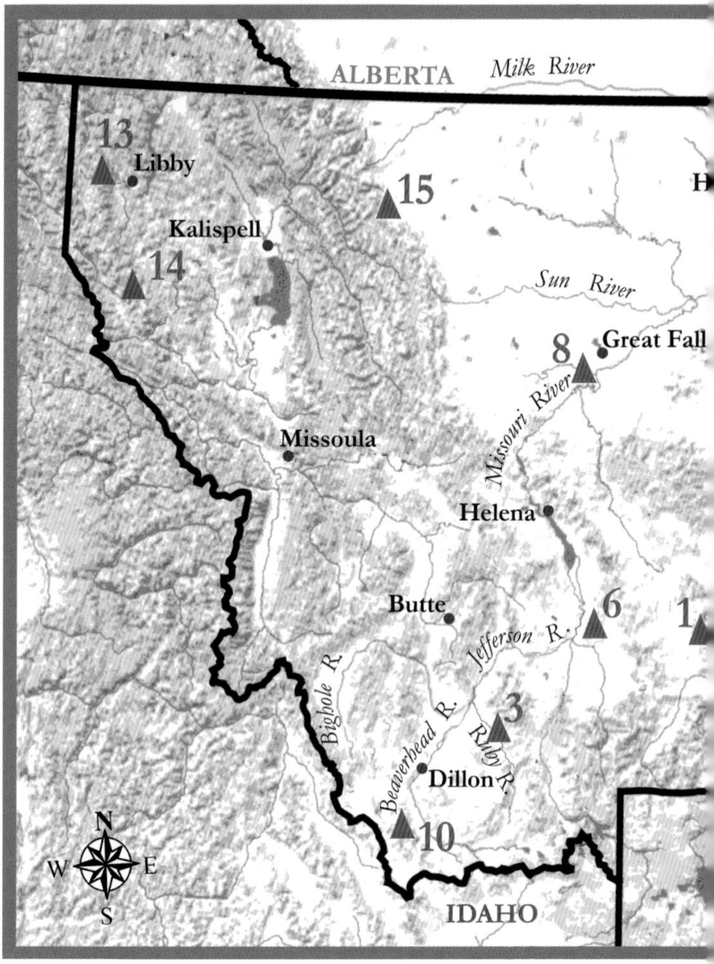

▲ Archaeological Sites & Traditional Cul

1 - Anzick Site
2 - Mill Iron Site
3 - Barton Gulch Site
4 - Spiro Pit House Site
5 - Pictograph and Ghost Caves Site
6 - Schmitt Quarry Site
7 - Bear Gulch Rock Art Site
8 - First Peoples Buffalo Jump
9 - Hagen Village Site
10 - Wickiup Cave Site
11 - Rosebud Battlefield Site

…perties (TCP)

12 - Absaroka Agency Site
13 - Kootenai Falls TCP
14 - Chicago Peak TCP
15 - Badger-Two Medicine TCP

0 100 200 km
0 100 mi

in the northwest corner of the state and the broad Beaverhead Valley in southwest Montana measure 2,096 and 5,545 feet above sea level, respectively.

The eastern two-thirds of the state belongs to the Great Plains physiographic province. This semi-arid region is a visually striking mosaic of rolling prairie grasslands, wide river valleys, heavily-eroded badlands, prominent sandstone escarpments, and isolated mountain ranges. Fed by snow from the eastern flanks of the Rocky Mountains, the Missouri and Yellowstone rivers bisect the region. By necessity the plants here are more drought-resilient than those in the western part of the state. Hardy cool- and warm-season grasses predominate on the open plains and mountain foothills. Lush grasses, sedges, and deciduous plants flourish only in the valley bottoms. Incessant prairie winds dry and cure native grasses and browse, providing winter forage for hungry animals. The Little Belt, Judith, Pryor, and other Rocky Mountain outliers rise up from the surrounding plains. Because of their elevations, these "island ranges" are better watered than the surrounding plains and support sage and grass covered foothills, upland meadows, alpine forests, and many springs and pothole lakes. The cooler seasonal temperatures and specialized resources of these areas attracted Native peoples for thousands of years.

Millions of bison once grazed the Montana plains, the Rocky Mountain foothills, and the intermountain valleys. This temperate grassland biome supported the immense herds on which Indian bands depended for food, hides, and other important products. Fescue grasses, in particular, provided protein-rich winter forage for the bison. In turn, bison dung fertilized the grasslands ecosystem and fueled people's campfires. After facing near extinction in the early twentieth century, today bison survive in small herds on private holdings, public ranges, Indian reservations, and in Glacier and Yellowstone national parks.

Montana is a well-known wildlife paradise for many species, including mule and whitetail deer, elk, pronghorn antelope, moose, bighorn sheep, mountain goat, bear, and mountain lion. For thousands of years, the state's first human residents depended on these and other large mammals for food, hides, bone, antler, sinew, gut, and other products. Like the bison, many of these big game species were nearly extirpated by the turn of the twentieth century. Their recovery today is due to modern wildlife conservation efforts. Big Sky Country is home to a wide variety of smaller mammals, carnivores, raptors, waterfowl, songbirds, and native fish. Indian peoples hunted and trapped these assorted creatures—large and small—to procure meat, eggs, pelts, feathers, and other body parts for food, clothing, implements, ornaments, and decoration.

The Columbia Plateau encompasses the Flathead and Bitterroot drainages of far western Montana, as well as parts of Idaho and Washington. Abutting the southwest corner of the state is the Great Basin of eastern Idaho. The Great Plains extend well north of Montana into Canada, south into the Wyoming Basin, and east to the Missouri River in the Dakotas. During the thousands of years in which they lived in these vast regions, Indian peoples continually adapted to their changing climates, landscapes, and resources. These distinctive adaptations produced what anthropologists call "culture areas." Over the millennia, people from the Columbia Plateau, Great Basin, and Great Plains came to this place we now call Montana to live, hunt, trade, raid, and socialize with each other, making the area a cultural crossroads. This convergence and interaction of Native groups from different regions over millennia is what makes Montana archaeology both fascinating and complicated—it tells not one story but many.

Time	Period	Epoch	Climate
150 yrs ago	**Modern-Anthropocene** - warming trend	MODERN/ ANTHROPOCENE	
700 years ago	**Little Ice Age** – cool and wet	HOLOCENE	
1,000 years ago	**Medieval Warm Period-Little Altithermal** – warm and dry		
5,000 years ago	**Medithermal-Neoglacial** – cool and wet		
9,000 years ago	**Holocene Climate Optimum-Altithermal** – warm and dry		
11,700 years ago	**Beginning of Holocene Epoch**-Interglacial Period		
12,800 years ago	**Younger Dryas climate reversal** – cold and dry	PLEISTOCENE	
19,000 years ago	**Beginning of continental glacier retreat** - gradual warming trend		
25,000 years ago	**Last Glacial Maximum** – cold and dry		
85,000 years ago	**Beginning of Wisconsin Glacial Period**		
2.5 mil years ago	**Beginning of Pleistocene Epoch**		

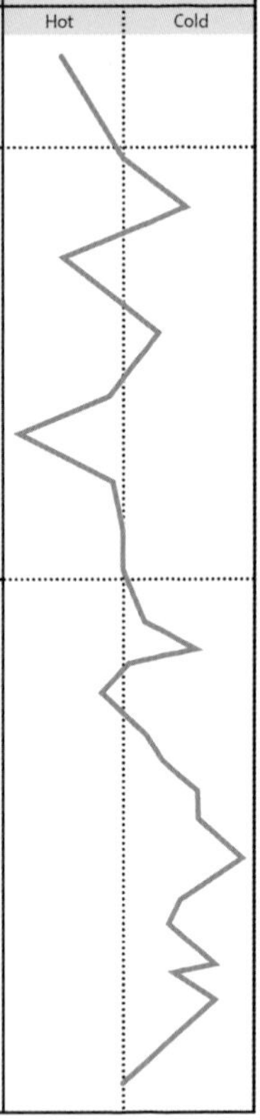

Climate variation is part of the natural world. Pleistocene and Holocene climate change, and the Ice Ages, were triggered by variations in the amount of solar radiation reaching earth due to cyclical changes in the earth's orbital geometry, volcanic eruptions, and other phenomena. Over the past 15,000 years, Montana's climate has varied between warm and cold periods, as shown here. Illustration by Eric S. Carlson.

CLIMATE PAST AND PRESENT

Wherever they lived, Montana's first peoples coped with the weather. One month might be cool and wet, while the next hot and dry. Climate is weather over an extended period of time—decades, centuries, and millennia. While yearly weather constantly challenged Montana's ancient residents, just as it does the state's modern ones, the climate determined how they lived and adapted to the environment over the long term.

Climate variation is part of the natural world. Cyclical changes in the earth's orbital geometry, caused by the gravitational pull of the Sun and other planets, are a major source of climate change. Called the *Milankovitch Cycles,* these oscillations occur roughly every 100,000, 41,000, and 23,000 years and affect the location of solar energy (called insolation) and thus seasonality.[5] They are responsible for the Ice Ages. Continental movement (plate tectonics), extraterrestrial impacts (asteroids, comets), air circulation patterns in the atmosphere, sunspots, ocean currents, volcanic eruptions, and modern industrial emissions also contribute to climate change.

Scientists can find out what ancient climates were like by looking at traces of those climates in Arctic ice sheets and marine sediment cores, glacial moraines (rocks and other debris piled up by glaciers), tree and sea coral growth rings, and other biophysical evidence. Fed with these and other data, powerful computers create models of past climates and predict scenarios for the future.[6]

Our climate story begins near the end of the Pleistocene geological epoch, dating from about 2.5 million to 11,700 years ago. During this epoch, continental and alpine glaciers advanced and retreated some 20 times. Over the last million years, major ice ages have occurred every 100,000 years when, thanks to the Milankovitch cycles, the earth's orbit resulted in the planet receiving the least amount of summer insolation. We now live in the Holocene epoch, a period of glacial retreat and warmer climate.

During the last, great Ice Age (ca. 100,000 to 11,700 years ago—called the Wisconsin Glacial Episode by geologists), the massive mile-thick Laurentide ice sheet covered all of Canada and the northern part of the United States. Cordilleran glaciers buried the Rocky and Cascade mountains. Pleistocene mammals like wooly mammoths and giant ground sloths grazed and browsed across the tundra-steppe in front of the ice sheets.[7] When continental glaciation was at its maximum reach some 26,000 to 19,000 years ago, the enormous Laurentide and Cordilleran glaciers pushed south into present-day northern Idaho and Montana, blocking the Clark Fork and Missouri rivers respectively with "ice dams" and creating vast glacial lakes.

About 18,000 years ago, the earth began to slowly warm, leading to the gradual northward retreat of the continental ice sheets. Meltwater from the ice sheets put enormous pressure on the glacial ice dams, periodically causing the dams to float. When this happened, massive amounts of water spilled out at enormous speed from underneath the dams. Catastrophic downstream flooding and erosion ensued, carving up the landscape of eastern Washington and parts of central Montana. Then the ice dams built up again. Scientists estimate that the Glacial Lake Missoula "ice dams" burst and flooded the region some 40 times or more between 15,000 and 13,000 years ago.[8] The old lakeshore lines are clearly visible on Mount Jumbo and

Mount Sentinel overlooking the city of Missoula. Glacial lakes Great Falls, Mussellshell and Glendive, which impounded substantial parts of the Missouri River Basin, also breached during the Late Pleistocene. There is, as yet, no solid archaeological evidence (at elevations above the maximum lake pools) showing that early Indian peoples used these vast lakes or their resources.

The gradual transition to Holocene conditions continued until about 12,800 years ago. Then the climatic event scientists call the Younger Dryas brought a 1,000-year return to unseasonably cold conditions. Scientists attribute the trigger for this sudden and relatively brief climatic reversal to melting ice sheets caused by a warming climate. Vast amounts of icy meltwater poured into the northern oceans. This influx of cold water slowed down or stopped the circulation of the warm North Atlantic Current, which normally produces temperate conditions in northern Europe. This sharp cold snap also impacted North America and probably stressed Montana's first Indian peoples (and the animal and plant resources on which they depended) but its actual effects are unknown. Once the ice sheets receded and the inflow of cold meltwater subsided, the North Atlantic Current reestablished itself, and the warming period began anew.

The Holocene began in earnest 11,700 years ago, bringing a climate markedly different from that of the last Ice Age. Early Holocene temperatures were as much as seven degrees Fahrenheit higher than during the Ice Age. The climate of the northwestern Plains and the Intermountain West became warmer and drier. As a result, habitats changed, and as a consequence of changing habitats, the giant Pleistocene fauna died out or evolved into smaller forms like the bison.

We think of the Holocene interglacial as a time of remarkable climatic stability, but this epoch actually experienced significant climatic variations, some of which greatly affected Native people's ways of life.[9] Foremost, between about 9,000 and 5,000 years ago, in what climatologists call the Holocene Climate Optimum or the Altithermal, the climate became extremely dry because there was less seasonal moisture. As shown later in the Barton Gulch and Spiro site chapters, Montana's Indian people adapted by becoming increasingly mobile and seeking out a wider range of resources.

A gradual cooling trend commenced 5,000 years ago. Summers remained dry but winters were wetter and warmer. This trend marked a period called the Neoglacial or Medithermal. At lower elevations, dry habitats transitioned into more temperate ones. The moderating temperatures of this period gradually peaked 950 years ago in what is called the Medieval Climatic Anomaly or Little Altithermal. This 300-year heat wave at northern latitudes famously allowed wine grape vines to grow in England and led to Norse explorations and settlement across the North Atlantic Ocean.[10] Archaeologists have yet to determine how a warmer climate affected Montana's mobile Indian hunter-gatherers, if at all.

The Little Altithermal gave way about 700 years ago to what scientists call the Little Ice Age—a renewed episode of climatic cooling and alpine glaciation.[11] On the Plains, prairie grasslands flourished in these milder wet conditions and supported vast herds of bison. Bison hunting became the economic mainstay of Montana's Indian peoples, as shown in the First Peoples Buffalo Jump chapter. Still, the effects of the Little Ice Age varied locally, with evidence of short, periodic dry spells and drought.

The Little Ice Age ended around 1850 A.D. Since that time, the Industrial Revolution, deforestation, and our modern fossil fuel-driven age have increased the input of the greenhouse gas carbon dioxide (C02) into the atmosphere well above the preindustrial average of about 280 parts per million (ppm). In 2017, the world's C02 level reached 410 ppm (recorded at the Mauna Loa Observatory in Hawaii), indicating the substantial role people now play in global warming, environmental change, and the extinction of organic life.[12] For this reason, many scientists believe we are entering a new geological epoch called the Anthropocene, the age of humans.

Today, winter temperatures in Montana average 27 degrees Fahrenheit while summer temperatures average 69 degrees Fahrenheit. Winters on the plains are severe, with the thermometer plummeting well below zero for extended periods. Montanans often call the area west of the Continental Divide the "banana belt" because of its generally milder weather. Harsh winter weather in central Montana is occasionally ameliorated by warm Chinook winds flowing east from the Rocky Mountains, which can increase temperatures by 30 or 40 degrees in a matter of minutes. The so-called Chinook Belt extends along the eastern front of the Rocky Mountains, where winter temperatures can be somewhat milder, with less snow compared to the frigid, windswept plains further east. Overall, precipitation statewide comes as winter snow and summer rainfall.

Archaeology is the study of past human life, culture, and behavior through the scientific recovery and analyses of material remains. During archeological excavations, a grid system (the small squares illustrated above) enables archaeologists to plot the exact location of artifacts and features. These mapped relationships provide vital clues to understanding how camps, hunting places, rock quarries, and other sites were used and for what purposes. Illustration by Eric S. Carlson.

HOW ARCHAEOLOGISTS LEARN ABOUT THE PAST

Archaeology is the study of past human life, culture, and behavior through the scientific recovery and analyses of material remains—ancient garbage! Because writing began only 5,200 years ago and wasn't widespread until recently, we need archaeology to extend our knowledge of the human past into the millennia before people started keeping written records. The field of archaeology as a science began around the turn of the nineteenth century when adventurers, explorers, soldiers, scientists, and antiquarians began recording and classifying Egyptian ruins, Greco-Roman antiquities, Neolithic monuments, Paleolithic caves, and Native American stone and earth works.[13] Eventually, archaeology became a profession in universities, museums, and similar institutions. Despite being a comparatively young science, it is highly technical and specialized today. Along with the historical context, it is useful to explore how archaeology is actually done today in order to better understand the site narratives that follow.

How are archaeological sites discovered in the first place? Prior to the 1960s in Montana, ranchers, hunters, hikers, and relic collectors passed along word of their discoveries to university professors, who then formally recorded the finds and sometimes commenced studies. These information sources have largely disappeared with the passage of time and the implementation of federal and state antiquities laws and cultural resource management programs.

Today, archaeologists walk carefully across the ground searching for telltale evidence—a broken stone tool laying on top of a gopher mound; fire hearth cobbles, charcoal bits, and bone fragments eroding from a stream bank; or an unusual geometric pattern of red pigment on a cliff face. Ground-penetrating radar, magnetometers, and other remote sensing methods assist archaeologists in detecting archaeological sites buried deeply in the ground.

Once an archaeological site has been discovered, the Montana State Historic Preservation Office (SHPO), formed by the NHPA, assigns a Smithsonian trinomial number as an identifier. This system allows archaeologists to communicate about specific places without the confusion of multiple state or local numbering, naming, and classification systems (a problem that besets all science). For example, the Smithsonian number 24BE601 signifies the state (24, Montana); county (BE, Beaverhead); and the 601st site recorded in that county. I've included Smithsonian numbers in the chapter titles.

To be perfectly clear, the goal of archaeology is not to find interesting or beautiful artifacts but instead to gather—using scientific methods—physical information about the ancient human past. Today, archaeologists frame their investigations with carefully considered research questions. For example, how did Indian hunter-gatherers adapt to the dry Altithermal period on the Plains? How extensively did Native people use mountain environments and for what purposes? When did people practice agriculture on the Plains? As the preeminent American archaeologist David Hurst Thomas famously said: "It's not what you find, it's what you find out."[14]

Archaeologists excavate sites using a grid system typically composed of one-meter squares (about one yard by one yard) or "units" laid out with wood or metal stakes and string. (Archaeologists use the metric system, but for reader convenience, measurements will also be expressed in feet and inches.) The grid system allows archaeologists to accurately plot and map artifacts and other cultural remains.

Think about it this way. Excavating an archaeological site is like investigating a crime scene. The relationships among artifacts, features, and areas of the site are crucial for interpreting what happened at the site in the past, which is why their locations are mapped so precisely. This job is more difficult when archaeological sites are disturbed and artifacts are removed—akin to a bystander taking the murder weapon from a crime scene before police investigators arrive. Archaeologists bemoan artifact collecting and uncontrolled digging because those activities (besides being illegal on public lands) undermine the integrity of the archaeological "scene" and remove valuable clues. Many archaeological sites in Montana have been ruined, or nearly so, by artifact collecting and amateur digging in the past, particularly in caves and bison kill sites.

Archaeological excavators use dental picks, brushes, trowels, shovels—and occasionally road graders or other heavy equipment—to slowly peel away layers of both culturally sterile and artifact-bearing sediment. It is slow, tedious work. Sites are dug downward in standard increments (usually 10 centimeters or about three inches) or by following natural sedimentary layers, or sometimes both. Excavated fill (soil, dirt) is sifted through screens with tight mesh. Water is often used to wash away the dirt, leaving artifacts, bone fragments, charred seeds, and other evidence of the human past glistening on the screen. These are all collected in labeled bags for laboratory processing and study.

Archaeologists use screens with tight mesh to recover stone, bones, and organic artifacts from excavated soil. Occasionally, water and hoses are used to both break apart dirt clods and improve recovery of tiny artifacts, as Kutoyis Archaeological Project students are doing here on the Blackfeet Indian Reservation. PHOTOGRAPH COURTESY OF BARA, THE UNIVERSITY OF ARIZONA.

During excavation, artifacts found *in situ* (in their original place) are plotted and mapped according to their placement or their coordinates within the grid. Archaeologists also carefully expose, measure, map, and photograph the features they find: fire hearths, storage pits, housing remnants, or other physical remains. Soil scientists and geoarchaeologists document the site's sedimentary and cultural layers in stratigraphic profile drawings and maps. The combined field notes, drawings, photographs, maps, artifacts, and final report are—and this cannot be emphasized enough—the archaeologists only true, reliable evidence from the excavation. Once a cultural level has been dug up, it is, for scientific purposes, effectively destroyed.

When excavations cease, the entire site is mapped with survey equipment. The grid is tied to a permanent datum, such as a metal survey stake pounded into the ground or an immovable boulder, so that the grid can be located again long after the initial excavation is finished. Plastic sheeting is often placed on the floor and sidewalls of excavated units and then buried with dirt from the screening piles. Covering things up protects the otherwise exposed sediments from the elements and vandalism. It also helps future investigators determine where to begin their work. In field camps and laboratories, artifacts are labeled, measured, and catalogued. Finally, the lead researchers compile, synthesize, and interpret the collected data in a professional report. Quality archaeological research is expensive, and it takes time. A final publication may take several years, although, regrettably, many take far longer.

When all of this is done, the field records and artifacts are carefully catalogued, labeled, and placed in museums and other official repositories. Given the huge popularity of the Indiana Jones movies and the resultant public misperception that archaeologists simply stash away the things they find in vast storerooms where they are never to be seen again—by anyone—I am compelled to say that prehistoric and historic artifacts are actually stored in university, federal, state, and tribal repositories. And that's where they should be—they belong to all of us.

In Montana, the BLM Curation Center in Billings, The Peoples Center in Pablo, Chief Plenty Coups State Park, the Museum of the Rockies-Montana State University, the University of Montana Anthropological Collection Facility, and state and federal offices and interpretive centers all house archaeological collections. The cultural materials are thus safeguarded in perpetuity for research, museum exhibits, educational programs,

Laboratory analysis is tedious but critically important work. Montana State University archaeologist Jack Fisher is studying the animal bones recovered from the Absaroka or Second Crow Agency. He determined that the Crow people butchered and consumed a wider range of wild animals than did non-Indian peoples at the old agency. PHOTOGRAPH COURTESY OF STEVE PLATT.

and ongoing traditional cultural uses. For example, the Crow Tribe safely stores medicine bundles in the Chief Plenty Coups State Park visitor facility within the Crow Reservation, for use by tribal members.

Beginning in the early 1990s to comply with the Native American Graves Protection and Repatriation Act, agency, museum, and repository officials returned artifacts with continuing cultural or traditional importance (called cultural patrimony) to Indian tribes. Still, every year academic research and agency projects conducted under the NHPA and the MAA generate new artifact collections. Repository space is limited and costly. Because of this storage issue, and in deference to the concerns of some Indian tribes about removing artifacts from archaeological sites, investigators increasingly practice what is informally called "catch and release archaeology." Artifacts located during fieldwork are plotted with Global Positioning System (GPS) instruments, photographed, described, and left where they were found. Sometimes the artifacts are covered with soil to hide them from casual or intentional collection, such as artifacts found along popular hiking trails on public lands.

But there are limits to what archaeologists can learn simply by digging things up. To overcome these limits, they draw on research in other fields and a growing repertoire of technologies.

ETHNOGRAPHIC RESEARCH

During the late nineteenth and early twentieth centuries, American cultural anthropologists recorded the customs of Indian tribes in the western United States in reports called ethnographies. Archaeologists draw on this rich resource to enhance their understanding of ancient Indian cultures and the ancestors of today's American Indian peoples. As shown in the site narratives in this book, archaeologists often use ethnographic research to infer social issues rarely revealed in the material record itself, such as gender, the roles of men and women, and their use of specific kinds of artifacts and spaces within an archaeological site. From cultural anthropologists we know that men made stone tools and hunted, but not exclusively; women did so too. Among hunter-gatherers, plant collecting and domestic tasks were largely the purview of women, but not always. Unfortunately, ethnographic research touches lightly on children, and children are difficult to detect in the archaeological record—their clothing and toys are hard to distinguish in surviving camp refuse. Because people's customs and lifeways change over time, archaeologists cautiously use ethnographic analogy to understand and interpret American Indian life in the far distant past.

Besides ethnographic data, archaeologists can better understand Montana's deep human past by paying close attention to the traditional cultural Indigenous knowledge of today's tribal elders and cultural specialists. But sharing this knowledge is a sensitive matter among Indian peoples who often look upon archaeology with deep skepticism and concern. In fact, for a long time archaeologists excavated sites and collected artifacts, including human skeletal remains, without regard for the wishes of Indian peoples. Given this troublesome legacy, many tribal members maintain that it is better to leave ancient places alone unless they are badly threatened by degradation or destruction. Some people believe that their tribe has lived here since the beginning of time and that there is nothing of value to be learned from archaeology and western science that cannot be taught by the elders. However, other tribal members feel that archaeological research, when conducted with sensitivity and respect, links the deep past with the present and strengthens tribal knowledge and identity.

Today, the National Historic Preservation Act, the Archaeological Resources Protection Act of 1979, the Native American Graves Protection and Repatriation Act of 1990, and other federal laws and regulations ensure that tribal people have a strong voice in historic preservation, including how cultural knowledge is shared and how archaeological research is practiced. American Indian anthropologists, archaeologists, historians, and traditional cultural specialists participate in all facets of historic preservation and academic research. Tribal oral traditions and ethnohistories (historical records, such as the journals of Lewis and Clark, containing information about the lives and customs of ethnic groups) are increasingly integrated into archaeological

American Indians now play an essential role in archaeology and historic preservation across Montana. Kutoyis Archaeological Project students are excavating a bison mandible and other artifacts in a bison kill site on the Two Medicine River near Browning. During excavation, archeologists dig one-meter-square pits, like this one, as part of an overall grid system. PHOTOGRAPH COURTESY OF BARA, THE UNIVERSITY OF ARIZONA

research.[15] Programs like the Kutoyis Archaeological Project on the Blackfeet Reservation now train American Indian students in field archaeology and cultural resource management. The Salish Kootenai College in Pablo offers tribal and non-tribal students courses in archaeology and historic preservation. Combining western science with traditional Indigenous knowledge is becoming the standard for archaeological research today. Still a work in progress, this collaboration is both long overdue and the future of archaeology in Montana and the United States.

THE TECHNOLOGY OF ARCHAEOLOGY

Archaeologists now use many kinds of technologies to study ancient sites. This book focuses only on radiocarbon dating because of its profound importance to archaeology. Developed by chemist and Nobel laureate Willard Libby in the late 1940s, radiocarbon dating is simple in principle but complicated in practice.[16] Plants absorb carbon dioxide (CO2) from the atmosphere through photosynthesis, and animals and humans acquire CO2 by eating plants. CO2 contains two isotopes that provide the key to determining the passage of time: carbon 12, a stable, unchanging isotope, and carbon 14, an unstable radioactive isotope. When the animal or plant dies, it stops absorbing carbon. Then the carbon 14 isotope begins to slowly decay into nitrogen at a half-life of 5,730 years. The ratio of the remaining carbon 14 isotopes to the stable carbon 12 isotopes tells us how long the plant or animal has been dead. Radiocarbon measurements are statistical probabilities around an average or mean, which accounts for the plus or minus number you see in radiocarbon dates; for example, 8,500 + 70 Radiocarbon Years (RCY) Before Present (B.P.), with "present" being pegged at 1950. This "before present" timescale—more straightforward than the Christianity-based "Before Christ/Anno Domini" (B.C. /A.D.) calendar—is widely used in science. (B.P. dates are easily converted to the B.C. /A.D. calendar by subtracting the year from 1950: 1950-8,000 = 6,050 B.C., then add 1 since there is no Year Zero.)

However, radiocarbon dates are skewed by past variations in the amount of carbon dioxide (CO2) in the atmosphere and the recent large-scale burning of fossil fuels. For this reason, conventional radiocarbon (RCY) dates are "corrected" or calibrated into modern (365 day) calendar years using instrumentally dated tree rings, marine coral and sedimentary layers, historical sources such as ancient Egyptian dynastic records, and complex math. Calibrated dates are statistical probabilities around the standard deviation (sigma) of the mean. The larger (but less precise) 2-sigma calibrated radiocarbon range is typically used by archaeologists since it has a 95% probability of accuracy.

Calibrated dates are technically written as: "9,497 $\pm$ 47 cal B.P." So that the reader can easily relate to the age of the artifacts and archaeological sites under discussion, this book uses calibrated or calendar dates, expressed simply as "9,500 years ago," for example. Note that this calibrated date is derived from the 8,500-conventional (RCY) radiocarbon example cited above. Calibration typically yields older calendar dates the further back in time one goes, so the 1,000-year difference above highlights calibration's role in precise time-related archaeological interpretations. Christian calendar dates are used when discussing Historic period archaeological sites.

Radiocarbon dates can reliably date organic materials up to about 50,000 years—a long time, but not nearly as long as humans have existed. To calculate the ages of artifacts older than 50,000 years, archaeologists turn to other kinds of "radioactive clocks." For example, potassium-argon dating is widely used in Eurasia and Africa to determine the age of archaeological remains that are hundreds of thousands or millions of years old. Since archaeological sites in the Americas do not, to the best of current knowledge, exceed 50,000 years old, archaeologists here rarely use these dating methods. Geologists, however, use them to understand landscape formation and change, and that knowledge, in turn, benefits archaeology.

ROCK TALK

Much of what archaeologists know about Montana prehistory was learned through the study of stone tools simply because hunter-gatherers left them everywhere and because stone tools have survived the ravages of time better than perishable artifacts such as hide clothing, shelter, and bags, and arrowshafts, cordage, and baskets made of cane, wood, plant fiber, and animal hair. Lithics (rocks that have been modified by humans) are the basis on which a ton of archaeology is done, especially in places like Montana where hunter-gatherer cultures predominate over more settled Indigenous groups. Understanding flintknapping—the art of making chipped stone tools—is crucial for interpreting the technologies and lifeways of ancient hunting-gathering people.

Archaeologists call the process of chipping useable tools out of lumps of rock "lithic reduction" because the knapper removed material from, or "reduced," the original piece of raw stone to make a tool.[17] Rock used for tool-making must be capable of breaking in a specific way, so not all rocks are suitable for tools. When struck with a cobble hammer-stone or antler baton, a good rock (what archaeologists call "raw material") does not break along its natural planes of separation. Instead, the energy from the blow emanates outward from the point of contact in rippling curves, allowing for the consecutive removal of stone flakes in a predictable and controlled way—in what mineralogists term a "conchoidal fracture." Fine-grained (siliceous) materials such as chert, flint, quartzite, and basalt share this trait, as do obsidian (volcanic glass) and porcellanite (baked clay shale, common to southeastern Montana coal country). Absent this trait, coarser-grained rocks struck with a hard blow literally explode into misshapen, unusable chunks.

At outcroppings of suitable rock, Indigenous flintknappers tested stones for quality and then removed the outer cortex (the weathered, outer surface of the rock) from stones that passed muster. Using river cobble or limestone hammer stones and antler batons or billets, they roughly shaped these stones on

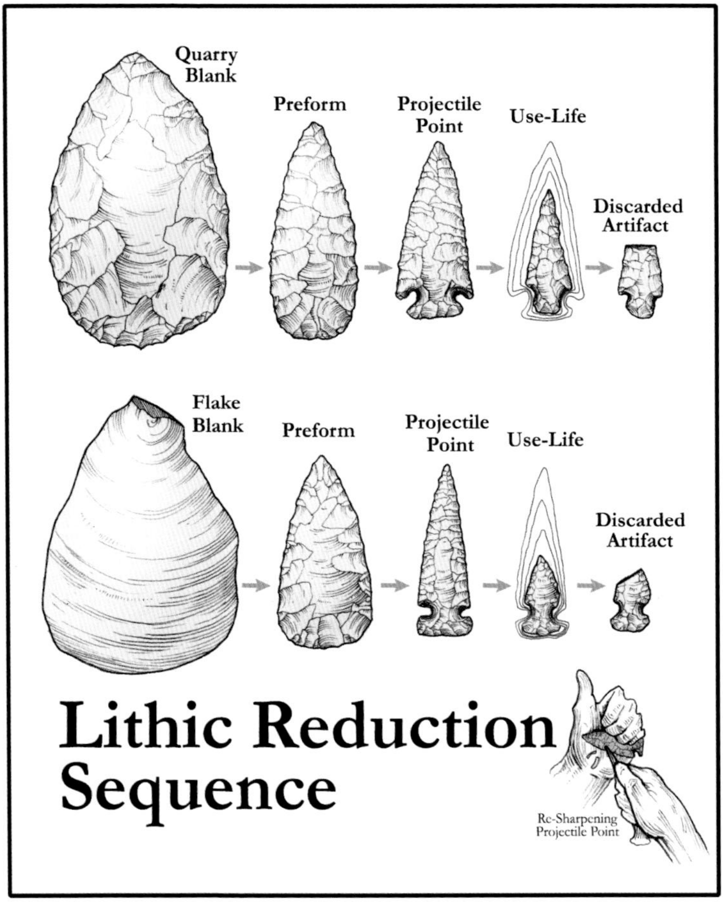

Indian flintknappers pared down raw cobbles into transportable forms called bifaces. In camps, flakes removed from bifaces, and the bifaces themselves, were made into projectile points, scrapers, knife blades, choppers, and other stone tools. The "use-life" drawings show how points became smaller as they were re-sharpened (by removing more flakes) until they eventually became unusable, resulting in the "discarded artifacts" found most often by archeologists. Adapted from Flenniken (1987).

both sides into leaf-shaped forms called bifacial cores or quarry blanks.[18] This flintknapping technique is called percussion flaking. Bifacial cores were easier to carry away from quarries in hide or fiber bags than cumbersome raw rocks. Once in their home camps, toolmakers removed flakes from the bifacial cores and fashioned the flakes and the bifaces themselves into various kinds of implements, including choppers, scrapers, knife blades, projectile points, engravers, and drills. For this reason, some modern flintknappers regard bifacial cores as the "original Swiss army knife."

Further percussion work with smaller cobbles or antler batons thinned and shaped the flakes into tool blanks or "preforms." Knappers then used pointed antler tines to pry off smaller flakes to give final shape, sharpness, and finish to the desired tool. This detail work is called pressure flaking. Once removed from the bifacial core, some flakes already had good, sharp, cutting or scraping edges without the need for further work. Such simple and expedient "utilized flakes" are common in archaeological sites throughout Montana.

The size and shape of a stone tool changed over its lifetime as the result of repeated tool sharpening—much as a pencil is continuously sharpened until it becomes an unmanageable stub and is discarded. So, what archaeologists typically find in ancient dwelling sites are discarded stone tools: well-used, broken, and misshapen. They are sorry representations of their former selves but certainly not the crude results of poorly skilled flintknappers or signs of a culturally backward people, as Indian relic collectors sometimes insensitively claimed in the past. Tools and artifacts found in "newly minted" condition are primarily from single-use animal kill sites, tool caches, and burial sites.

Called "lithic debitage" by archaeologists, "waste flakes" are the most technologically diagnostic byproduct of flintknapping. But analysis requires great patience to accurately sort and identify thousands of large, small, and micro-sized flakes. More daunting, some lithic analysts refit flakes on discarded tools to document where they were made, used, refurbished, and discarded in ancient campsites (akin to tracking all the places in your house where you and your family used your hammer). Use-wear patterns on stone tools shed light on the kinds of work people did. For example, a nibbled or polished edge of a scraper tells us whether the tool was used on a hard object such as bone or a soft material such as hide. Ancient blood residue removed from stone tools allows specialists to identify the genera, if not the species, of the ancient hunter's prey—fish, birds, and mammals. Finally, the geographical origin of the stone used for the tool can be traced, a topic discussed in the Schmitt Chert Mine chapter.

HUNTER-GATHERER ARCHAEOLOGY

Prior to 13,000 years ago, all of our ancestors, everywhere on earth, were hunters and gatherers. They obtained food by hunting, plant foraging, and fishing, rather than by agriculture. Hunter-gatherers lived in small groups and bands made up of extended families, numbering from 30 to 50 people in winter camps.[19] Band movements were determined by the seasons and the availability of food and other resources. The identity and location of habitually used seasonal camps, subsistence areas, religious sites, and other important places were passed down from one generation to the next in oral tradition, creation stories, and places names (as they are even today among tribal people). The seasons, sacred time, oral tradition, myths, and geography all blend together in hunting-gathering societies.

Ethnographic data further show that these societies were egalitarian with few differences in influence, power, and wealth. Sharing and reciprocity were essential to survival. Individuals became leaders by consensus or because group members recognized that certain people had special knowledge and skills. In Montana, ethnically related Indian bands gathered at certain times of the year into larger populations (tribes), averaging (ethnographies tell us) anywhere from about 700 to 950 people, for annual hunts, socializing, trade, ceremonies, and mutual defense, and then dispersed again into their individual group and band territories.

Throughout most of the world, hunter-gatherers developed into more complex societies where resource-rich environments enabled intensive plant foraging and eventually agriculture. At these locations, population densities increased, specialization of activities occurred, and permanent settlements were established. On Montana's plains and in the Rocky Mountains, however, food resources were always seasonal and patchy—even bison herds were constantly on the move—so hunter-gatherer survival depended on an intimate understanding of the land and a great deal of mobility.

The seasonal mobility of Montana's ancient hunter-gatherers makes archaeological investigations challenging. Early nomadic bands carried the necessities of life on their backs, with pack dogs pulling small pole sleds called travois. (Horses became available on the Plains in the early 1700s.) Everything these nomadic peoples owned—what archaeologists call "material culture"—had to be economical and portable. In contrast to the rich archeological sites of sedentary villages, transitory hunter-gatherer camps frequently contain only scattered stones, fractured hearth cobbles, bones representing meals, and a bit of flintknapping. This meager evidence does not mean that just a few cultural activities (eating, tool making) took place, but only that these activities form the only surviving refuse. A good archaeological axiom is that "absence of evidence is not evidence of absence."

Any refuse not picked over by the Indian's dogs—and later by bears, coyotes, wolves, and other scavengers—eventually decayed. Only the most durable artifacts—stone tools and the densest bone scraps—survive in most of the camps investigated by archaeologists. Furthermore, erosion, flooding, burrowing animals, freezing and thawing, wildfire, and (in contemporary times) plowing, livestock grazing and development all wreak havoc on the ground surface and the sediments below that might contain artifacts and other cultural evidence. As a result, our picture of hunter-gatherer life in Montana is invariably skewed by poor site preservation and the near absence of perishable artifacts—tools, clothing, bags, cordage and toys made of hide, plant fiber, or wood.

Despite these challenges, archaeologists have developed artifact typologies and cultural chronologies to assist in the interpretation of Montana's ancient Native American past. Typologies classify artifacts by their physical and technological traits—shape, size, material, and so forth. A cultural chronology organizes those diagnostic artifacts and other characteristics into a meaningful time sequence. What enables archaeologists to build a chronology are archaeological sites containing evidence of successive periods of human habitation over a long period of time. We can date these successive periods by radiocarbon analysis, artifact typology, and other methods, giving us a strong sense of how ancient cultures changed over time.

Unfortunately, so-called "deep sites" containing evidence of human use over millennia are few and far between in Montana. The Myers-Hindman site near Livingston contains eight habitation layers dating back some 9,000 years. Just across the Continental Divide from southwestern Montana, the Bison and Veratic rock shelters in the Birch Creek Valley of eastern Idaho have equally long records, as does the culturally rich Mummy Cave near Cody, Wyoming, with 36 occupational levels.[20] Montana archaeologists compare and reference these and other long-inhabited, multi-layered sites to put their own sites into context.

Archaeological chronologies for the Plains and Intermountain West rely heavily on chipped stone projectile points because they are ubiquitous and changed stylistically through time. Projectile point is a catchall term for the fashioned stone tip attached to the end of a spear, dart, and arrow shaft.

Millennia ago, hunter-gatherers made leaf-shaped, stemmed and notched stone projectile points that they attached to dart shafts and propelled with a throwing board called an atlatl. The atlatl provided more accuracy, speed and distance than hand-thrown spears. Its tongue-twisting name is derived from the Aztecs, who were still using this weapon during the Spanish conquest of Mexico in the early 16th Century. Upper Paleolithic cultures in Europe began using atlatls some 17,500 years ago, and Eurasian hunter-gatherers carried this weapons technology to the Americas.

The bow and arrow replaced the atlatl on the Northwestern Plains around 1,500 years ago. So-called "bird points" (a term coined by artifact collectors, not archaeologists) are actually arrowheads suited to killing bison and other big game but are smaller than the points for spears or atlatl darts.

New weapons technologies did not completely replace the preceding ones. Lances tipped with stone and, later, metal blades were used well into historic times, though it appears that Montana hunter-gatherers abandoned the atlatl well before A.D. 1000. Bows and arrows complimented the use of muskets and rifles throughout the late 18th and 19th centuries.

In the 1940s, William Mulloy, a pioneer figure in Montana archaeology, developed the first chronology for northwestern Plains cultures up to the arrival of Euroamericans in the eighteenth century.[21] Plains archaeologists have since modified Mulloy's cultural chronology.[22] These newer chronologies benefit from an abundance of data generated by academic studies and, especially, cultural resource compliance work (under the

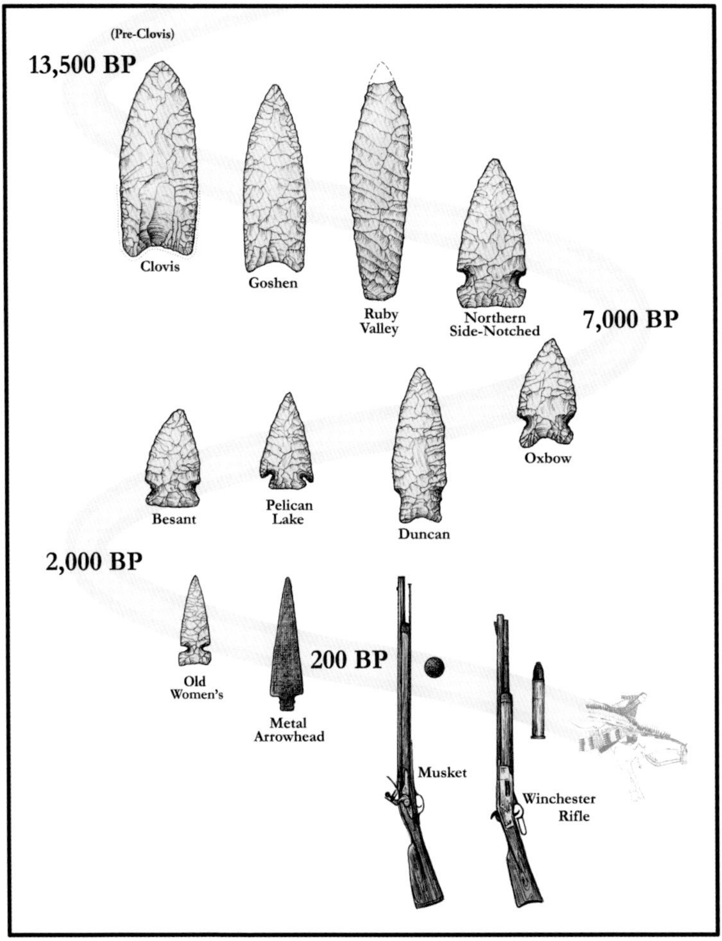

Projectile point styles reflect changes in Native American weaponry over time. Paleoindians used leaf-shaped points on their atlatl darts and lances (Clovis, Goshen, and Ruby Valley points above). These shapes gave way to stemmed and notched atlatl dart points during the Holocene (Northern Side-Notched through Besant). (Similar-looking dart points often share more than one name depending on geographic location.) The bow and arrow replaced atlatls and darts around 1,500 years ago and required smaller arrowheads. Metal arrowheads and guns were used in the Historic period.
Illustration by Eric S. Carlson.

National Historic Preservation Act and other legislation) completed in advance of ground-disturbing developments during the past 50 years. Out of this federally mandated archaeological work (with its added cost to the land developer and government agencies) has come a benefit to academia and the American public—an increased scientific and humanistic understanding of the peoples who occupied this land through time.

Archaeologists have given various names to collectively describe ancient Indian societies that shared similar material cultures and lifeways but whose ethnic identities are usually unknown. A few of the most popular archaeological monikers—like the ancient Clovis culture or Pelican Lake people—crop up in this book, but for our purposes, all of these archaeological terms denote American Indian hunting-gathering peoples.

The atlatl or spear-thrower was widely used throughout the Americas before the advent of the bow and arrow some 1,500 years ago. The narrow wood or bone throwing board or rod (atlatl), with a small projection or hook on its rear end to hold a dart shaft in place, provided the extra power of a second elbow, substantially increasing dart speed and distance. The atlatl, held with leather thong straps, occasionally had small attached stones, whose weight steadied the throw. Throughout the Holocene, different styles of leaf-shaped, stemmed, and notched projectile points were attached with sinew and pitch to the ends of dart shafts or foreshafts. Illustration by Eric S. Carlson.

COMING INTO THE COUNTRY

When, where, how, and why people came to inhabit the Americas is one of the most intriguing and controversial topics in archaeology. Colonization is best appreciated in a global bioevolutionary perspective.

All modern peoples—*Homo sapiens*—originated during the Pleistocene geological epoch. Regardless of physical appearance, language, or culture, we all are of the same biological order and share the same genetic code or genome.[23] Humanity's collective ancestral homeland is Africa, where paleoanthropologists and archaeologists have discovered an abundance of fossils of our Great Ape (hominid) cousins and archaic human (hominin) relatives dating back millions of years. No indisputable archaic hominin fossils (like the Neanderthals) have ever been discovered in the Americas; only fossils of anatomically modern people have been found.

Genetic and fossil evidence shows that modern humans (*Homo sapiens*) evolved in Africa some 200,000 years ago. Perhaps forced out by severe drought, small hunting-gathering bands eventually left their eastern African homeland some 130,000 or more years ago to colonize the Near East and Asia, then Europe (some 60,000 years ago), Australia, and eventually the Americas by at least 15,000 B.P. In Eurasia they replaced archaic Hominins already living there, like the well-known Neanderthals and the recently discovered Denisovans, although,

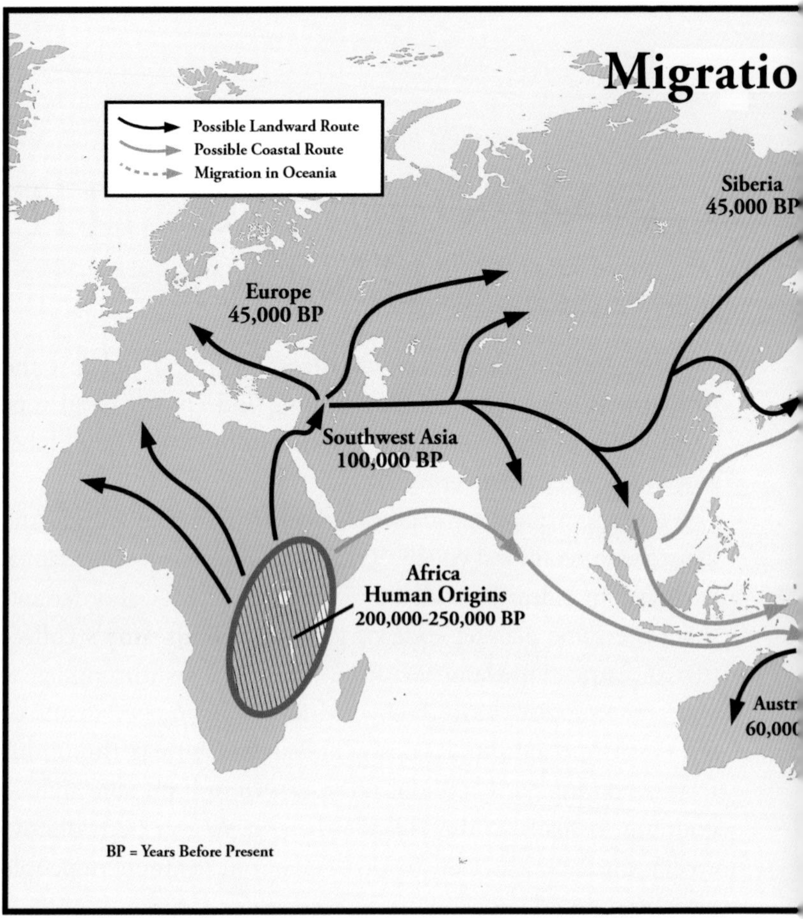

Fossil, genetic, and archaeological evidence enable scientists to map the timing and routes used by anatomically modern humans (*Homo sapiens*) to colonize the earth after evolving in Africa some 200,000 years ago. This map shows the two likely routes into North

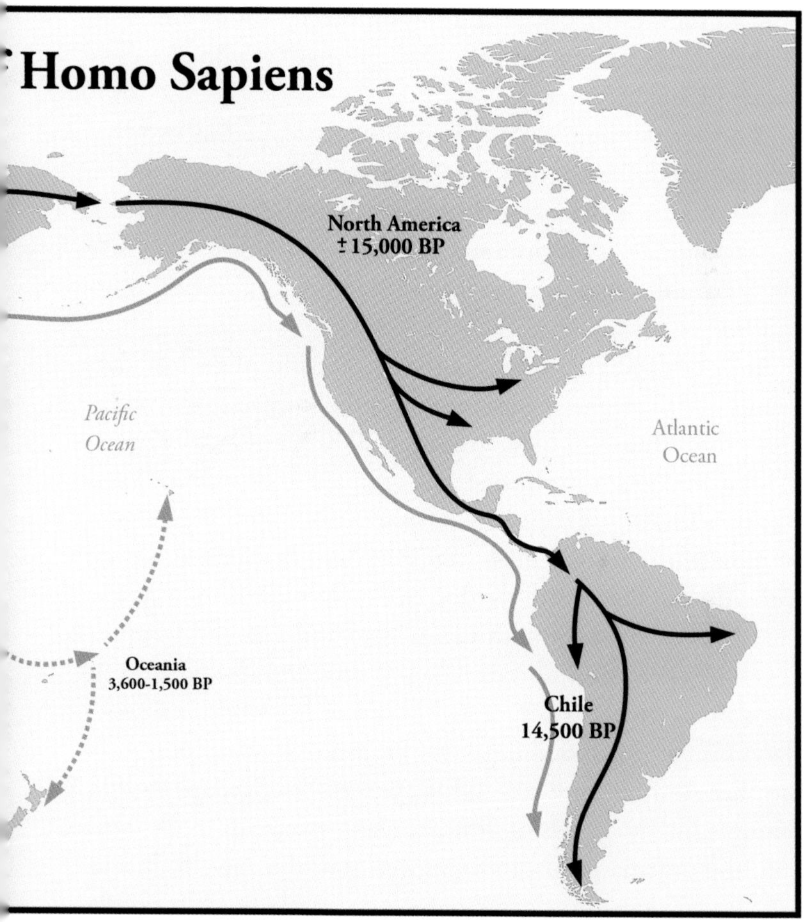

America: an overland migration from Siberia and a coastal route requiring boats. Genetic evidence now demonstrates that human migrations to and within the Americas were more complicated than once thought by archaeologists. Illustration by Eric S. Carlson.

prior to their extinction, these ancient species added a tiny bit of their DNA to our genome through mating with the early modern humans.[24]

Whether the human colonization of the Americas involved a single migration or multiple migrations is a long-standing debate among archaeologists, linguists, tribal experts, physical anthropologists, geologists, and geneticists. Consensus is elusive but, as of this writing, a widely accepted line of thinking is explained here.

American Indian peoples are the descendants of ancient Eurasian Upper Paleolithic hunting and gathering societies who inhabited northeastern Siberia some 35,000 years ago.[25] During the last Ice Age, a band, or bands, hunted and gathered their way eastward across the grassy Siberian "mammoth steppe" and eventually arrived at a huge stretch of land that joined Siberia with Alaska. This relatively dry, 600-mile-wide land mass existed because the enormous Cordilleran and Laurentide continental ice sheets tied up vast amounts of water, lowering ocean levels by as much as 400 feet. The lower sea levels exposed a "land bridge" identified today as "Beringia" or more popularly the "Bering Strait land bridge." Hunter-gatherer groups lived in Beringia for thousands of years, surviving on mammoth, caribou, and other large mammals, as well as wild plants, birds, and fish. In this harsh but game-rich land, people lived in tightly sewn animal-skin shelters and fueled their campfires with scrub wood and animal bone.

During their long tenure in Beringia, these hunter-gatherers genetically separated from their Eurasian relatives. (Today, American Indian genomes show only trace evidence of this ancient Asiatic connection.) These pioneering peoples, called Paleoindians by archaeologists, eventually crossed the entirety of Beringia, arriving in northwestern Alaska and the Yukon Territory of Canada, where the mile-high Cordilleran ice sheet blocked further travel eastward into continental North America. Unfortunately, evidence for the first presence of Paleoindians is hard to come by. Seawater now inundates Beringia, and Alaska and northwestern Canada are vast and rugged places in which to look for archaeological sites. However, archaeologists have found sites in Alaska at Swan Point, Nenana Valley, and other locations and dated them to between 14,000 and 12,000 years ago.

The routes that these hardy Paleoindian bands traveled southward into North America are speculative because scientific evidence is scarce and frequently controversial.[26] One long-standing interpretation is that they migrated southward in an ice-free corridor between the Cordilleran ice sheet to the west

Paleoindians hunted wooly mammoths and other Ice Age fauna. Archaeologists are unsure whether the death of the Lindsay mammoth found near Glendive is due to Paleoindian predation or other natural causes. The Lindsay mammoth tusks and bones shown here are on elevated soil blocks so that archaeologists can excavate beneath them. PHOTOGRAPH COURTESY OF CHRISTOPHER HILL.

and the Laurentide continental ice sheet to the east. This corridor existed just east of the Rocky Mountains in Canada. Eventually Paleoindian peoples emerged from this migratory funnel in a bountiful new land, and they headed east, west, and south to settle all of the Americas.

The ice-free corridor hypothesis hinges on when the corridor opened and closed during and after the last Ice Age and thus was available for passage. Some scientists question whether this ice-bound route would have provided enough food to sustain migrating animals and the bands of humans that followed them. Clearly, it would have been passable after 13,000 years ago when the continental ice sheets and immense glacial lakes were in full retreat. But now there is evidence that people were living here at least several thousand years before that date, as evidenced in the Anzick site chapter.

A popular alternative to the ice-free-corridor hypothesis is that of a route southward along the Pacific Coast.[27] Although the Cordilleran ice sheet caused sea levels to drop, its tremendous weight pressed down so heavily on the land from Beringia to northern Washington State that the continental shelf remained submerged.[28] Thus, people could have paddled southward along the "kelp highway" in open boats made of wood and sewn animal skins ("umiaks"), landing on and inhabiting islands along the southern Alaska and Canadian coasts. On their way, these daring peoples lived on seals, fish, and other marine resources.

Once south of the huge Cordilleran ice sheet, some Paleoindian groups left their boats and proceeded on foot along the coast and adjacent lands. Their foot travels led them inland, ascending the Columbia River drainage and other major watersheds further south, and then across the mountains, basins, plains, and woodlands of continental America. The coastal route more easily explains the presence of Late Pleistocene archaeological sites in distant South America, such as the famous 14,500-year-old Monte Verde Paleoindian site in southern Chile.

Unfortunately, evidence for the coastal route is nearly as scarce as evidence for the ice-free-corridor route because when the glaciers melted, possible archeological sites were inundated by rising sea levels. Undaunted, archaeologists are modeling the topography of the continental shelf with the optimistic goal of finding submerged archaeological sites. Recent archaeological evidence demonstrates that Indian people occupied the islands off coastal British Columbia at least 13,000 years ago.[29]

In fact, the ice-free corridor and coastal routes might not be mutually exclusive. Recent genetic evidence suggests that there were at least two Late Pleistocene migrations of Eurasian hunter-gatherers to the Americas.[30] The first migrants traveled south from Beringa along the Pacific Coast some 16,000 years ago, which accounts for the surprising presence of the well-preserved, 14,500-year-old Monte Verde Paleoindian site in southern Chile and other early sites. A second migration occurred around 13,500 years ago once the ice-free corridor had opened. These slightly later Paleoindian migrants, possibly Clovis "culture" hunter-gatherers, expanded rapidly throughout North America, either displacing or, more likely, genetically mixing with pre-Clovis peoples. However, this intriguing hypothesis requires DNA testing of currently non-existent pre-Clovis skeletal material and the consent of American Indian peoples if it is found.

A third and entirely different possible route is across the North Atlantic Ocean. The evidence for this hypothesis rests on the close similarities between European Solutrean and American Clovis stone tool technologies. In this scenario, Upper Paleolithic Solutrean people traveled by land and perhaps boat along the exposed continental shelf from northern Europe to the eastern seaboard of North America.[31] As on the West Coast, marine resources facilitated their cold, Atlantic-bound journey.

Sadly for the proponents of this theory, genetic data from the Anzick site in Montana and the Paisley Five Mile Point

Caves in Oregon support the Asiatic origin of America's earliest peoples. But archaeologists Dennis Stanford and Bruce Bradley, two of the Solutrean hypothesis's proponents, point out that unexplained genetic signatures found in eastern North American Indian populations have no counterpart in Asiatic populations. Moreover, the number of genetic samples from ancient Indian populations are minuscule, making it difficult to draw absolute conclusions. The Atlantic route remains contentious among archaeologists.

That Upper Pleistocene peoples would trust their nomadic fates to small hide and wood boats may seem far-fetched. In fact, there is no direct evidence of these maritime migrations: we have no boat ruins, paddles, or depictions of sea voyages in rock art on either the Pacific or Atlantic coasts. Nevertheless, we do have evidence showing that the earliest ancestors of the Aborigines colonized Australia some 50,000 to 60,000 years ago[32] and that Polynesians settled many far-flung islands in the South Pacific millennia later. In both cases, little direct evidence of ancient seafaring exists, but there is no other explanation for the presence of people on these islands.

As the search for the First Americans continues, researchers will continue to find new evidence that modify or further illuminate the colonization scenarios depicted above. Even now, archaeologists claim to have found the remains of a 130,000-year-old mastodon kill site in California.[33] Does this mean an archaic Hominin group or an early wave of anatomically modern peoples came to the Americas that far back in time? At first glance, this claim seems doubtful. Rest assured, the scientific community will carefully scrutinize this paradigm-blowing claim and any others to follow.

Clovis sites, like Anzick near Wilsall, are extremely rare in Montana and across the West. As depicted here, the body of a child is buried in a talus slope above a small creek, accompanied by stone-and-bone hunting equipment necessary to ensure a successful Late Pleistocene afterlife. To date, human burials associated with Clovis tool caches are unknown in North America except at Anzick. Illustration by Eric S. Carlson.

ICE AGE MONTANANS

ANZICK SITE
24PA506

13,100 YEARS AGO

Millennia ago, grieving parents placed the red ocher-covered body of a two-year-old child into a shallow grave at the base of a sandstone escarpment in what is now southwestern Montana. We will never know what ceremony accompanied this small child's journey into the Upper Paleolithic afterlife. Perhaps a shaman conducted a ritual. But the child's people, the Late Pleistocene Clovis people of the Northwestern Plains and Intermountain West, are no mystery to American archaeologists.

Archaeologists in the 1930s first identified the Clovis culture from excavations at Blackwater Draw in New Mexico. (The site name derives from the nearby town of Clovis.) Used with the spear-thrower or atlatl (and possibly lances), the culture's distinctively shaped projectile points were found among the bones of mammoth, bison, horse, and other late Ice Age fauna in what was once a spring-fed marsh or lake. (It is now a gravel quarry.)[34] Later Indian camps lie above the 12,900 to 12,500-year-old Clovis level, indicating that this was an enduring place to hunt and live.

For a long time, archaeologists considered the Clovis people to be America's earliest human inhabitants, arriving here from northeastern Asia around 13,500 years ago. (Archaeologists call this idea the "Clovis First" hypothesis.) Beginning in the early 1970s, however, a handful of carefully excavated archaeological sites in North and South America clearly demonstrated that people arrived in the Americas at least 1,000-2,000 years before the Clovis-point hunter-gatherer bands. The 14,500- to 15,000-year-old layer (II) at the Monte Verde site in Chile revealed the frames of wooden structures; clay hearths; butchered mastodon meat and vegetable foods; shellfish remains; and stone, fiber, wood, and bone tools.[35] Meadowcroft Rockshelter in southwest Pennsylvania yielded pre-13,500-year-old cultural remains of a hunter's camp in a large rockshelter above Cross Creek.[36] A handful of equally early sites have now been found in other states.[37] At present, archaeologists don't know much about these earlier people, so they are simply called "pre-Clovis."

Pre-Clovis sites have yet to yield human skeletal remains from which ancient DNA might be extracted. However, Paisley Five Mile Caves in southeastern Oregon produced DNA from human coprolites or feces, predating 14,000 years ago.[38] Like the Anzick site, the DNA evidence supports a genetic connection with Eurasian peoples. All told, the genetic and cultural relationships among pre-Clovis, Clovis, and post-Clovis peoples are, for the moment, unclear. Early skeletal material is exceptionally rare and DNA analysis is controversial among American Indian peoples. Small non-Clovis and Clovis groups may have co-existed for an unknown period of time over truly enormous hunting-gathering territories. If the single early migration theory into the Americas holds true, then pre-Clovis peoples were the progenitors of later Clovis and non-Clovis bands.

At present, we don't know much about pre-Clovis in Montana because no very early sites have been found. One possible exception is the Lindsay mammoth site near Glendive in eastern Montana, which dates between 14,000 and 15,000 years ago—definitely pre-Clovis.[39] Here, incisions and breakage pattern on the bones of a single excavated mammoth seem to suggest human predation and butchering. Unfortunately, it is unclear whether the stones found in the silts associated with the mammoth bones are of cultural or geological origin. Only further work will determine whether Lindsay qualifies as one of America's oldest archaeological sites.

Thankfully, Plains archaeologists know a good deal more about what came next: the Clovis people. Anzick is Mon-

The late Ice Age landscape of the Shields River Valley was colder and harsher than today, with alpine glaciers present on the Crazy Mountains shown in the distance. Anzick Clovis people buried several small children at the base of the escarpment on which this photograph was taken. Some 13,500 years later, the remains of two of the Paleoindian children were reburied here in a poignant, multicultural ceremony.

tana's premier Clovis site. Located in the Shields River Valley of southwestern Montana, the site was discovered accidently in May 1968 by two local men using a front-end loader to excavate gravel from a sandstone escarpment and talus slope adjacent to Flathead Creek. Upon seeing a large stone tool in one of the bucket loads, the men hastily dug out more ancient stone and bone tools from what seems to have been a three-foot-deep pit in a layer of finely weathered sandstone within the talus slope. The extraordinary artifacts were caked in rusted-red colored hematite (iron oxide) or ocher, a pigment that early humans gathered and applied to tools, rock walls (in drawings or rock art), and perhaps to their own bodies.

Over the following week, the men returned to uncover more artifacts, as well as the similarly red-stained skeletal fragments of a one- to two-year-old child near the bottom of the pit. They also found cranial fragments of a six- to eight-year-old child without red ochre staining in the talus slope some 20 feet away. When the news of the discovery leaked out, the landowner, Dr. Melvyn Anzick, stopped the amateur digging and buried the cache pit under several tons of talus. Because these slightly later human remains and a bison kill are found near the same spot, the earlier child burial and tool bundle were eventually designated as Anzick-1.

Recognizing the scientific importance of this astonishing discovery, archaeologist Larry Lahren and Melvyn Anzick enlisted the help of Dee C. Taylor of the University of Montana, who hoped to find evidence directly linking the Clovis-age tools to the Anzick-1 child burial.[40] To his great dismay, Taylor could not establish a clear relationship because the amateur digging had mixed up the talus. The university crew found a few more artifacts by sifting the backhoe spoils piles, bringing the total to some 115 specimens.

Larry Lahren and other scientists later investigated Anzick to try to pin down the exact stratigraphic relationship between the tools and the Anzick-1 burial and better understand the local geology. Success was limited, although they did find a red ocher zone and a red-stained human clavicle at the site of what have might have been the child's grave.[41] Geological work suggested that the escarpment possibly contained a small alcove before being covered by talus sometime in the distant past.

All of the available evidence (including interviews with the discoverers) convinced most archaeologists that the stone and bone tool bundle and the tiny Anzick-1 child were from the same time period and were part of an ancient Clovis burial rite. The remarkable Anzick tools were so described in a few scientific journal articles and even graced the cover of a 1979 issue of *National Geographic Magazine.*[42] Thanks to Lahren's persuasion, the collectors and landowner, who had divided up the artifacts, loaned part of the Anzick collection to the Montana Historical Society Museum, where it can be seen today.

As a comprehensive report about all of the work at Anzick never materialized, professional interest in the site languished, but in 2014 the publication of the Anzick-1 child's genome put Anzick squarely in the Paleoindian spotlight.[43] Geneticist Sarah Anzick (granddaughter of the property owner), colleague Morten Rasmussen, Paleoindian expert Michael Waters, and a large research team successfully sequenced the Anzick-1 child's mitochondrial DNA (mtDNA). This highly stable part of our DNA is passed down solely through the female line.[44] When compared with the genomes of 143 contemporary non-African populations, including 52 Native American populations, the mtDNA analysis showed a statistically closer affinity to the Native American groups than to the other populations. The Anzick-1 child also showed a closer genetic affinity to Native populations in Central and South America than to the Native Americans of Canada and the Arctic. After some head scratch-

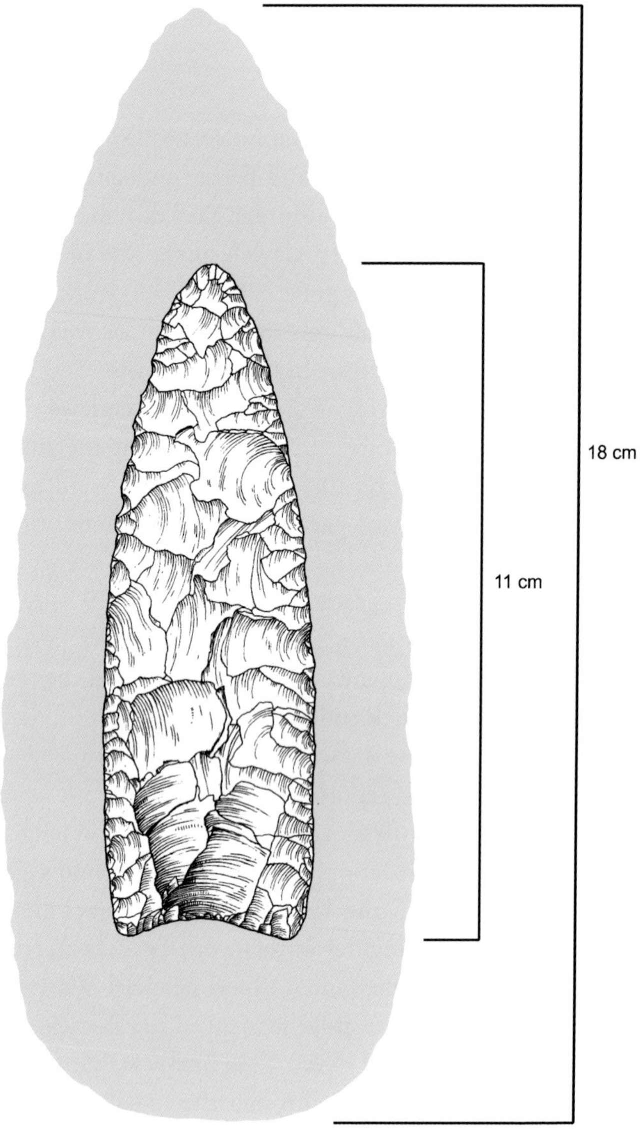

Clovis flintknappers used large-sized, high quality raw material to make distinctive projectile points. This illustrated Anzick Clovis point (4.3 inches or 11 centimeters in length) was manufactured from a bifacial core (7 inches or 18 centimeters in length), as shown in outline form, in the Anzick collection at the Montana Historical Society. ILLUSTRATION BY ERIC S. CARLSON.

ing, the researchers concluded that North and South American lineages genetically diversified prior to Clovis times.

Discovered on private lands, the Anzick human remains could not be repatriated under the federal Native American Graves Protection and Repatriation Act (NAGPRA) of 1990. (Repatriation is the legal return of human burials and funerary artifacts to their area of geographic origin and to the appropriate cultural groups.) Nor did the Montana human burial law strictly apply because the Anzick children were discovered prior to the law's enactment. Nonetheless, a coalition of archaeologists, geneticists, and tribal people cooperated in the genetic research and the reburial of both sets of ancient human remains in an intertribal ceremony in June of 2014.

Over the years, archaeologists obtained about a half-dozen radiocarbon dates from the Anzick skeletal material and the beveled, tapered, and pointed bone rods, some proving to be more reliable than others for technical reasons (contamination, use of older antler) that need not concern us here. According to recent assays, the red ochre-covered rib of the Anzick-1 child dates to circa 12,800 ago.[45] Two of the bone rods date to 12,900 to 13,100 years ago. The bone rods easily fit within the Clovis time frame—about 13,300 to 12,800 years ago—while the Anzick-1 child dates to near the end of the Clovis period. (The age discrepancy between the rods and Anzick-1 child is disconcerting but the dates generally overlap within the 2-sigma statistical range.)[46] The bleached skullcap of the older child is younger by about 2,000 years.

Uniquely, no other Clovis tool caches found in the United States are accompanied by human burials as at Anzick. Stratigraphic relationships, often reckoned in millimeters in bona fide archaeological digs, are unknown at Anzick. The original discovers' recollections can take us only so far. So, in fact, the exact relationship between the stone and bone tool bundle and Anzick-1 child burial remains ambiguous. Nevertheless, over time, the inferred association of the tools and the tiny Anzick-1 child led to the site's substantial reputation as the only known Clovis-age burial in the entire Americas associated with grave goods—what archaeologists call a mortuary or funerary assemblage.

The skillfully knapped Anzick stone artifacts are beautiful: leaf-shaped bifaces, point preforms, basally thinned Clovis points, scrapers, and flake tools. Some are made of fine-grained chert-chalcedony from quarry sources in central and southeastern Montana. Other lithic material comes from south-central Wyoming. Whether these far-flung tool stones were obtained directly by Anzick band members or through trade with other Paleoindian groups is, of course, impossible to know.

Oregon State University graduate student J. Scott Jones studied the Anzick stone tools as his Master's thesis, discovering that most were abraded and battered from use and transport.[47] His research proved these were functional tools, not specially made funerary items. Such items would have suggested social stratification or ranking among the Anzick people and the high status and prestige afforded this particular Clovis child. Instead, Jones and his mentor Robson Bonnichsen imagined that the tools were part of a "heirloom burial assemblage," whereby functional Clovis tools, handed down from generation to generation, were left in a simple burial pit following the death of the Anzick-1 child.

Anzick also yielded 15 complete and fragmentary elk antler rods.[48] Jones suggested that the rods, along with some of the stone tools, were deliberately broken as part of a Clovis mortuary ritual. The Anzick rods are similar to about 30 other specimens from a dozen archaeological sites across the United States, mostly in the American West. The function of these bone rods, long considered a hallmark of the Clovis culture, has puzzled archaeologists for a long time.

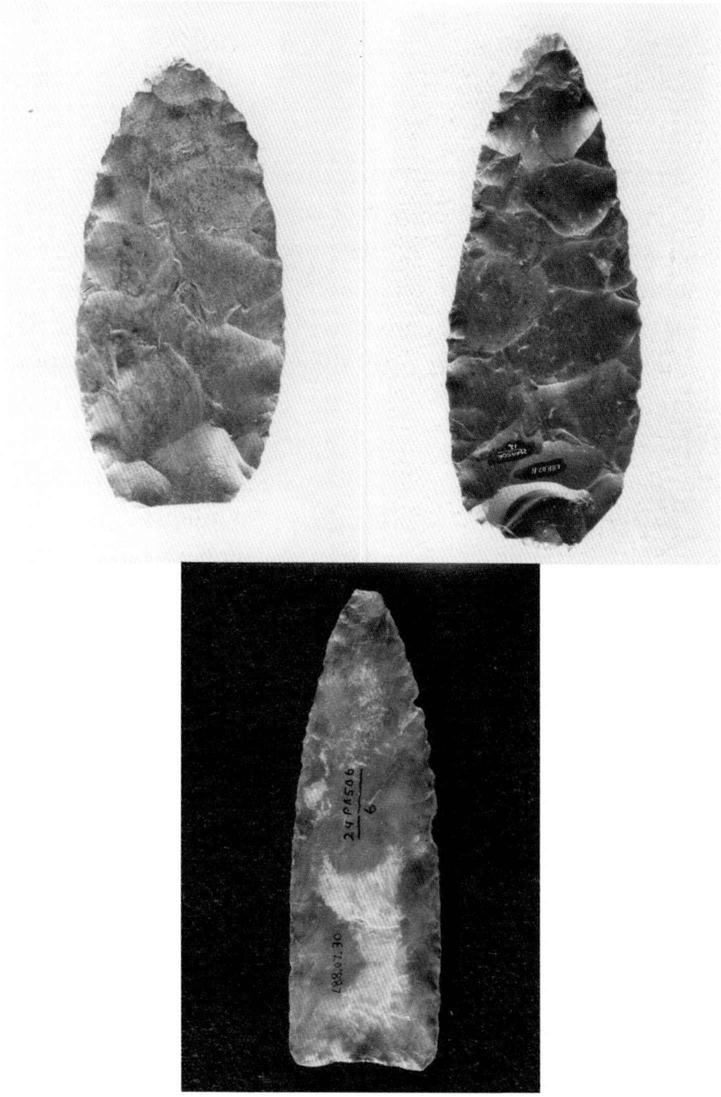

Many of the impressive Anzick Clovis artifacts are on display at the Montana Historical Society in Helena. Anzick Clovis projectile performs (top) and points (bottom), such as the ones shown here, were basally thinned and roughened on their lower lateral edges to facilitate hafting onto a lance or dart shaft. The nature of its discovery; dispersal of artifacts; and lack of a comprehensive report all hamper our understanding of the Anzick site. PHOTOGRAPHS COURTESY OF PHIL WILKE.

Anzick investigators Larry Lahren and Robson Bonnichsen first proposed that the bone rods served as lance foreshafts.[49] Similar to Eurasian Upper Paleolithic weaponry, the beveled end secured a stone projectile point in a mastic (pitch) and sinew wrap, while the rounded end was inserted into a socket of the main spear or dart shaft. Once thrust or thrown inside an animal, the embedded foreshaft detached from the main shaft and caused more internal slicing and hemorrhaging as the wounded animal moved. Paleoindians used these formidable composite weapons to bring down Pleistocene megafauna. Experimental hunting and butchering of dead and mortally wounded African elephants by modern archaeologists during herd culling at Hwange National Park in Zimbabwe reinforced this popular interpretation.

Other archaeologists see it differently. Based on their experimental replication work, Phil Wilke and his colleagues argued that the beveled Anzick rods were the handles of sturdy, composite pressure flakers—flintknapping tools—used with attached antler bits which have long since decayed.[50] In contrast, Lee Lyman and Michael O'Brien believe that the sinuous-edged points from the Richey-Roberts Clovis site in Washington (now known as the East Wenatchee Clovis site) were used as butchering saws. When tied on a bone handle, the tools were used to carve up Pleistocene bison and mammoth carcasses (no bone rods were found here).[51] In this scenario, bone rods like at Anzick served as hafting inserts or wedges to tighten up the sinew binding of well-used Clovis saws. The bindings have long since decayed away.

Archaeologists working at the Upper Sun River Site in the central Tanana River basin in Alaska have recently found evidence that may shed light on this long-standing debate. Here, four beveled bone rods were discovered in direct association with a child burial, one of which dated to 11,600 to 11,230

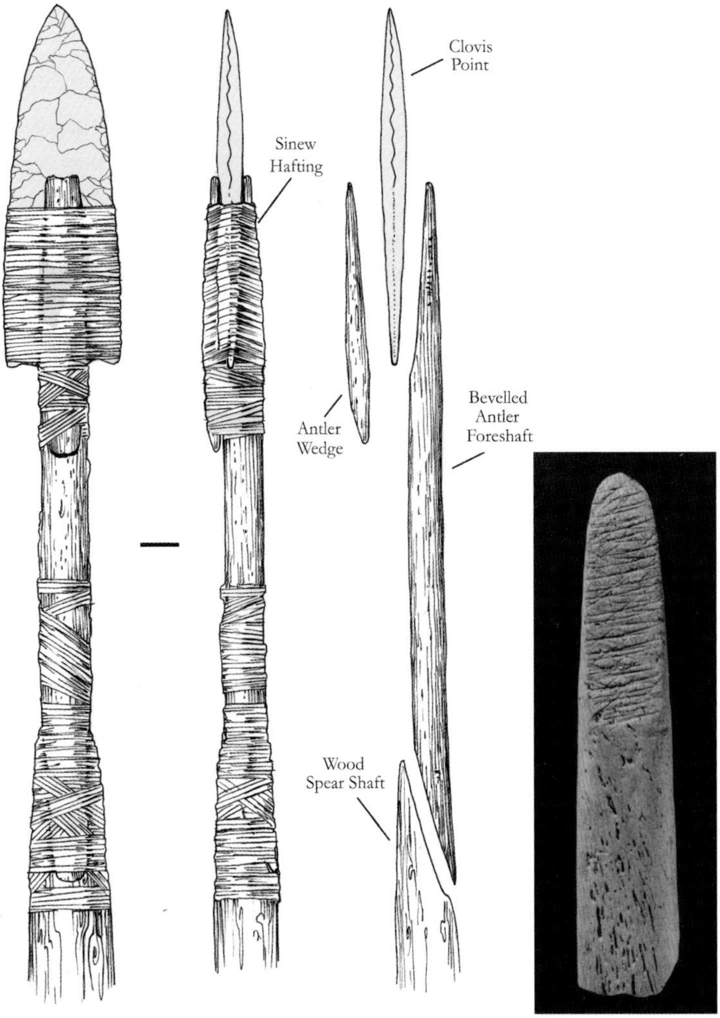

Beveled rods made of bone, antler, and ivory are considered a hallmark of the Clovis culture. The beveled or tapered ends of fifteen complete and fragmentary rods from Anzick were cross-hatched or scored with incised lines (photo). Among several interpretations, the most popular is that they were parts of detachable spear or atlatl dart foreshafts. Drawn in front and side view here, a sticky mastic (aided in gripping by the scored surfaces) and sinew wrap held the multi-piece foreshafts and Clovis points together. Adapted from Lahren and Bonnichsen (1974).

years ago (so a bit later than Clovis).[52] Two bifacial points were positioned at the beveled ends of two rods, suggesting that they functioned as atlatl darts or thrusting spear tips attached to bone foreshafts. Still, as Lyman and O'Brien point out, a "one size fits all" explanation may be misleading given the many kinds of tools used by Late Pleistocene peoples.

With their diverse stone and bone tool kits, Clovis people hunted and scavenged Pleistocene megafauna. Under deteriorating Late Pleistocene climatic conditions, Paleoindians hunted mammoths, mastodons, bison, and other Pleistocene fauna in ever-constricting refugia areas, according to Clovis authority Gary Haynes.[53] This hunting strategy may have triggered the migrations of Paleoindian bands across the grassy steppe of northeast Asia and Beringia, and then across North America.

Archaeologists also believe the pervasive focus on Clovis hunting of large Pleistocene megafauna is overblown, and that a myriad of cultural and ecological factors were the causes of population migrations. After all, mobility is a defining characteristic of hunter-gatherers, if not of humankind. Furthermore—in a now familiar theme—a wide range of cultural activities using non-durable or perishable technologies—animal and plant fiber string, cordage, hunting and fishing nets, baskets, bags, and so forth—have simply not survived. A portrait of Clovis lifeways remains incomplete.

Nonetheless, across the West, Clovis people preyed upon mammoths, mastodons, gomphotheres (another elephant-like creature), camels, giant ground sloths, and bison. Using analogies from modern African elephant behavior, archaeologists believe Pleistocene hunters deliberately targeted juvenile mammoths that occasionally strayed from small family herds. A wandering and vulnerable mammoth was surrounded and perhaps deliberately trapped by hunters in an arroyo, snowbank, or sand dune, and then dispatched with atlatl darts and lances.[54] This opportunistic hunting strategy intentionally reduced the chances of encountering the highly protective and aggressive herd matriarch or other mature elephants. Hunters may have returned several or more times to the same watering hole or browsing patch favored by mammoth herds. The relative scarcity of mammoth kill sites suggests that these hunts were not routine events, leading some archaeologists to jest that a band of Clovis hunters killed one mammoth and then spent the rest of their lives talking about it!

The "Pleistocene overkill hypothesis" claimed that highly successful Clovis Paleoindian hunting led to the extinction of Ice Age megafauna.[55] Most specialists now agree that rapidly changing Late Pleistocene climate and deteriorating periglacial habitats (the lands adjacent to glaciers) were the causes of their demise, with human hunting being only the *coup de grace*. After all, by the beginning of the Holocene somewhere between 40 and 60 genera and species of animals had disappeared globally, an amount which surely cannot be attributed to the hearty appetites of small, nomadic, Paleoindian bands.[56] In any case, Pleistocene megafauna were extinct by 10,000 years ago, with only a tiny surviving population of dwarf mammoth on Wrangel Island, Alaska, off the tip of Siberia. They survived until 3,600 years ago.

Clovis-age hunting and living sites have proven hard to find in Montana, although a small number of isolated Clovis projectile points have been discovered across the state by archaeologists and artifact collectors. The finds may be the only surviving evidence of sites that have long since eroded away, or they may be weaponry that was either lost or discarded after a hunt. In any case, Clovis (and pre-Clovis) sites are probably buried under many feet of sediment, hindering their easy discovery and investigation. Other sites no doubt eroded away millennia ago. Unlike their Upper Paleolithic counterparts in Eurasia, Clovis people apparently did not live in caves and rockshelters, for little evidence has yet been found in such places. Thus, Clovis shelter is poorly known.

Worldwide, Upper Pleistocene survival at northern latitudes depended on tailored hide clothing, shelters, bags, and other accouterments. Clothing that was tightly sewn with slender, eyed-bone needles and sinew thread gave anatomically modern (Cro-Magnon) people a cold-weather advantage over the archaic Neanderthals whose clothing was less tightly sewn together (with sinew and stone awls) and therefore less insulating.[57] One hundred or so bone needles have been recovered from a sprinkling of Clovis and later Paleoindian sites in the United States. At several such sites, bone needles found in spatially discrete areas hint at "sewing circles" and the important role of women in Late Pleistocene life.

Clovis people were adept hunters and foragers, moving about the Ice Age landscape with an intimate knowledge of animals, plants, fish, bird, and other biological and natural resources. Their pursuits brought them into new territory, which they settled, passed through, or passed by. In this way, the Clovis culture came to occupy most of the Americas. Specialists debate whether this widespread evidence reflects the actual movement of Clovis people or simply the transference of Clovis technology and ideas to existing pre-Clovis groups. It was probably both. Some experts (like Haynes) call Clovis a "fugitive culture" because its place of origin is elusive. However, other archaeologists now speculate that Clovis origins lie in the southeastern United States, where numerous Clovis camps are found, rather than in the American West where animal kill sites predominate.

Clovis disappeared archaeologically around 12,300 years ago. While some Clovis bands may not have survived the 1,000-year-long Younger Dryas cold snap, others are surely the genetic and cultural ancestors of succeeding Paleoindian peoples described in the Mill Iron and Barton Gulch chapters that follow. Wherever Clovis bands died out or evolved, the archaeological evidence suggests their successors were more technologically diverse and populous, acknowledging that estimating ancient hunter-gatherer population size is a precarious business and that better natural preservation may account for the increase in post-Clovis archaeological sites.

Clovis holds a strong spell on archaeologists as one of the most ancient and widespread cultural manifestations in the Americas. Clovis people made exquisite stone weaponry and hunted Ice Age megafauna. Although their role as the founding population in the Americas is now disputed, Clovis people led a rich Late Pleistocene hunting-gathering lifeway just like their Upper Paleolithic counterparts in Eurasia. Clovis is still the Late Pleistocene hunter-gatherer benchmark for the significant environmental, cultural, and technological changes that soon came to the Americas and Montana.

Pleistocene animal hunts required careful planning, coordination, and execution. At the Mill Iron site in southeastern Montana, depicted here, Paleoindian hunters lured a small group of *Bison antiquus* into a badlands arroyo, trapping and dispatching about 30 cows and calves with spears and atlatl darts while others escaped. Illustration by Eric S. Carlson.

HORNS AND SPEARS

MILL IRON SITE
24CT30

12,500 YEARS AGO

Tangling with large, unpredictable Ice Age bison would be unimaginable today without the benefit of a modern hunting rifle and the safety of a pickup truck. Yet millennia ago, Paleoindian hunters brought down these formidable Pleistocene beasts with stone, bone, and wood weaponry in countless places across Montana and the Northwestern Plains. Unfortunately, because they are so old, most Paleoindian animal kill sites have not survived the passage of time.

In the late 1970s, a proposal to repair a livestock-watering reservoir on Bureau of Land Management (BLM) rangelands near the small town of Ekalaka in far southeast Montana required archaeological review. As archaeologists often do, BLM staff wandered over to inspect a nearby butte while monitoring reservoir construction. Here they discovered bits of bone and several finely made Paleoindian projectile points, called Goshen, eroding out of the ground. (Goshen points are finely flaked points with straight or concave bases; the term also identifies the Goshen Paleoindian "culture.")

The soft sediments of the Fort Union Formation badlands have eroded and changed shape over the millennia, but pollen analysis revealed that the rolling sagebrush-grasslands habitat surrounding Mill Iron today would have looked familiar to Paleoindian peoples. PHOTOGRAPH COURTESY OF THE BLM BILLINGS CURATION CENTER.

The discovery of what became known as the Mill Iron site led to an important multi-year excavation by the University of Wyoming from 1984 to 1988. George Frison, the preeminent Plains Paleoindian expert at the University of Wyoming, led the dig with the support of the BLM, university students, and local archaeological society volunteers. No shoestring operation, the BLM, National Geographic Society, and the National Science Foundation funded the project. Mill Iron is a landmark study of Late Pleistocene archaeology in Montana.[58]

The environments of Anzick and Mill Iron could hardly be more different. Mill Iron lies on top of a low butte in the stark badlands of southeast Montana. Nearby Humboldt Creek, which is dry much of the year, drains northward into the more reliable, though sluggish, Box Elder Creek some miles away. Pine and juniper on the nearby Humboldt Hills provide a bit of shade. The soft sediments of the Fort Union Formation have eroded and changed shape over millennia. But pollen analysis by Linda Scott-Cummings revealed that the plants of the sage and grassland area have not changed all that much since the last Ice Age. Today's vegetation would have looked familiar to the Mill Iron Paleoindian peoples.

Excavations at Mill Iron first revealed an ancient campsite containing delicate but lethal Goshen projectile points, stone tools, and butchered bison bones buried beneath four and a

BLM archaeologists discovered the Mill Iron camp at the base of a badlands butte while monitoring construction of a livestock watering reservoir (shown in the distance). The multi-year excavation project revealed a 12,500-year-old Goshen "culture" campsite and bison kill site containing Goshen-style projectile points, stone tools, and butchered bison bone. Photograph courtesy of the BLM Billings Curation Center.

half feet of sediment. The large amount of butchered bones led the investigators to speculate that a bison kill site was located nearby. Anxious to see the condition of Mill Iron after a long, cold Plains winter, George Frison visited the dig in the early spring of 1987. By then, the team had collected enough data to warrant buttoning-up the project. (Today, archaeological sites are only partly dug in order to allow opportunities for future investigations with new technologies and research questions.) As luck would have it, Frison saw the remnants of an old bone bed eroding from a small drainage channel near a previously closed excavation trench. His fortuitous discovery prompted another season of fieldwork at Mill Iron.

Under a hot badlands sun, the archaeological excavators used bamboo picks and hand brushes to clear away soil from the highly weathered and fragile bison bone bed, which covered an area 12 feet by 15 feet. The bone bed was buried in slope wash and debris flows from the terrace above. The crumbly bone required chemical stabilization before it could be removed for analysis. Goshen points and other stone tools were mixed among the butchered bone. At first, the investigators thought the bone bed might simply be a secondary butchering area near an undiscovered bison trap. They also considered a natural die-off of bison, opportunistically scavenged by Paleoindian hunters. But careful study of the Mill Iron faunal assemblage led the investigators to conclude that the site was an actual kill location, although a poorly preserved one.

The first radiocarbon dates from charcoal in the camp and bone bed clustered around 12,600 and 13,200 years ago, respectively, both within the time ranges of Clovis and the early Folsom culture (a slightly later Paleoindian people who made smaller, delicate "fluted" points). But the bone bed dates were uncomfortably old for Goshen and the disparity between the dates from the camp and kill areas was also disconcerting. So

The student excavator shown here is carefully mapping the friable Mill Iron bone bed before it is stabilized and removed to a lab for analysis. By studying the Mill Iron bison remains, project faunal experts determined the age and sex of the killed bison; the season they were killed; Paleoindian butchering practices; and the extent of post-depositional damage by scavengers and natural processes. PHOTOGRAPH COURTESY OF THE BLM BILLINGS CURATION CENTER.

Frison's team thought that stratigraphic mixing and coal contamination from the underlying Fort Union Formation might have compromised some of the radiocarbon dates—a definite problem with this dating technique in coal country. Three radiocarbon dates recently obtained on bone (rather than campfire charcoal) from the bone bed ranged from 12,500 to 12,250 years ago.[59] These dates more closely align with the camp's timeframe and also show that the Goshen culture was a bit later than Clovis but is contemporaneous with (middle and late) Folsom Paleoindian groups on the Plains.

The camp and bone bed yielded stone points, knives, scrapers, and debitage (debris from tool making). The project's lithic experts concluded that few tools were actually made at Mill Iron other than expediently manufactured flakes whose sharpened edges were used in butchering and other camp tasks. Mill Iron peoples used a variety of local toolstone: Tongue River Silicified Sediment, porcellanite, chert, and other material. Knife River flint and other high quality toolstone are poorly represented. Unlike earlier Clovis and Folsom peoples, Goshen flintknappers did not create a central channel (flute) on both sides of their elegant dart points, for reasons unknown. (Many archaeologists think that thin bases and central flutes on Clovis and Folsom points facilitated hafting onto a foreshaft or main shaft.) Like changes in manufactured products today, projectile point styles changed for technological, aesthetic, and cultural reasons.

The Mill Iron excavators unearthed two unique bone artifacts. One is a tool handle or part of a lance shaft made from a mammoth rib. The investigators emphasized that this rare artifact doesn't necessarily indicate the presence of living mammoth during Goshen times. Rather mammoth carcasses and bones would have been available to scavenge for some time after their extinction, as even now they are occasionally discovered in the permafrost of Alaska and Siberia. The other item is an egg-shaped piece of bone that may have been part of a pendant, perhaps lost during the messy business of butchering bison or other camp work.

Today, faunal specialists can tell the species, age, and sex of the killed animals, the season in which they were killed, how they were butchered, which meat parts were carried away, and the extent of damage done by scavengers and nature to the butchering areas and spoil piles after the hunters departed. Faunal expert Larry Todd concluded that Goshen peoples at Mill Iron killed and consumed parts of at least 30 bison belonging to an Ice Age species called *Bison antiquus,* which had large skulls and horns. This formidable species descended from Eurasian

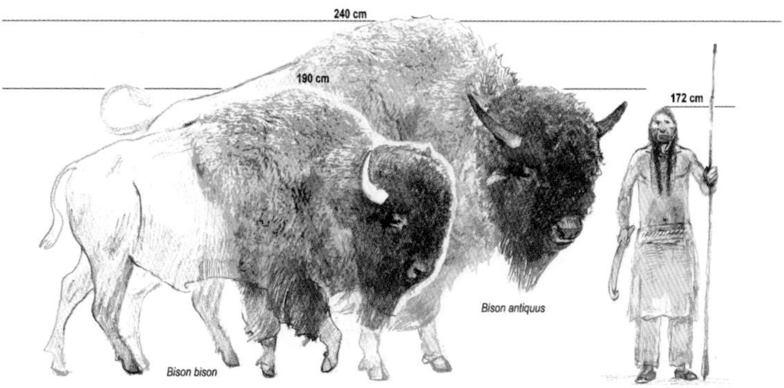

The formidable *Bison antiquus* from the Mill Iron site are descendants of Eurasian bison populations that migrated across Beringia to North America during a glacial period some 250,000 years ago. Modern bison (*Bison bison*) are descended from *Bison antiquus* and a later, intermediary form called *Bison occidentalis*. Illustration by Eric S. Carlson.

populations that had migrated from Siberia to the Americas across Beringia during a previous glacial period some 250,000 years ago. *Bison antiquus* disappeared about 10,000 years ago. The smaller, curved-horn *Bison bison* are descended from *Bison antiquus* and from a later intermediary form, *Bison occidentalis.* The ancient Mill Iron bison were mostly cows, killed in one or more episodes in the spring or early summer.

In his many fine books about ancient Plains Indian archaeology, George Frison describes the tricky and dangerous enterprise of ancient bison hunting. To be successful, hunters shared an intimate knowledge of animal behavior, landscape topography, and weather conditions, just like proficient hunters do today.[60] Unlike domestic cattle, and often forgotten by visitors to Yellowstone National Park, bison are temperamental, agile and

This mammoth bone fragment is one of two unique bone artifacts recovered from the Mill Iron site. A conical hole drilled into one end of the bone led investigators to speculate that this bone fragment is a remnant of a lance or dart shaft that once held a foreshaft. (The foreshaft and attached Goshen point shown here are replications.) The bone was probably scavenged from a long-dead mammoth carcass. PHOTOGRAPH COURTESY OF BILLINGS BLM CURATION CENTER, BILLINGS.

fleet afoot. How the hunters operated the Mill Iron bison kill is speculative because there is little surviving evidence of the hunting event itself. The topography of the badlands has changed over the millennia, effectively erasing older geomorphic features like deep arroyos. Furthermore, there is no evidence of postholes in the bone bed area to indicate the presence of a timber pound or corral (used by later Indian peoples, as discussed in the First Peoples Buffalo Jump chapter). However, the area partly lies within an old stream channel so the steep banks might have formed a natural enclosure or trap.

Mill Iron peoples knapped delicate but lethal Goshen-style projectile points and attached them to dart (and probably spear) foreshafts and mainshafts. Unlike earlier Clovis points or later Folsom points, Goshen points lacked the basal or central flute. Point styles changed and spread in prehistory for largely unknowable technological and cultural reasons. The Mill Iron camp and bonebed are linked by the mutual presence of exquisite Goshen points. PHOTOGRAPH COURTESY OF THE BLM BILLINGS CURATION CENTER.

If so, we might imagine that, over the course of an early spring morning many thousands of years ago, Mill Iron Paleoindian hunters separated a small group of cows and calves from the larger bison herd and slowly drove them toward the creek bottom and adjoining arroyo. A young hunter disguised in a bison robe mimicked the bleating of a lost calf, attracting the attention of the cows and drawing them even closer. Once at the mouth of an arroyo, other hunters, heretofore hidden behind rock piles and tall sagebrush, stampeded the bison into the confined space of the arroyo and began hurling atlatl darts and lances at the trapped and panicked herd. When the killing was done, hunters skinned the bison and transported large pieces of the carcasses to the nearby camp for processing. It is unlikely that such communal hunts were spontaneous events. The Mill Iron hunt was no doubt conceived, planned, and executed according to specific ritual practices and under the instruction and guidance of skilled hunt leaders and religious specialists or shamans.

By no means is Mill Iron the only Paleoindian *Bison antiquus* kill site on the Plains. But it is one of the oldest. The landmark discoveries in the 1920s of stone artifacts directly associated with extinct Pleistocene fauna at places like Folsom and Blackwater Draw, New Mexico, and Lindenmeier, Colorado, established, after a lot of academic controversy, the Pleistocene presence and antiquity of humans in the Americas.[61] Excavations also demonstrated that Paleoindian peoples brought the Eurasian tradition of tricking, trapping, and killing large mammals with them. However, as the Pleistocene megafauna (mammoth, mastodon, camel, and ground sloth) eventually became extinct due to climate and habitat change, possibly hastened by human predation, hunters broadened their focus to a wider range of game and plant resources.

By 11,000 years ago, Agate Basin, Hell Gap, Alberta, Cody, and other Late Pleistocene-early Holocene Paleoindian groups succeeded the widespread Clovis, Goshen, and Folsom cultures.[62] Apparently going their separate technological if not cultural and linguistic ways, these Paleoindian hunter-gatherers made exquisite and deadly leaf-shaped and stemmed atlatl dart points, which have long fascinated Plains archaeologists and, unfortunately, relic collectors too. (However obtained, there is still an active trade in American Indian artifacts, especially highly sought "paleo-points.") Specialists are able to identify subtle differences in the stone tool kits of these different Paleoindian

Goshen points and Goshen "culture" archaeological sites are rare in Montana but archaeologists know that Goshen succeeded the Clovis culture across the northern and southern plains millennia ago. The effects of the cold Younger Dryas climate reversal on Clovis and Goshen lifeways remains an intriguing but unresolved archaeological problem. Clearly, Goshen people continued to rely on bison as a food staple, as demonstrated at the Mill Iron site. PHOTOGRAPH COURTESY OF THE BLM BILLINGS CURATION CENTER.

cultures, but to the untrained eye they are simply the same homogenous blend of points, bifaces, scrapers, gravers, and flake tools used since Clovis times, if not well before.

Dogs accompanied Paleoindian hunting-gathering bands in their travels throughout what is now Montana. Genus *Canis* has a long and complex genetic history around the world.[63] Domesticated from wolves, dogs first appear in the archaeological record of Western Europe and East Asia between 33,000 and 18,000 years ago. (When and where dogs were first domesticated by humans during the Late Pleistocene is disputed.) Scientists speculate that wolves first tagged along behind Pleistocene hunting parties, scavenging left-behind carcasses and gut piles.

Emboldened, they later came to rest warily in the darkness at the edge of firelit caves and camps hoping to scavenge meat and bone scrap. This tentative human-wolf relationship offered mutual protection from denning Pleistocene animals like the fierce short-faced bear and the saber-toothed cat. "Self-taming" by wolves eventually allowed Pleistocene hunter-gatherers to capture, nurture, and train the now human-tolerant wolf pups. The first domesticated northern breeds may have looked like the Siberian husky or modern Samoyeds. By the early Holocene, dogs had become an integral part of hunter-gatherer life, serving as pack animals, hunting companions, camp sentinels, and food.

Dog bones are found in Montana archaeological sites but so far, none have been associated with the Paleoindian period. This lack of evidence is due to the very few Paleoindian sites excavations in Montana combined with the difficulty of distinguishing wolf, coyote, and domesticated dog bones in the archaeological record. Domesticated dog bones recovered from the Paleoindian Agate Basin site in neighboring Wyoming have led archaeologists to assume that dogs also accompanied early hunter-gatherer bands in Montana. Domesticated dogs are present in Montana sites dating to more recent time periods (the Hagan village site).

In contrast to Clovis groups, later Paleoindian peoples inhabited caves and rockshelters. They also built sturdy hide and pole lodges with slightly excavated floors, as inferred from the patterning of archaeological refuse, cobble rings, and dark sediments from fires and charcoal in well-defined depressions. More substantial housing may reflect a longer commitment to well-established hunting and gathering territories. This bigger archaeological "footprint" may equate with increasing human populations, although better site preservation also is a factor. While big game hunting was still the norm, the archaeological record shows a diversification of Paleoindian hunter-gatherer lifeways and subsistence strategies to accommodate early Holocene warming, environmental changes, and perhaps population growth and pressure, as indicated in the next chapter.

The Barton Gulch site offers a rare glimpse into Paleoindian diet beyond the pervasive focus on hunting and meat. As depicted here, charcoal was first made in open pits or braziers, shown by the woman with the stirring stick. The woman in the background is pouring hot charcoal into the bottom of a rock-lined roasting pit. The two women in the foreground place lamb's quarters on top of a layer of leafy greens in a roasting pit, as children look on. The plants were then sealed and cooked under another layer of greens, rocks, and soil. Popped seeds from charred lamb's quarters plants were ground on flat stones into meal and stored in hide or fiber containers. Located away from the smoke and activity, the Barton Gulch Paleoindian's camp is located in the distance. ILLUSTRATION BY ERIC S. CARLSON.

NOT BY MEAT ALONE

BARTON GULCH SITE

24MA171

9,800 YEARS AGO

Given the great importance of plants in the cultures of hunter-gatherers, archaeological evidence of their collection, processing, consumption, and use should be common in the archaeological record of Montana. Surprisingly, it is not. That the Barton Gulch site was spared the devastating effects of nineteenth and twentieth century placer mining in mineral-rich southwestern Montana is thus a preservation miracle, for this remarkable site tells us about the diets and culinary practices of early Holocene Indian peoples beyond their pervasive focus on hunting and processing of wild game.

Barton Gulch sits in the timber- and sage-covered foothills of the Greenhorn Mountains within the scenic Ruby River Valley. Located on both private and BLM lands, it covers a large, open terrace above a heavily mined perennial stream. Local garnet collectors first brought the Barton Gulch site to the attention of Montana State University (MSU) archaeologist Tom Roll. Their tip subsequently led to excavations under the direction of Leslie Davis and MSU crews in the late 1980s and early 1990s.[64]

The MSU research team uncovered three distinct Indian occupations buried within some 24 vertical feet of terrace sediments. The team first enlisted a dragline excavator (machinery with a large mechanical bucket suspended from a boom) to remove the placer mining overburden, making it easier to efficiently excavate the deep, underlying living surfaces containing chipped stone tools, animal bone, fire hearths, and cooking features. The Alder Complex, the oldest habitation, produced calibrated dates from 8,700 to 10,700 B.P., with the majority clustering between 9,200 and 10,000 years ago. The slightly later Hardinger Complex produced a thin scatter of stone artifacts and bone refuse, and the significantly younger Middle and Late Holocene (4,000-to 2,000-year-old) occupations lay on top of it.

The Alder Complex's cultural remains are important and unique. Its exposed "living floor" comprises four spatially discrete areas. Spaced uniformly about 12 feet apart, each area contained a shallowly excavated, fire-reddened basin surrounded by one or two unlined charcoal-filled pits. Small stains or "post molds" formed an approximate 18-foot-diameter circle around the basins. The investigators hypothesized the large circular features in the center of each of the four areas were open hearths or braziers used to make charcoal for cooking. The adjacent pits were earth ovens heated by the processed charcoal. The small surrounding stains may be the remnants of postholes supporting windbreaks or drying racks. The investigators did not think that the pattern of depressions and stains resembled the ruins of covered, subterranean pithouses (see the Spiro site chapter). Some style of stationary or transportable pole and hide lodges must have been built near the processing area.

How did the charcoal pits and roasting ovens function together? Steve Armstrong pondered this question as his Master's thesis project.[65] An "experimental archaeologist," Armstrong

Placer mining destroyed many archaeological sites during and after Montana's Gold Rush. Luckily, the Barton Gulch site was spared this fate, allowing Montana State University archaeologists to conduct important research here in the 1980s and 1990s. A dragline excavator was first enlisted to remove the overburden. Then the student excavators carefully excavated the Paleoindian-age Alder and Hardinger occupations buried deeply in terrace sediments. The gravel piles across the draw, opposite the excavations, are from placer mining. PHOTOGRAPH BY LESLIE B. DAVIS.

replicated the fire hearth and pit features at three different locations, including Barton Gulch. At each test site, he built hearths and roasting pits using templates of the originals; collected sagebrush and other fuels for charcoal production; gathered leafy insulating materials; and cooked cactus pods and seeds, popcorn, and rabbit and beef stew meat in the roasting pits. Armstrong's experiments did not precisely replicate either the appearance of the archaeologically recovered seeds (most were undercooked rather than charred or burned like

MSU archaeologists determined that this maze of dark soil stains and pits in the Alder Complex cultural layer were the residues of Paleoindian plant food processing. The largest circular features were open hearths or braziers used to make charcoal. The numerous small pits were below-ground earth ovens heated by the processed charcoal. The vast majority of the charred seeds recovered in the roasting ovens were slimleaf-goosefoot or lamb's quarters and prickly pear cactus. PHOTOGRAPH BY LESLIE B. DAVIS.

the originals) or the pit and hearth features. He suggested that some intermediary processing steps, invisible now in the archaeological record, lent to more thorough cooking. But Armstrong's work nonetheless sheds light on how wild plant food was cooked many thousands of years ago.

The Paleoindians of Barton Gulch clearly arranged their camp to allow ample workspace for processing and roasting wild plants. Large, open, fire hearths created charcoal out of sticks and branches of sagebrush, pine, birch, cottonwood, and willow. The Paleoindians placed hot charcoal in the bottom of the nearby roasting pits, followed by a layer of dirt and a layer of green, leafy, insulating material. Food, perhaps held in a wet hide or fiber pouch, was laid atop the leafy bed and covered with another layer of leafy material and soil. Ancient cooking times are unknown—seasonal temperature, wind velocity, and other factors would have all come into play. When the roasting pits were opened, the Barton Gulch cooks removed the "popped" seeds from the charred plants; ground them up; and then stored them either as meal or dried cakes in hide or fiber containers.

Roasting plants in subsurface ovens has a long history in ancient North America. These cooking features ranged from shallow depressions to deeper pits lined with cobblestone that held up the pit walls and captured the heat. The Alder Gulch Complex ovens contrast with later roasting pits in Montana by their lack of cobblestone linings. However, "hot-rock cooking" is not a common Paleoindian practice so the unlined roasting pits at Barton Gulch obviously worked well enough. Archaeologist Alston Thoms hypothesized that increasingly elaborate roasting features indicate efforts to recover more food to feed growing populations within defined, and possibly contested, hunting and gathering territories.[66] Roasting camas roots and bitterroot came to be a critical subsistence practice among the Indian tribes of western Montana and the Columbia Plateau. Roots and tubers were dug up with a 2-3 feet long, fire-hardened wood digging stick with an attached antler handle. Using ethnographic analogy, the strong focus on plant food collection and preparation at Barton Gulch demonstrates the important role of women in Paleoindian life.

Archaeologist Steve Aaberg processed a sample of charcoal-rich fill from the Alder Complex fire hearths, roasting pits, and postholes—about 273 gallons total—in a laboratory procedure called flotation, whereby lighter seeds and other herbaceous parts float to the surface of a water-filled tub. (Flotation, which models industrial milling and recovery of metals, became a common archaeological technique in the late 1960s.)[67] Aaberg recovered several thousand plant macrofossils representing 36 major plant groups. Nearly all of the recovered material comprised complete or fragmentary charred seeds, with the vast majority coming from the roasting pits.

Aaberg found that almost 90 percent of the recovered seeds were from slim-leaf goosefoot or lamb's quarters (*Chenopodium*) and prickly pear cactus (*Opuntia*). A small but diverse number of other kinds of seeds was also present, including ragweed, sedge, spurge, sunflower, chokecherry, limber pine, wild rose, and blue gamma. Chokecherry, wild rose, and other edible fruits, plants, and seeds were deliberately brought to camp, though apparently not in great numbers. Other weedy plants and grasses may be "camp followers," that is, plants which naturally thrived on trampled camp soils, inadvertently becoming part of the Barton Gulch archaeological record. Aaberg determined that the majority of recovered plants were gathered and processed during the summer or early fall.

Lamb's quarters, a fast-growing weedy annual, was an important economic plant for Plains Indians. Gathered when young and tender, lamb's quarters was cooked in pottage or else baked and "popped" to produce seeds that were ground into coarse meal. (Baking also ensured that the seeds did not sprout, making them less prone to spoilage.) Masticated leaves served as teas for stomach ailments and as a poultice for cuts, bites, inflammation, and arthritic pain. Prickly pear cactus, a common sight throughout dry southwest Montana, was also a nutritious food and medicine among Plains Indian groups. The fruit was eaten raw, boiled and sliced, dried, or roasted to yield seeds. Even the stickers were used as needles and for decoration.

Palynologist Glen Fredlund studied the ancient plant pollen and opal phytoliths (the silica structures of decayed plant tis-

Agitating hearth dirt in water-filled tubs (a process archaeologists call flotation) yielded abundant charred lamb's quarters seeds. The fast-growing weedy annual was an important economic plant for Plains and Intermountain Indian peoples. Lamb's quarters was gathered and eaten when young and tender or baked in earth ovens to produce "popped" seeds which were then ground into coarse, transportable meal. PHOTOGRAPH BY LESLIE B. DAVIS

sue) in the Barton Gulch sediments. Fredlund's work showed that the vegetation community was much like that of southwest Montana today: open parklands, sagebrush and grasslands, and upland pine-fir forest.[68] But he also noted several differences. Lodgepole and limber pine forest had expanded into lower elevations at the expense of ponderosa pine and Douglas fir, and there was a higher frequency of weedy vegetation and prickly pear cactus—all pointing to a drier climate. Pine species and cool season grasses—wheat grass, needle and thread, and wild rye grass—dominated the phytolith sample. The unusual presence of prairie junegrass, wild onion, and prickly pear phytoliths

The flotation process at Barton Gulch also yielded an abundance of prickly pear cactus seeds. A common sight in dry southwest Montana, prickly pear cactus was eaten raw, boiled and sliced, dried, or roasted to yield seeds. Its stickers were used as needles and for decoration. PHOTOGRAPH BY LESLIE B. DAVIS

led Fredlund to suggest that these plants were deliberately gathered and used by the occupants of Barton Gulch.

Alder Complex hunters returned to camp with mule and white-tailed deer, jackrabbit, cottontail rabbit, and porcupine. Bison are notably absent in the faunal sample. Deer were the game of choice, which is not surprising given that the sage-covered foothills of southwestern Montana are popular for deer hunting even today. Most of the mammal bone was crushed and pulverized with stone cobbles to extract iron-rich marrow "butter"—a common practice among Montana's first peoples. Faunal analysis showed that much of the game was killed and processed in late spring. With atlatls, Alder Complex hunters launched small- to medium-sized leaf-shaped Ruby Valley dart

Barton Gulch hunters returned to camp with mule and whitetail deer, brought down with Ruby Valley atlatl darts in the surrounding sage-covered foothills of the Greenhorn Mountains. Butchering evidence—cobble hammers and smashed bone—shows that deer bones were extensively processed to obtain iron-rich marrow "butter."

points to bring down big game. Many of these points and other artifacts were made of grainy quartzite—a popular raw material of Indian groups in southwestern Montana.

During the early Holocene, the Barton Gulch Paleoindians foraged in well-defined territories along the foothills and interior valleys of the Rocky Mountains. Investigator Les Davis estimated that bands seasonally inhabited strategically situated base camps like Barton Gulch, where as many as several hundred people may have lived for an extended period of time—no small crowd even by today's standard. Moreover, Barton Gulch was used intermittently for hundreds of years, reflecting its popularity as a base camp. Other archaeological sites in southwestern Montana share this same localized Paleoindian lifestyle but lack, as far as we know, an elaborate "kitchen" set-up as at Barton Gulch. Archaeologists have not determined whether this mountain-foothills cultural tradition evolved in place from Clovis, Folsom, and other early Paleoindian populations or is the result of migratory peoples moving in from the Plains or the Columbia Plateau.

Thanks to the modern technique of flotation, we can identify many of the specific plants harvested and used at Barton Gulch. Palynology and plant phytolith analysis provide an understanding of the vital role of plants in the cultures of Holocene hunter-gatherers. Still, these provide, at best, only fortuitous and seasonal snapshots. We must turn to ethnographies and tribal cultural specialists to appreciate the incredible range of plants used by American Indians, past and present, as food, spices, painkillers, sedatives, salves, anti-inflammatories, expectorants, diuretics, laxatives, stimulants, poultices, douches, soaps, insecticides, and tanning agents, as well as for a myriad of religious, social, and ceremonial purposes.[69] Plants were fabricated into arrow shafts, cordage, fish weirs, baskets, mats, and a wide array of other, now largely unrecoverable, gear.

Today, there is little archaeology to see at Barton Gulch. Although we know a lot about this critically important archaeological site, we must await a published report for the final word. Barton Gulch is documented in a VHS video produced in 1993 by the Museum of the Rockies in Bozeman entitled, *People of the hearth: Paleoindians of the Northern Rockies*. Shown widely in Montana school classrooms, this well-done video is a testament not only to the late Les Davis and his team's skills in examining the lives of Montana's Paleoindian hunter-gatherers, but also to their vision and dedication to archaeology education across the state.

Montana's early hunter-gatherers built different kinds of shelter to protect them from the elements. Living at the northern margin of the dry, exposed Bighorn Basin near the Montana-Wyoming border, Spiro hunter-gatherers built pithouses, which were shelters partly dug into the ground and roofed with poles, hide, brush, and dirt. Jackrabbits, shown being skinned and butchered in this illustration, were an important food source for Spiro people.
Illustration by Eric S. Carlson.

WINTERING OVER

SPIRO SITE
24CB1332

5,000 YEARS AGO

Montana's Plains Indian peoples are popularly known for their colorfully painted hide and pole tipis. Nomadic hunting and gathering lifeways required portable housing, and the tipi was the ideal solution. However, American Indian peoples of antiquity also constructed stationary wood, brush, and earthen abodes across the Plains and Intermountain regions. The least known of these housing styles is the subterranean pithouse, which was a shallow excavation roofed with poles, hide, brush, and earth. The Spiro Site is the only pithouse found thus far in Montana, though many others have been excavated in neighboring Wyoming. That mobile hunting-gathering peoples would invest in such substantial housing—and then abandon it altogether—is an intriguing aspect of Montana archaeology.

In 1996, archaeologists surveying the route of a proposed oil pipeline on BLM lands in south-central Montana discovered ancient pithouses.[70] Their discovery happened using remote-sensing equipment, which is frequently used to identify buried archaeological sites where there is little or no surface evidence. In this case, ground-penetrating radar, which uses radar pulses to create images of objects and features in the ground, revealed evidence of the pithouses. Because of this significant discovery, archaeologists quickly excavated part of the Spiro site as a way to mitigate the impacts of the pipeline trenching. Data recovery (once called "salvage excavation") is an accepted practice for ground-disturbing projects when preservation is not a viable option. Sunday Walker-Kuntz and her colleagues dug some 200 one-meter squares within the area to be impacted by the pipeline trench. Their work revealed pithouses, hearths, roasting pits, and camp debris. Spiro dates to about 5,000 years ago and was intermittently occupied over a span of 1,000 years.

The ecological setting of the Spiro site is telling. It covers an open, sage-covered slope overlooking Sage Creek to the north, which flows through the upper end of the dry Bighorn Basin. Even 5,000 years ago, shelter from the sun, snow, wind, and bad weather would have been important to anyone living in this beautiful but stark and challenging landscape for any length of time.

Nine pithouses, evidenced by shallow, elliptical-shaped pits and measuring six- to eighteen-feet across and one- to two-feet deep, were identified. Spiro people probably used wooden sticks to dig—an idea supported by the marks of digging sticks in the floor but not the walls of the Medicine House site in Wyoming. The exterior pit edges were easy to see on some of the Spiro pithouses but were less evident on others due to overlapping pits and hearth features. The village was repeatedly rebuilt over a long period of time. Heavily fire-reddened areas in pithouse interiors were the result of warming or cooking hearths, collapsed and burnt superstructures, or both.

Unfortunately, there is little evidence to indicate the type of superstructure covering the Spiro pithouses. At Wyoming pithouse sites, smallish, outlying reddened stains are thought to represent postholes of timber superstructures. But no reddened stains of posts were found at the Spiro site so lightly embedded poles obtained from nearby riparian areas may have supported

Federal historic preservation law allows land managers to conduct data recovery in order to mitigate the impacts of ground-disturbing projects to significant archaeological sites. At Spiro, archaeologists excavated 200 one-meter (3 feet by 3 feet) pits to remove a representative sample of artifacts and other evidence from the path of the Express pipeline corridor. PHOTOGRAPH COURTESY OF THE BLM BILLINGS CURATION CENTER.

brush or hide covers. Investigation of the Two Medicine House site in Wyoming revealed pieces of clay, which may be remnants of mud packing used to hold branches and brush together atop the roof. But, again, archaeologists found little evidence for this level of work investment at Spiro. This variability in pithouse construction no doubt reflects the ease of digging in tough prairie sod; the availability of building material; the season of use; and cultural, if not family, preferences. One pithouse at Spiro is larger than the rest and has an earthen bench around its interior perimeter. It had a large, central fire hearth. The investigators thought this feature might have been the only living structure at the site or, alternatively, may have served some special but unknown purpose, possibly as a place for group, clan, or kin ceremonies or events.

Three styles of fire hearths and ovens are found inside and around the Spiro pithouses. One type heated rocks for stone boiling and cooking. Stone boiling involves placing heated stones inside a hide "pot" containing water and food to be cooked. The hot stones slowly bring the water to a boil and thus cook the food. Another type is the unlined, roasting oven similar to those at Barton Gulch. Three deeply baked and hardened "cylindrical" pits containing massive amounts of charcoal were probably the source of the fuel used in the roasting pits, again like those at Barton Gulch.

Spiro women, and perhaps men, used flat mealing stones or *metates* and hand-held *manos* to grind seeds, dried roots, and possibly even insects like grasshoppers into a course meal or flour. Pollen and floral analysis revealed the presence of biscuit root, slim leaf goosefoot, prickly pear, and various grasses. This evidence and the roasting pits clearly show the importance of wild plants in the diets of the ancient Spiro people.

Spiro hunters supplied their small village with rabbit, deer, antelope, bison, and fish. Jackrabbit was the most common

Jackrabbits were an important food for Spiro peoples living at the northern end of the Bighorn Basin some 5,000 years ago. In addition to protein, rabbits provided warm, soft pelts that could be sewn into clothing such as capes, hats, and belts. Historically, Great Basin Indian peoples hunted rabbits with bows and arrows, traps, snares, and capture nets made from plant fiber. Unfortunately, no direct evidence for clothing styles or rabbit hunting methods survives in the archaeological record at Spiro. PHOTOGRAPH BY CHRISTOPHER CAUBLE.

meat. The preponderance of jackrabbit remains in the faunal record suggests that the rabbits may have been communally hunted, which involved men, women, and children walking across a small basin and beating the vegetation in order to drive the skittish creatures into a corral made of long, woven, plant fiber nets.[71] Here they were dispatched with wood clubs. (Ancient rabbit nets and clubs are found in well-preserved Great Basin cave sites.) Up to the historic period, Great Basin Indian peoples hunted rabbits in this way, as well as with an assortment of snares and traps. Great Basin and Plains Indians also hunted antelope in a similar way but used timber and brush "fences" rather than twisted fiber nets. Besides being a tasty meat source, rabbit pelts may have been woven into warm robes or capes like those worn by Great Basin Indian peoples, although this is only speculation because there is no direct archaeological evidence for fiber hunting nets or clothing at Spiro due to poor preservation.[72]

The patterning of camp debris shows that Spiro people worked inside and outside their covered lodges. Different kinds of stone tools were found but simple flake tools, probably used in many different tasks, predominate. Men and women crafted bone awls, abraders, and beads for tools and decoration. Pollen analysis indicates the presence of grass inside the lodges, which could represent floor insulation or bedding, or it could simply be intrusive and non-cultural.

Based on their sturdy construction, presence of food storage pits, and the floral/faunal evidence, archaeologists think pithouses were primarily used during the winter. During this harsh season in the Bighorn Basin, Indian peoples ate stored seeds, dried tubers, and coarse meal complimented by dried and fresh rabbit, deer, and other game hunted on sage- and juniper-covered winter range. But here Spiro becomes problematic because it lacks storage pits, at least in the excavated area, and the floral evidence points to a late summer to early fall habitation. So, the Spiro pithouses might have been built for cooling summer shade rather than protection from freezing winter winds and blizzards. Whatever the case—and archeologists aren't sure with Spiro—pithouses are clearly responses to local environmental conditions.

Pithouses took time and effort to build. They were constructed in environments that gave Indian peoples easy access to foothill and basin landscapes with reliable food resources. This more sedentary way of life may give the impression of a busy Indian

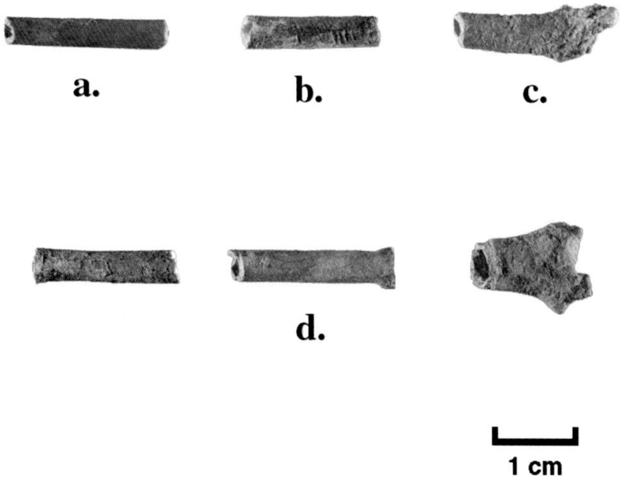

Stone tools and decorative shell items, such as these tubular bone beads, indicate that a variety of domestic activities occurred at Spiro. Still, the small amount of camp refuse indicate that pithouses were occupied only intermittently and relatively briefly by Spiro hunter-gatherers during their seasonal movements. PHOTOGRAPH COURTESY OF THE BLM BILLINGS CURATION CENTER.

village—a "Spiro Town" if you like. Not really. The relatively scarce cultural remains at Plains pithouse sites like Spiro indicate these places were only longer stops in the seasonal rounds of nomadic peoples. By comparison, the pithouses of the well-known Puebloan (Basketmaker Culture) people of American Southwest and Native Alaskan villagers were far more elaborate and occupied semi-permanently.

Northwestern Plains pithouses date between 8,000 and 1,000 years ago.[73] They are often buried under several feet of subsequent sediment, and thus leave few traces on the ground surface. Many in Wyoming were discovered in deep trenches excavated for oil and gas pipelines. More than 50 pithouse sites are now known on the northwestern Plains, but only one, the Spiro pithouse, has been found in Montana. Others may be found as university and CRM research continues across the Plains and Rocky Mountain foothills.

Pithouses are most strongly associated with the Altithermal period of 9,000 to 5,000 years ago. Hot, dry conditions may have placed a priority on group territories with reliable plant and animal resources.[74] Indeed, as prolonged heat and drought across the Plains reduced the size of subsistence areas, hunter-gatherers migrated to the wetter valleys and basins or cooler mountain foothills. Animal and human populations may have declined. In fact, there is a noticeable drop in the number of known archaeological sites dating to this time period, but this may be due to archaeological site loss in parched, erosion-prone landscapes. In any event, people lived in pithouses on basin floors during the frigid winters, or hot summer months, or both. A return to a cooler climate and better environmental conditions allowed nomadic groups to spread out again.

Of course, Montana's ancient hunter-gatherers did not live exclusively in covered pithouses during or after the long Altithermal. They also inhabited caves and rockshelters as temporary stopovers and base camps, as discussed in the Pictograph and Ghost caves chapter. Outside of caves, the patterns of archaeological refuse—stone tools, chipping debris, bones, cobbles, hearths and other refuse—are the footprints of long-vanished, portable, and stationary Indian lodges.

About 3,000 years ago the pole and hide tipi became the shelter of choice for Montana's hunter-gatherers.[75] These transportable lodges are evidenced today by circular patterns of stones called tipi rings. (Some Indian peoples part ways with archaeologists and consider these stone rings to be ceremonial circles,

Pole and hide tipis came into widespread use on the Plains about 3,000 years. The transportable lodges are evidenced archaeologically by circular patterns of stones called tipi rings, one shown here. Tipi rings range from 15 to 30 feet in diameter. Cobbles and wood stakes held down the hide covers. Thousands of tipi rings are identified throughout Montana. PHOTOGRAPH COURTESY OF THE MONTANA STATE HISTORIC PRESERVATION OFFICE.

not evidence of tipis.) Rock cobbles and wood tent stakes held down the bottom of the tipi covers and interior frost liners, which hung from the lower poles inside the lodge to provide both insulation and interior storage space.[76] Ranging from 20 to 30 feet in diameter, tipis could comfortably hold a single extended family. Rings typically have a central fire hearth. Made of a dozen or more tanned bison hides sewn together, tipi covers lasted several years. Artifacts are often scarce inside tipi rings, suggesting that many tasks were done outside the tipi or perhaps hide robes on the floor held the interior debris, which was then tossed aside when the camp moved on.

Tipi rings proliferate in number around 2,000 years ago, possibly correlating with a more temperate climate, flourishing grasslands, growing bison herds, and human population growth. Tipi rings number in the thousands across the plains and foothills of northern Montana, which also has the richest concentration of bison kill sites in the state. Indian bands camped in tipis on the open plains throughout much of the year. To escape the harsh cold and the snow- and sleet-laden winds, Indian bands wintered in sheltered valley bottoms where firewood and horse pasturage (once horses had become a part of Plains Indian life) were readily available, as Charlie Russell's paintings and Edward Curtis' photographs from the late 19th and early 20th centuries evocatively depict.

Not all stone arrangements represent tipi rings. Smaller, low-walled rock circles are fasting beds used by initiates during vision quests, as known from ethnographies and tribal informants.[77] Others are hunting blinds, and some are stone forts in strategic locations such as mountain passes. Larger, more elaborate boulder formations include raised mounds, large human effigies, serpents, animal, and geometric designs, and circles or wheels with spokes or rays, like the famous Bighorn Medicine Wheel located on top of the Bighorn Mountains of Wyoming.[78] The boulder arrangements were apparently built for ceremonial, astronomical (solstice), and religious purposes whose cultural content and meaning varied from tribe to tribe.

When cold Montana weather descends, it is hard to imagine living year-round in the outdoors without a substantial shelter. Or, for that matter, surviving Montana's summers, months on end, of often intense heat, dust, smoke, and pesky insects without recourse to screened or air-conditioned spaces. Yet, living in a wide range of stationary and portable shelters, Montana's Indian peoples survived and flourished. Their shelters were not simple either, for as Spiro attests, they required an investment of time and energy to build and maintain. In any case, the many different kinds of shelters used by Indian bands provided protection from the elements, warmth, shade, sleeping quarters, storage, social space, and a secure place to nurse infants and corral young children. It is no wonder that many Plains Indian peoples were reluctant to move into dark, cold, smoky log and adobe cabins during the reservation period of the late nineteenth and early twentieth centuries.

Plains Indian hunting-gathering bands intermittently occupied Pictograph and Ghost caves from about 5,000 years ago into the historic period (ca. 1800 A.D.). This illustration shows an extended family band arriving at Pictograph Cave some 1,000 years ago. Prior to the adoption of the horse in the early 1700s, nomadic hunter-gatherers carried the necessities of life on their backs, using dogs to pack loads and to pull small pole sleds called travois. Illustration by Eric S. Carlson.

PINE PARKLAND LIVING

PICTOGRAPH AND GHOST CAVES

24YL1 & 2

4,000 YEARS AGO

Much of what archaeologists know about world prehistory is derived from caves. The bones of our hominin relatives and ancestors lie deeply hidden in natural shelters from the tip of South Africa to the China Sea. The early modern peoples of Africa and Eurasia took up residence inside caves or used them for ceremonies. In the Americas, over the millennia, hunter-gathers came to rely on caves as home bases and temporary shelters.

As one consequence, the discarded refuse of ancient hunters and gatherers accumulated within layer-cakes of sediment in favored caves, preserving, to the delight of modern archaeologists, long sequences of human habitation. These natural shelters enable archaeologists to recover evidence about past climate and environment and how hunting-gathering societies responded, interacted, and changed over time. Evidence from caves gives scientists the "long view" of ancient environments and human cultures.

Cave dwellings and rockshelters dot Montana's landscape.

Much of what archaeologists know about world prehistory is derived from cave excavations. In Montana, few are of the size or archaeological importance as Ghost and Pictograph caves, which are now part of Pictograph Cave State Park near Billings. For centuries, Ghost and Pictograph caves were occupied by nomadic Indian bands. PHOTOGRAPH COURTESY OF MONTANA STATE PARKS.

Few are of the size or archaeological importance as Pictograph and Ghost caves near the city of Billings in southeastern Montana. The scientific importance of these caves is recognized by their inclusion in the Montana State Park system and their National Historic Landmark status. (Landmarks are nationally significant historic places designated by the Secretary of the Interior-National Park Service.) The human history of these caves is at once a story of the very beginnings of professional archaeology in Montana and a window into the foraging ways of native hunter-gatherers who were finely attuned to the pine parklands region, beginning some 5,000 years ago.

Montana archaeology owes its professional beginnings to the Great Depression of the 1930s. As one way to ease the severe economic hardship, President Franklin Roosevelt's Works Project Administration (WPA) employed young men and women in archaeological fieldwork.[79] In the late 1930s, Melville Sayre, a geologist with the Montana School of Mines in Butte, organized

During the Great Depression of the 1930s, the Works Project Administration (WPA) employed workers in archaeological survey and excavation projects around the country (nearly all were untrained in archaeological field methods prior to their employment). At Ghost and Pictograph caves, Melville Sayer, Oscar Lewis, and William Mulloy supervised the WPA crew shown here. The crew lived in Ghost Cave and Empty Gulch, excavating year-around. PHOTOGRAPH COURTESY OF HALCYON LAPOINT, CUSTER-GALLATIN NATIONAL FOREST.

WPA archaeological projects across eastern Montana. In one instance, rainwater gushing over a sandstone rimrock near the city of Billings exposed Indian artifacts inside a spacious "painted cave." Several locals reported their discovery to Sayre and his WPA foreman Oscar Lewis. WPA excavations were planned immediately at the newly named Pictograph Cave in cooperation with the Montana Highway Commission, Yellowstone County, the City of Billings, and the Billings Chamber of Commerce—a unique but necessary collaboration to receive WPA funding.[80]

Surprisingly, how Ghost Cave got its name is unclear. One possible explanation is that it derives from the general Crow term for places with "ghost writing" or rock art. No rock art is

Caves can be notoriously difficult to excavate because of their complicated layering of sediments, or stratigraphy. Digging through sandy sediments and around roof-fall (boulders) of all sizes, the WPA crew dug Pictograph Cave to a depth of 28 feet, removing most of its cultural deposit and resulting in the final, complex stratigraphic profile shown here. PHOTOGRAPH COURTESY OF HALCYON LAPOINT, CUSTER-GALLATIN NATIONAL FOREST.

found in Ghost Cave but it is abundant in nearby Pictograph Cave. This Crow appellation may have been shortened and adopted by the WPA crew (but that is a guess).

Even with modern technology, caves are notoriously difficult to excavate. Archaeologists must decipher a complex arrangement of sediments laid down by wind, water, and roof disintegration, and disturbed by these very same processes plus burrowing and denning animals and the activities of ancient peoples and modern relic collectors. From the start, problems plagued the WPA excavation of Pictograph and neighboring Ghost caves. Relic collectors had pockmarked the caves' floors with their uncontrolled diggings. Neither Sayre nor his WPA workers had formal archaeological training, although Oscar Lewis was an adept recorder of the dig's progress. WPA field

methods were unrefined—the caves were excavated in one-foot vertical levels rather than by natural stratigraphy or in the tiny centimeter, if not millimeter, increments used today. Controversy ensued over laboratory locations and the disposition of the artifacts. A fire burned down a small museum built near the caves, destroying equipment and records. Proving to be an enthusiastic archaeology salesman but a poor project manager, the WPA relieved Sayre of his duties in 1938, and Oscar Lewis took over supervision.

As Depression-era excavations progressed at places like Pictograph Cave, WPA program administrators became alarmed by the lack of work quality and pushed for professionally trained supervisory staff. Thus William Mulloy arrived on the scene as director of the Montana Archaeological Survey and WPA projects. A professional archaeologist, later famous for his work on Easter Island in the South Pacific, Mulloy took charge of excavations at Pictograph Cave in 1941. By then, WPA excavators had removed all of the cultural deposit in Ghost Cave and most of it in Pictograph Cave. Nonetheless, Mulloy managed, in less than a year, to work out the stratigraphic sequences of both caves using his own records and Oscar Lewis's careful field notes. World War II military service interrupted Mulloy's research, but in 1958 he published the first prehistoric chronology of the Northwestern Plains using his data from Pictograph and Ghost caves and surrounding sites. It is one of the most widely read and enduring archaeological works on the northwestern Plains.[81]

WPA workers recovered an extraordinary collection of stone, bone, and perishable artifacts in 23 vertical feet of sediment in Pictograph Cave. They excavated through 40 vertical feet of sandy deposit in Ghost Cave, but only the upper eight feet contained cultural material. Mulloy's stratigraphic reconstruction led him to infer that caves were used by Indian peoples from the Middle Prehistoric to the Historic periods (that is, from the mid-Holocene onward). He puzzled over the few so-called "Yuma" points found by the WPA crew, suspecting they represented either an ephemeral Early Prehistoric Period occupation or were picked up elsewhere and "curated" by later Indian peoples at Pictograph Cave.

Recent research by Montana State Parks archaeologist Sara Scott helps clarify the cultural chronology at Pictograph Cave.[82] Using a 3-D computer model of the original excavation grid, Scott obtained radiocarbon dates from a small sample of precisely plotted bone artifacts taken from various depths within the cave's sediments. The oldest dates cluster around 4,300 years ago while others occur later in the Holocene. The dates match the kinds of projectile points and other cultural material found in the cave. Scott's dating sample is very small and an earlier Paleoindian ("Yuma") habitation may be mixed with later ones. Also, earlier cultural deposits may have washed or eroded out of the cave. For now, however, the radiocarbon evidence suggests that the first well documented occupation of the cave began during the mid-Holocene, around 5,000 years ago.

Throughout 5,000 years, the inhabitants of Pictograph Cave hunted bison, deer, antelope, rabbit, turkeys, grouse, and other

Three bone harpoon points, one shown *in situ* here during WPA crew excavations, are rarely found in Montana. This fishing tackle was apparently used to catch channel catfish, paddlefish, and bull trout in the lower Yellowstone River. The WPA crew did not find any fish bones in Pictograph Cave, but this was due to their coarse recovery methods. Harpoons indicate that fishing complimented hunting and plant food gathering in the late Holocene. PHOTOGRAPH COURTESY OF THE MONTANA HISTORICAL SOCIETY RESEARCH CENTER-PHOTOGRAPH ARCHIVES, HELENA, MONTANA.

pine-parklands species, following the same broad foraging pattern described at the Spiro site. Worn-out projectile points, dull or broken butchering knives, and discarded dart and arrow shafts (several with projectiles and sinew wrapping still attached) were distributed throughout the cultural deposit. The success of the hunters may have coincided with cooler climatic conditions and improved animal habitat following the hot Altithermal. Bone harpoon heads suggest that catfish, bull trout, and other species in the Yellowstone River and its tributaries were speared or caught with traps and weirs made of willow. Fish bones were not recovered, but this is likely due to poor preservation and the selective recovery of artifacts by inexperienced WPA workers.

Pictograph Cave people collected raw materials and plants from nearby riparian areas.[83] Artifacts of willow, cottonwood, and common reed (all found in wetlands) were made into arrow shafts, tool handles, snares, and other items. The abundant husks of the prairie turnip—a starchy tuber—suggest this was an important food source. Nearby pine, juniper, willow, and sage stoked campfires and food roasting pits. Although none are present in the existing collection, Oscar Lewis reported seeing abundant chokecherry pits in the cave. If ever excavated or cored, the small amount of remaining intact sediments at Pictograph Cave could someday yield plant macrofossils, pollen, and phytoliths, providing more complete knowledge of the plants eaten and used by the people living in Pictograph Cave.

The cave's inhabitants used wood, bone, and antler to create a wide assortment of digging sticks, awls, knapping tools, fleshers, scrapers, chisels, gaming pieces, pendants, whistles, beads, bow guards, and shell bracelets. Several dozen pieces of stitched wood bark may be remnants of a vessel. Camp artisans crafted river mussel shells into disks, pendants, rings, and bracelets. Olivella and dentalium shells were made into fine beads. Women made hide moccasins, clothing, bags, and other articles

The peoples of Pictograph Cave started their warming and cooking fires with hearth sticks, shown here, and drills or spindles. By vigorously spinning (by hand or with a small bow and hide) the drill in the socket, the friction created extremely small coal, which was carefully blown into flame and fed with small bits of grass and kindling to create tinder. The flaming tinder was then used to start camp fires. Three juniper hearth sticks were recovered from Pictograph Cave. This one is about 520 years old. PHOTOGRAPH COURTESY OF SARA SCOTT.

This shredded branch of limber or ponderosa pine is called a tinder stick. Its matted clump of pitchy shavings probably provided the tinder for starting fires with hearth sticks and drills. The tinder stick is about 960 years old. PHOTOGRAPH COURTESY OF SARA SCOTT.

with bone fleshers, awls, needles, and sinew. Sometime within the last 500 years, people used pottery containers to store food, carry water, and cook pottages and stews on open hearths in Pictograph Cave. In sum, this is the surviving refuse of daily domestic life.

Fires in the hearths found throughout the cave deposit were started with a wooden drill (spindle) spun in the socket of a hearth stick. This created enough friction and heat to ignite grass or wood tinder.[84] One juniper specimen is more than 500 years old. The tinder may have come from a shaved tinder stick similar to a 950-year-old pine specimen found in an older layer. Saturated with pitch, tinder sticks are excellent fire starters.

Ghost Cave also yielded an extraordinary artifact collection. Archaeologist Dave Schwab identified distinct material concentrations within the cave, including spots where river mussels were processed for food and their shells for ornaments.[85] From the number of arrow points and knife pieces, Schwab thought that Ghost Cave served as place to retool and repair equipment in anticipation of communal bison hunts. In a broader perspective, the material culture of Ghost Cave resembles the contents of other sites scattered across southeastern Montana that date between 1,500 and 800 years ago.[86] At such places, these culturally related, but ethnically unidentifiable, Indian groups (called Beehive by Plains archaeologists) occasionally occupied squat log and stone slab houses on top of prominent sandstone buttes.

Some Ghost Cave artifacts indicate far-reaching trade networks. A fragment from a coiled basket or seed-parching tray from Ghost Cave is 1,370 years old and closely resembles those made by northern, semi-agricultural Great Basin Fremont peoples. Gaming dice, shell ornaments, and other artifacts may also be trade goods obtained from distant peoples. Some archaeologists speculate that the Beehive peoples were ancestral Kiowa or Athabascan peoples who once lived in

Indian basketry is uncommon in Montana due to its poor preservation qualities and the wide use of animal hides for containers and gear by Plains Indians. This 1,370-year-old coiled basketry fragment from Ghost Cave, and a small sample of similar basket fragments from archaeological sites in canyons and mountains south of Ghost Cave, suggest far-reaching trade contacts, possibly with northern Great Basin peoples. The fragment shown here may have been part of a tray used to parch plant seeds. PHOTOGRAPH COURTESY OF SARA SCOTT.

Montana before migrating southward to the southern Great Plains and American Southwest.[87]

Pictograph Cave is best known for the hundred or so multicolored paintings covering its back wall. Mulloy recorded them on large sheets of butcher paper, which now safely reside in the archives of the University of Montana Library. Painted in black, red, and white with fingers, "crayons" (lumps of pigment mixed with animal fat), and brushes, the paintings range from nondescript images to depictions of warriors carrying large, circular shields and weaponry (described in the Bear Gulch chapter). There are animal figures such as bison, bear, elk, birds, and turtles, one of which (painted in black charcoal) is radiocarbon dated to about 2,100 years ago.[88] Rather than portraying a food

Pictograph Cave is best known for its colored paintings, or pictographs. Today, most of the pictographs are faded and difficult to see. Some, such as a charcoal turtle figure, have spalled off the cave wall. For the benefit of visitors, Montana State Parks staff developed this photographic overlay to more clearly show part of the original artwork, including shield-bearing warriors, elk and bison, and guns. The artwork spans hundreds of years. PHOTOGRAPH COURTESY OF MONTANA STATE PARKS.

source, scholars believe that the water and land dwelling turtle symbolized travel between the natural and supernatural worlds.

Some 250 years ago, an artist used a short, peeled sagebrush or cottonwood applicator to paint red images in Pictograph Cave. The applicator's reddish end is embedded with sand grains, indicating it was pressed hard against the wall of the cave rather than on a portable wood or hide object. Images of flintlock guns and riders on horses document the use of the cave well into the historic period.

Many of the pictographs are fading and hard to see. Others are falling in fragments off the cave wall. Sadly, rock art conser-

Tools used to paint pictographs (such as brushes and crayons) are not often preserved in archaeological sites. This rare 250-year-old paint applicator from Pictograph Cave is made from a peeled sagebrush or cottonwood stick. The applicator was used to paint red images on the back wall of the cave. Photograph courtesy of Sara Scott.

vation experts and engineers conclude that little can be done to arrest the paintings' (or cave's) deterioration and spalling.

The ethnic identity of the Pictograph Cave artists is speculative. The famous "bear dancer" figure comprises a rectangular body, long neck, a round head with tufted ears, large eyes with tear streaks, and bear claw moccasins. This figure carries a bow-spear and arrows. Rock art experts Julie Francis and Larry Loendorf attribute this impressive figure, called a therianthrope or shapeshifter, to bear ceremonialism, which was common among Plains Indian groups such as the Assiniboine and Crow.[89] These ceremonies were held to honor the bear, heal sickness, and prepare for war. Shape shifters, shield figures, animals, and other pictographs likely imbued Pictograph Cave with special significance to hunter-gatherer groups, though apparently not of the sort that precluded living there. Today, the Crow people of southeastern Montana regard most ancient rock paintings and carvings as "ghost art" and steer clear of them, believing their supernatural power will bring bad luck to anyone who visits them.[90]

WPA excavations in Empty Gulch, located below the caves, uncovered the remains of a simple "house" structure evidenced by an ovoid arrangement of 15 postholes, a hard-packed earthen floor, and fire hearths. This structure may be associated with decorated pottery unearthed in Empty Gulch, which Mulloy labeled Tradition A, Mandan-Hidatsa ceramic ware. If the pottery sherds are the trash of Middle Missouri River migrants, the house may date to within the last 600 years. (Earth lodges are discussed further in the Hagan Site chapter.) Alternatively, local groups using timber poles, hide, earth, or other materials may have built the house among the broken pottery of Middle Missouri River traders or visitors. Without further excavation, there is no way to tell.

Pictograph Cave is a useful reminder of how ideas evolve and change in archaeology and science. For a long time, a focus on hunting preoccupied Plains archaeologists, due to ready access to hundreds of animal kill and butchering sites containing thousands of stone tools scattered across the landscape. Academic volumes were dedicated to "hunters of the distant past," leaving women largely on the sidelines, possibly due to the fact that (for nearly a half-century) men dominated the field of American archaeology.

Beginning in the 1960s, three things changed. First, new field and laboratory methods (like flotation) enabled the recovery of plant and other fragile evidence hitherto unknown or ignored. Suddenly women's activities such as gathering plant foods and domestic tasks could be seen in the archaeological record. Second, studies of contemporary hunting and gathering societies led to a realization that these groups were adept "broad-spectrum" foragers who relied on a wide range of natural resources. Ethnographic fieldwork showed that women and children did many of these foraging tasks. Third, a growing number of women archaeologists brought attention to long neglected areas of inquiry and the inherent male bias in archaeological interpretations. Today, intensively occupied archeological sites like Pictograph and Ghost caves are no longer seen primarily as staging areas for hunting expeditions and other masculine tasks, but rather as base camps from which any number of socioeconomic activities took place among all band members.[91]

Long aware of the caves' tourism potential, the City of Billings leased Empty Gulch as a city park in the early 1960s. Montana State Parks eventually agreed to incorporate Pictograph and Ghost cave into its system in 1969. Today, popular Pictograph Cave State Park has a fine visitor center, interpretive trails, and knowledgeable interpreters. Although its delicate paintings are fading, Pictograph Cave and its companion Ghost Cave still tell the remarkable story of Montana's ancient hunter-gatherers. It is one of the few places in Montana solely dedicated to the state's archaeological past, and visiting the caves is an educational experience absolutely worth the stop.

Stone quarrying and tool manufacturing is nearly as old as humanity itself. Native American tool stone quarries, large and small, are widely distributed throughout Montana. As depicted here, at the Schmitt Chert mine near Three Forks, Pelican Lake peoples dug deep into the ground with antler digging tools to remove desirable chert nodules from the soil and limestone matrix. ILLUSTRATION BY ERIC S. CARLSON.

ROCK KNOCKING

SCHMITT CHERT MINE

24BW559

3,000 YEARS AGO

Stone tools have been around nearly as long as humanity itself. The simple pebble tools and stone hand axes made by our earliest hominin ancestors gave way to the small core and flake tools of the Neanderthals. Then, around 50,000 years ago, the early modern peoples (*Homo sapiens*) of Eurasia began knapping sophisticated bifacial knives and blades with thin, sharp, cutting edges. An array of bone and antler tools—harpoons, billets, wrenches, awls, and punches—complimented their elaborate stone tool kits. Eurasian hunter-gatherers carried these highly effective technologies with them into Beringia and the Americas.

Geological deposits of fine-grained chert, flint, quartzite, and other types of toolstone are found in thousands of places across Montana and neighboring states. In many areas, toolstone was simply collected by hunters and gatherers from exposed outcrops or in gravel terraces and streambeds, sometimes only as small pebbles. A sparse scattering of chipped stone flakes is often the only archaeological evidence that Indian peoples exploited these places at all.

Large nodules of quality toolstone were harder to come by. In the places where they could be found, the archaeological evidence is far more abundant (and frequently overwhelming). Thousands of waste flakes, bifacial cores, cobble hammer stones, and other debris lie everywhere. At these major quarry sites, raw material was not only collected from the surface but dug out of the ground with bone and antler digging tools, creating a maze of open pits. There are dozens of major toolstone quarries in Montana. The Schmitt Chert Mine near the Three Forks of the Missouri River in southwest Montana is a good example of how ancient Indian toolstone quarries once operated.

The Schmitt Chert Mine lies just west of the community of Trident at the northern margin of the Three Forks Basin, about 30 miles west of Bozeman.[92] The quarry covers the top of a bare knoll overlooking the Missouri River and the Horseshoe Hills. A rugged topography of juniper-covered ridges, steep-walled canyons, and barren limestone outcrops surrounds the mine. The knoll provides sweeping vistas of the Missouri River Valley and the surrounding Big Belt, Bridger, Gallatin, and Tobacco Root mountain ranges. The area's topography is capped by Madison Group limestone. This geological deposit yields nodules of white to gray to orange-brown chert—a high quality toolstone.

Ancient toolstone quarry pits are frequently mistaken for exploration holes of nineteenth- and twentieth-century hard-rock miners. For this reason, many Indian quarries go unrecognized and unreported. Bill Kolokotrones of Three Forks suspected that something else had happened on a particular limestone knob above the Missouri River. He dug there in the 1930s and found stone chips, bone fragments, and river mussel shells. He returned again in the 1960s with a front-end loader. Shallow cuts with the loader revealed more stone and bone artifacts, convincing Kolokotrones that this was an Indian camp of considerable importance. He contacted archaeologist Les Davis at nearby Montana State University in Bozeman, who began field investigations at Schmitt in the 1980s.

Indian quarriers dug open, relatively shallow pits to obtain suitable raw material. At Schmitt, the unexpected discovery of a small, excavated cavern within the limestone indicated that Indian quarriers had "gophered" their way downward into cracks between solid rock to pry out desirable chert nodules. MSU students excavated a deep trench in order to trace the ancient diggings, recovering antler digging tools and many other artifacts. Photograph by Leslie B. Davis.

The Schmitt Chert Mine was found to be part of a larger quarry complex. Multiple chert outcrops, ancient prospect pits, and stone circles or tipi rings formed what Les Davis named the Three Waters Quarries. Initially, Davis' crews focused on the shallow prospect pits, but the chance discovery of a small underground cavern revealed that ancient quarriers had "gophered" their way downward through spaces between fractured bedrock. Digging with split rib, bone splinter, and antler-tine prying tools, wedges, and picks (such tools are found throughout the rock and soil fill in the Schmitt Chert Mine), these miners found quality chert nodules in manganese-stained limestone fissures and cavities.

As the miners dug, they gathered up their waste rock or tailings, probably on hides, and dumped the waste back into excavated areas and beneath dangerous underground bedrock overhangs, thus shoring them up to prevent collapse. (Davis's crews used wood posts.) The subterranean digging, tailings dumps, and large limestone blocks maneuvered by the quarriers, coupled with natural infilling of sediment, rodent burrowing, and other natural disturbances produced a very complex stratigraphy at Schmitt.

An unusual aspect of the Schmitt Chert Mine is its paucity of flintknapping debris. As mentioned in the Rock Talk chapter, stone flakes, cores, and hammer stones occur in abundance at most quarries as smaller, more portable bifaces and other tools were made on site. Why not at Schmitt? The investigators believe the anomaly is due to the mine's geology. The subterranean chert occurs as cobbles whose quality was superior to the weathered and fractured nodules found above ground. Furthermore, the cobbles were already worn and rounded, making them easier to transport. Substantial knapping on-site was not necessarily required.

An ancient campsite surrounds the Schmitt Chert Mine.

At toolstone quarries, flintknappers pared down raw material into transportable bifaces by using hand-held stone cobbles and antler billets. The paucity of flintknapping debris at Schmitt, and the great effort expended at quarrying below ground, led the investigators to infer that the buried cobbles were high quality and required little paring down or shaping prior to their transport to distant camps. ILLUSTRATION BY ERIC S. CARLSON.

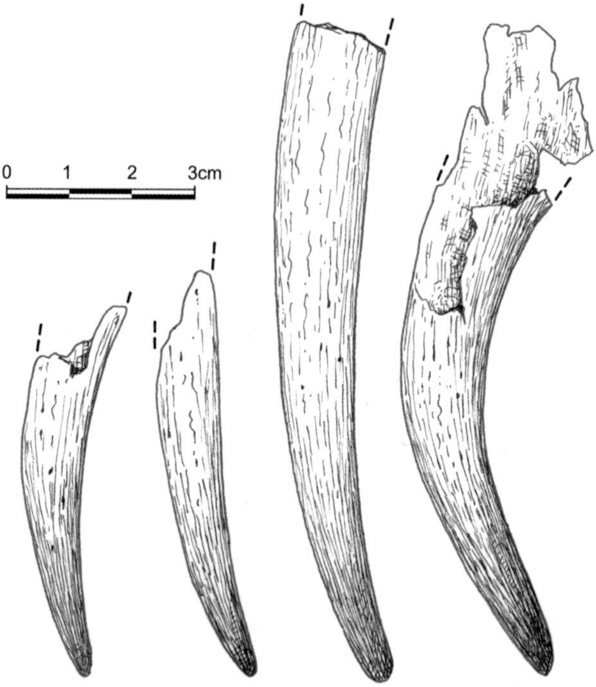

Digging tools are rarely preserved at ancient quarry sites in Montana. At Schmitt site, deer and elk antler tine picks were used to pry out chert nodules from the soil and limestone matrix. Illustration by Eric S. Carlson.

Here, Davis's crews dug up flintknapping debris, projectile points, tool blanks and preforms, scrapers, drills, perforators, cobble hammer stones, antler tine knapping tools, and an antler shaft wrench (used for straightening dart point shafts). The tools were scattered around warming and cooking fires. Butchered bones within the kitchen areas came from bison, antelope, elk, deer, jackrabbit, cottontail rabbit, skunk, beaver, and turtle—all common to the area today. Bone awls and needles, river mussel

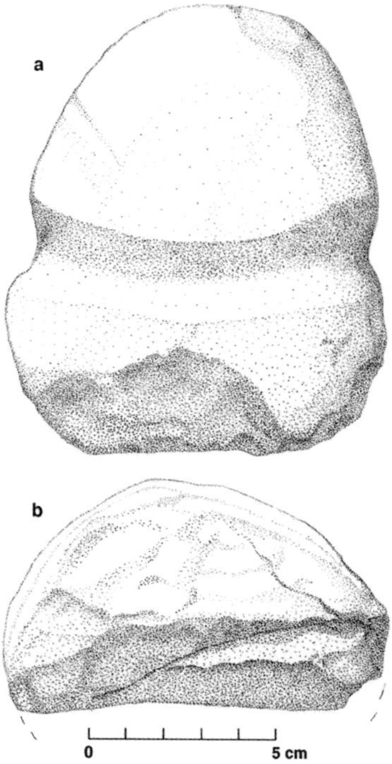

Grooved stone mauls are common throughout Montana. This example from the Schmitt site is made from a river cobble that has been carved around its center by pecking and abrasion with a harder stone. The split end of a wooden handle was placed in the groove and bound tightly to the maul with rawhide wrappings. Breakage and use-wear patterns indicate that mauls were used in tool stone quarrying (as inferred at Schmitt), domestic tasks (pounding tipi stakes, smashing animal bones for marrow) and as deadly war clubs (called "pogamoggans"). ILLUSTRATION COURTESY OF LESLIE B. DAVIS.

and perforated snail shell ornaments, and an incised soapstone bead indicate the Schmitt people were in no hurry to leave. They had time to sew clothing and craft ornaments. Stone tipi

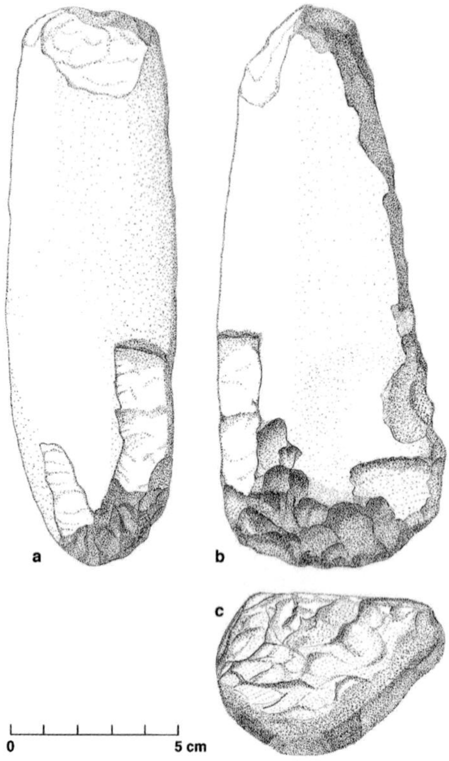

Long hammerstones were another kind of heavy-duty tool used by Indian peoples at Schmitt. Investigator Les Davis speculated that these kinds of tools, either hafted or hand-held, were used by Pelican Lake peoples to break the limestone matrix and extract chert nodules. He further suggested that many of these heavily battered quartzite and basalt pounding tools were carried to the Schmitt mine specifically for that purpose. Illustration courtesy of Leslie B. Davis.

rings indicated that the Schmitt people probably lived in pole and hide lodges.

Projectile point styles and 3,500- to 2,000-year-old radiocarbon dates show that Indian groups—called Pelican Lake by archaeologists—mined chert at the Schmitt site. These peoples moved between winter camps in sheltered river valleys and summer camps on the hot, windy plains. They were skilled bison hunters. Pelican Lake bands maintained widespread travel networks and trade contacts, as indicated by the presence of distant raw materials, including Knife River Flint from North Dakota, porcellanite or baked shale from southeastern Montana, obsidian from the Yellowstone Plateau, and Pacific coast Olivella seashells. Although the quantity of chert mined at Schmitt is unknown, it is likely that any surplus moved along these same trade routes and networks.

Whether Pelican Lake people controlled access to the Schmitt Chert Mine as part of their band (or tribal) territory is unknown. Resource ownership or control varies widely among contemporary hunter-gatherer societies so it is impossible to assess this kind of social behavior so far back in time. The number of people who dug out toolstone is also speculative. Intuitively, mining underground in cramped quarters probably allowed for only a few diggers and rock haulers at any given time. A "support team" from the nearby camp may have supplied digging equipment, encouragement, food and water. After some 50 generations of use, Schmitt Mine was abandoned. Archeologists don't know why.

The ethnic identity of the Schmitt quarriers is equally ambiguous because there are few culturally diagnostic clues in the surviving quarry and camp rubbish. The ancestral Assiniboine, Blackfeet, Kiowa, and Salish are some of the potential candidates since they are known to have occupied or used the Three Forks of the Missouri area. Whatever their ethnicity, the faunal evidence indicates the camp was used intermittently by Indian bands year-round—made possible because snow quickly blew away or rapidly melted on top of the wind-swept, south-facing ridge. Indeed, Schmitt was strategically located in an area that could supply game and plant foods, water, fuel, and other resources any season of the year.

The Schmitt site is similar in most ways to other, generally less explored, Indian toolstone quarries across the state. The Devils Eyebrow chert quarry in western Montana, the Cashman basalt and Camp Baker chert quarries in central Montana, and the Bear Gulch obsidian and South Everson chert quarries in southwest Montana all contain pits and knapping refuse.[93] Most appear to have been used intermittently throughout the Holocene, in contrast to the concise 1500-year aboriginal history at Schmitt.

Toolstone is now routinely traced to its geological origin, or quarry source. These instrumental data are exceptionally helpful to archaeologists working with the typically sparse cultural remains of mobile hunter-gatherers. Geochemical "fingerprinting" provides direct evidence of the movement of specific toolstone (and thus people) across the landscape and trade networks. Called X-Ray fluorescence (XRF), this technology irradiates obsidian artifacts with X-ray beams to map the presence of their component minerals, such as zinc and iron.[94] Their XRF profiles can then be compared statistically with a master list of all known obsidian quarries to pinpoint their exact sources.

Abundant XRF data generated over the past four decades identify Bear Gulch obsidian, situated in the Centennial Range on the Idaho-Montana border near Yellowstone National Park, as the primary obsidian source for hunter-gatherers in Montana. Obsidian Cliffs in the park was also widely used. Other obsidians were imported into the state in smaller amounts from numerous quarries in Idaho, Oregon, Wyoming, and elsewhere, reflecting both commerce (trade) and the back and forth journeys of Columbia Plateau, northern Great Basin, and Plains Indian peoples. Obsidian also moved through near-continent wide aboriginal trade networks. Tools made of Obsidian Cliff glass turn up in Hopewell ("Mound Builder") culture sites of several thousand years ago, indicating trade that reached all the way from present-day Yellowstone National Park to Ross County, Ohio.[95]

Based on these same geochemical principles, chert-chalcedony artifacts can be similarly analyzed, but at present, chert gives less precise results. Obsidian derives from local volcanic magma flows so their "fingerprints" are geographically restricted and chemically unique. In contrast, limestone replacement cherts occur across major geological formations so their chemical signatures are more homogenous and widespread, making it far harder to pinpoint an exact quarry. Thus, archaeologists often "source" chert tools on visual characteristics—an inexact method at best (though some material like Knife River flint or Phosphoria chert is very distinctive in appearance, making correlations more reliable). However, the Madison Formation Schmitt chert is not particularly distinctive, and thus it is currently difficult to know how widely it was used and traded across Montana's plain and mountain regions.

Many toolstone quarries eventually fell out of popular use as Euroamerican trade goods trickled into the economies of Indian hunter-gatherers in the 18th and 19th centuries. Arrowheads, lance points, and knife blades made of metal replaced stone tools; wood and metal buckets replaced hide and ceramic containers; and so on. Native peoples also acquired muskets and then rifles, augmenting their bow and arrow, lance, mace, and club weaponry. Still, some kinds of stone tools like hide scrapers were popular well into the early 1900s.

Indian stone artifacts are tangible and often exquisite reminders of bygone days. Montanans collected many thousands of them for the better part of the twentieth century. "Keepers" were cleverly displayed in glass-covered frames on living room, café, and local museum walls, while broken or unremarkable specimens were relegated to cabinet drawers and cigar boxes. Inevitably, with the passage of time, private artifact collections were forgotten, lost, sold, discarded, or given away to museums,

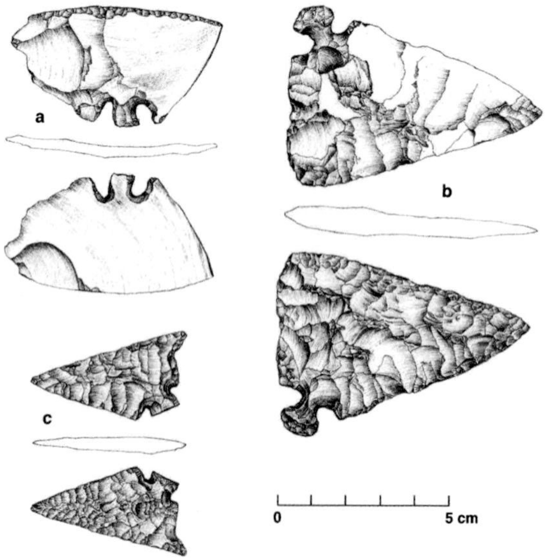

The distinctive corner-tang knife is one hallmark of the Pelican Lake culture. The triangular-shaped tool has a hafting element or "tang" on one corner. When tied to a wood or bone handle, corner-tang knives became effective all-purpose cutting tools analogous to modern kitchen knives. Incurved and irregular-shaped blade edges opposite the tang indicate repeated re-sharpening. ILLUSTRATION COURTESY OF LESLIE B. DAVIS.

often with little locational information attached. Fortunately, artifact collecting on public lands is largely a thing of the past, thanks to the passage and serious enforcement of antiquities laws and a more enlightened public historic preservation ethic. But a significant amount of scientific information has been lost over the years.

In the Northern Rockies and on the Plains, Indian groups made and used stone tools from the far distant past well into the nineteenth century. Thus, an ancient technology, first developed in the Upper Paleolithic of Eurasia, never completely died out among Montana's first peoples. Today, amateur and professional flintknappers carry on this ancient tradition in scientific, artistic, and commercial venues, as a stroll through any archaeology lab, community craft fair, or tribal powwow will quickly attest.

Bison jumping was a complex and dangerous band enterprise. This illustration is highly compressed and dramatized to show the different roles of band members. The woman waving the bison robe and other band members first encircled part of a bison herd and gently spooked it into stone drive lanes. When the bison were near the jump precipice, Indians stampeded the herd. Young men disguised as panicked bison calves sometimes ran ahead of the herd, leading the animals directly to the precipice, and then scrambled to safety, as shown by the boy in the bison calf robe. At First Peoples, Blackfeet hunters used spears to ceremonially kill the first bison to run over the precipice. ILLUSTRATION BY ERIC S. CARLSON.

"DEEP BLOOD KETTLE"

FIRST PEOPLES BUFFALO JUMP

24CA1012

1,000 YEARS AGO

Bison were the staff of life for Plains Indian peoples. These shaggy, temperamental animals were a major source of meat, organs, hide, horn, bone, gut, sinew, and other raw materials—a veritable walking superstore. Ancestral Blackfeet, Cheyenne, and other Indian groups gave up settled ways of life in their distant Upper Midwestern homelands to take up year-round residency on the Plains and pursue a nomadic, bison hunting economy. Their seasonal travels were determined, in part, by the annual migrations of the bison herds. Farmers from the Middle Missouri River region of the Dakotas and hunter-gatherers from the Columbia Plateau and northern Great Basin journeyed to the Montana Plains to fill their larders with bison meat and hides. As shown at Mill Iron, this bison-human relationship has deep roots in North America.

Bison and buffalo are members of the same family, *Bovidae*, but they are not of the same genus or species. Bison evolved in the Americas (*Bison bison*) and Europe (*Bison bonasus*). In contrast, the water buffalo of Asia and the Cape buffalo of Africa are

Bison were the staff of life for Plains Indian peoples, providing meat, hide, horn, gut, sinew, and other raw materials. Native peoples also traveled from their Middle Missouri River, Columbia Plateau, and northern Great Basin homelands to the northwestern plains to harvest bison. Photograph by Christopher Cauble.

true species of buffalo. Unaware of this taxonomic distinction, European and American explorers used the words interchangeably and the term buffalo has stuck in American vernacular and imagination.[96] The term "bison" is used throughout this book.

The journals of early European and American explorers give the impression of teeming masses of bison roaming everywhere across the western Great Plains and Rocky Mountain foothills. Indeed, bison numbered in the millions—literally spread out "as far as the eye can see" as many historical sources accurately recount. However, the huge bison herds actually comprised innumerable smaller groups of several hundred or more females and their immature male and female offspring—analogous to cow-calf herds in modern ranching operations. Males formed small, widely dispersed bull groups for much of the year, only mixing with cow-calf herds during the rut.

Like wildebeest and other large herd animals of the Serengeti Plains in Africa, bison seasonally migrated across the vast Great Plains and well into the Rocky Mountains. Bison aggregated during the summer when grass was plentiful and dispersed in the winter in search of reliable graze, water, and shelter. Drought, range fires, freezing blizzards, mass drownings (from attempting to cross frozen rivers), disease, insects, carnivore predation, and hunting by humans all affected the health and vitality of the herds and influenced their yearly movements. Indian bands actively searched for bison herds or awaited their arrival in productive grasslands—bison were not simply everywhere for the taking as Hollywood movies might suggest.

American Indian peoples used their knowledge of landscape ecology and bison behavior to great advantage, killing millions of bison over thousands of years. Thus, it is no great surprise that the bone piles of ancient bison kills are good places to find Indian arrowheads and tools. Throughout the better part of the twentieth century, artifact collectors dug up bison kill sites across Montana, leaving these interesting places pockmarked with abandoned holes, dirt piles, and broken digging equipment. Enforcement of state and federal antiquities laws, especially the Archaeological Resource Protection Act of 1979, eventually eliminated much of the artifact collecting on public lands. But this unfortunately time-honored recreational pursuit continued well into the 1980s in Montana.

As if to add insult to archeological injury, bison kill sites in northern Montana and across the border on the Canadian plains were commercially mined for bone during the 1930s and 1940s.[97] Operating under government-issued permits, and with little awareness of or regard for the precious archaeological heritage they were destroying, mining companies bulldozed deep trenches into the thick bone middens. Immense piles of excavated bison bones and skulls were transported to on-site drying tanks. The bone was then shipped in railcars to distant markets for use as agricultural fertilizer and livestock feed additive.

Thankfully, this destruction of ancient bison jumps did not go unnoticed. In 1945, amateur archaeologist Maynard Shumate watched in despair as miners dug up bison bone at the base of a prominent sandstone escarpment called Taft Hill near Great Falls. Shumate collected arrowheads and other Indian artifacts from the huge bone piles and even placed small test pits in the bottom of some of the mining trenches, thereby discovering underlying, still intact layers of bison bone. Shumate published his finding on the Taft Hill kill site, originally called Ulm Pishkun (pishkun or pisskan is a Blackfeet word meaning "deep blood kettle") in the state's archaeology journal, arousing professional interest and public awareness of the scientific value of this extensive bison jump and its devastation.[98]

The Frost Fertilizer Company mined Ulm Pishkun for two more years before local preservation pressure finally brought it to a halt. The area became a state park in 1974 but had minimal visitor facilities and little agency presence. As a result, recurrent artifact digging and vandalism prompted the Great Falls Optimists Club to "adopt" Ulm Pishkun. The group eventually became the Ulm Pishkun Support Group under the auspices of the Cascade Historical Society. This group lobbied the Montana State Parks to instigate archaeological survey, excavation, and protection. To say the least, Ulm Pishkun is testimony to the tremendous importance of community advocacy in historic preservation.

Today, Ulm Pishkun is called First Peoples Buffalo Jump State Park and is located 10 miles southwest of Great Falls near the small community of Ulm. The park includes the base and top of Taft Hill. Overlooking the valley bottoms of the Missouri and Sun rivers, Taft Hill offers stunning vistas of the Rocky

Mountain Front, Square Butte, and the Highwood and Little Belt mountains. The park's starkly beautiful landscape is a treeless expanse of prairie grass. In 1988, Montana State Parks built a visitor center near the base of Taft Hill, and a road and interpretive trails now provide access to the main jump. The significance of First Peoples Buffalo Jump State Park is recognized by its listing on the National Register of Historic Places and its designation as a National Historic Landmark.

The first extensive investigation of the First Peoples Buffalo Jump occurred in the 1990s under the direction of Montana

Bison kills are impressive places to visit. First Peoples Buffalo Jump State Park encompasses prominent Taft Hill and its bottomlands near Ulm, Montana. Over a period of two millennia or more, Indian bands ran many thousands of modern bison off the prominent cliff and butchered them on the grassy bench below. PHOTOGRAPH COURTESY OF MONTANA STATE PARKS.

State University archaeologists Jack Fisher, Tom Roll, and Steve Aaberg.[99] Because of the jump's immense scale, efforts were focused on the south side of Taft Hill, which faces the Visitor Center today. Backhoe trenches exposed the most extensive bone deposits in this part of the jump. Excavations with shovels and trowels then commenced in the most promising areas. The "fall and kill" zone directly under the cliff revealed a mass of bison carcasses, stone arrowheads, and butchering tools. There are unexplored, older bone deposits below the university's work.

Montana State University archaeological crews excavated parts of the First Peoples bison kill and butchering area on the southside of Taft Hill. Here, Avonlea and Old Women's (Blackfeet) bands orchestrated various jump events from 1,000 to 570 years ago. Archaeologists estimate that more than 10,000 bison were killed during this 500-year period in this area of the jump alone. This area of the jump was used primarily during the fall through early spring. Square Butte can be seen in the distance. PHOTOGRAPH COPYRIGHT BY JACK FISHER., USED WITH PERMISSION.

The excavated areas date from 1,000 to 570 years ago. Indian groups, called Avonlea and Old Women's by archaeologists, orchestrated the various jump events. Fetal bison and teeth showed that hunters used this area of the jump during the fall through early spring. Investigators estimated that more than 10,000 bison were killed over a 500-year period in this area of the jump alone. Since other bone middens at First Peoples have yet to be excavated, bison mortality figures could easily double or triple. Still, this quantity pales in comparison to the Highwood bison kill in central Montana, where archaeologists estimate that 238,000 bison met their demise over several centuries of communal bison hunting.[100] In fact, over thousands of years, millions of bison were killed at hundreds of sites scattered across the Plains from Fort Collins, Colorado, to Calgary, Alberta.

For much of the Holocene, individual bison were stalked and killed, or small groups were trapped and killed in steep arroyos or in pole corrals and impoundments constructed by Indian bands. Driving bison over cliffs as a predominant mass hunting strategy came into widespread practice only during the past 2,000-3,000 years. The trigger for this cultural change may have been favorable climatic conditions and expanding grassland habitats. Such ecological circumstances enabled ever-growing and well-nourished bison herds to aggregate in huge numbers and for extended periods of time on the Plains and Rocky Mountain foothills (the Chinook belt) during the winter months. Pedestrian hunter-gatherer bands armed with atlatls and darts, and later with bows and arrows, communally hunted bison in grass-rich and well-watered basins.

The ecological and spiritual knowledge of powerful religious societies within the Indian bands dictated the placement, construction, and use of kills sites and their associated stone features and monuments. Topography, grass conditions, and weather all factored into their planning and decisions. No longer the work

Over the millennia, Plains Indian peoples used their sophisticated knowledge of landscape ecology and bison behavior to successfully kill millions of bison by various hunting methods. About 3,000 to 2,000 years ago, the stampeding of bison herds over cliffs and precipices became a predominant mass hunting strategy. Hundreds of bison kill sites, large and small, are scattered throughout Montana's plains and intermountain valleys. The terrain at many sites often slanted slightly uphill or downhill so that the bison could not easily see the precipice until it was too late. PHOTOGRAPH BY CHRISTOPHER CAUBLE.

of a single hunter or a handful of hunters, communal bison jumping became a serious, periodic, and highly dangerous band (or multi-band) enterprise. It became deeply embedded in the ecological knowledge, religious practices, economies, and social structures of Plains Indian groups.[101]

Bison jumps did not require high cliffs but only small prominences with a steep escarpment or "drop-fall" and a sizeable grazing basin or "catchment area" behind it. Converging,

V-shaped drive lanes made of low-lying rock piles rigged with brush and pole flagging, sometimes extending a mile or more across the open prairie, funneled the bison herd from the grazing area to the jump. Using the drive lanes both as vantages and reference points, band members (adults and older children) encircled the targeted bison and slowly herded them inside the converging drive lanes.

Finally, when hunt leaders deemed the herd to be close enough to the jump apex, the band members quickly closed on the herd, shouting, waving robes, and creating enough commotion to start a stampede. The terrain at jumps like First Peoples often slanted slightly uphill or downhill so that the bison could not easily see the precipice until it was too late. To further draw the bison to the exact jump spot (for bison are surprisingly fast, agile creatures that can change directions quickly), brave young men disguised in bison calf robes sometimes raced aside and ahead of the stampeding herd, leading it to the very edge of the cliff where the men tucked themselves safely below the ledge or behind large boulders. The now massed and colliding bison either ran over the precipice or were pushed over it by other bison, crashing helter-skelter into the kill zone below.

Mayhem then ensued below the cliff as hunters quickly dispatched the crippled but still dangerous animals with darts, arrows, and lances. Drawing on earlier hunting methods, impoundments made of brush and timbers were occasionally built at the base of jumps to improve the hunters' chances of containing and dispatching the injured animals. (There is no evidence yet of such a containment structures at First Peoples.)

Naturally, hunter-gatherers could neither predict nor control the precise number of bison charging off a jump. Sometimes bison mortality far exceeded the band's needs and wastage was not uncommon. Such "over-kill" was the inevitable by-product of a mass hunting technology that was designed to produce large,

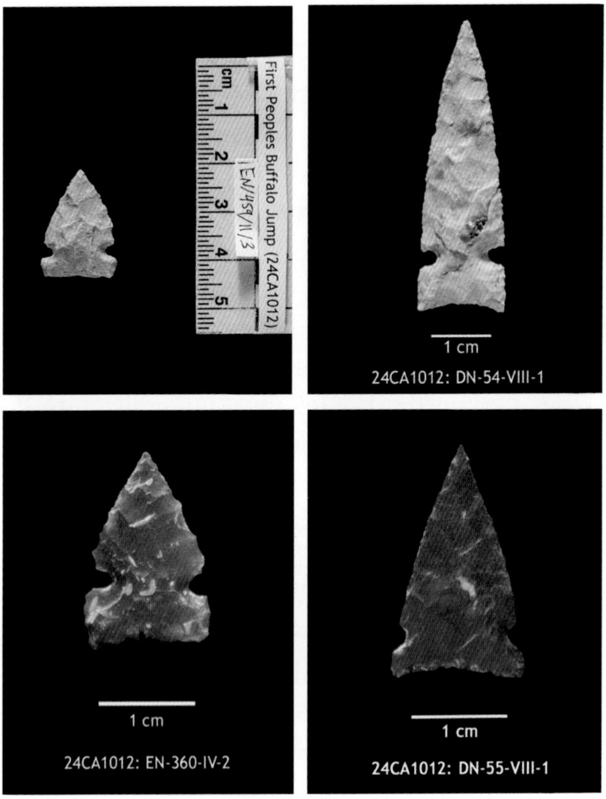

MSU archaeologists recovered an abundance of arrow points manufactured by Avonlea and Old Women's archaeological culture groups from First Peoples Buffalo Jump. Sometimes erroneously referred to as "bird points" by artifact collectors, these small, side- and tri-notched points were widely used to hunt bison and other large game, beginning about 1,500 years ago. Archaeologists distinguish arrow-point styles by minor differences in shape, finish, and raw material, and even attribute (with caution) some types to specific ethnic groups like the Blackfeet and Shoshone. Top left: Old Women's point with on-site archeological labeling protocol. Top right and bottom left: Old Women's points. Bottom right: Avonlea point. PHOTOGRAPHS COPYRIGHT BY JACK FISHER, USED WITH PERMISSION.

transportable quantities of meat, hides, and other animal products in a region blessed with enormous bison herds. It was not an indication of the ecological or conservation values or ethics of past Native peoples.[102]

Band members carried and dragged partly butchered carcasses away from the blood and gore at the base of the cliff to a processing area on a nearby grassy bench. Men and women stripped the meat from the bones, cracked open and crushed large bones to extract the iron-rich marrow, and boiled crushed bones in hide containers and pottery vessels to render grease and to make nutritious blood pudding. Women pounded fat and berries into meat strips and then dried the strips on pole racks to make portable stores of pemmican jerky. At some jumps, though not at First Peoples, Indian bands burned the remaining bison carcasses and offal. Archaeologists speculate that burning alleviated the powerful stench and made the rotting mess less attractive to scavenging and potentially troublesome wolves and grizzly bears.

Besides bison butchering and processing at First Peoples, bone beads and ornaments, refurbished tools, and other evidence led investigators to conclude that hunter-gatherer groups remained for some time before, during, and after the jumping event. Plenty of other domestic tasks were done here. Bands camped in nearby areas, now dotted with stone tipi rings. Indian bands traveled from a long way to hunt at First Peoples, as indicated by the geographic origins of stone tools found there. (Of course, toolstone from distant sources also could have been obtained through trade.)

Cultural factors may have contributed to the strong shift to communal mass bison hunting during the last 2,000 years. Some archaeologists believe that the growing size of Native populations, heavy reliance on bison jerky or pemmican, and a vibrant trade with Indian farmers in the Middle Missouri region of the Dakotas, and even the urbane Native cultures of the lower Mississippi River valley, intensified Plains Indian bison hunting economies late in prehistory. In contrast to earlier time periods, bison were intensively harvested and processed to obtain large quantities of dried, transportable meat, rendered bison fat, and hides for both personal use and trade.

The Two Medicine River Valley on the Blackfeet Indian Reservation of north-central Montana is rich with bison jumps, drive lanes, butchering areas, rock cairns and alignments, and camps. Archaeologists Maria Zedeño and Jesse Ballenger and Blackfeet anthropologist John Murray regard it as a "culturally engineered landscape."[103] Old Women's groups—the ancestral Blackfeet—constructed many of these features as a way to establish their long-term presence in this highly productive bison hunting territory and to discourage or deter competing, non-Blackfeet bands. Bison hunting knowledge passed from generation to generation through traditional (ecological-zoological) knowledge, stories, sacred medicine bundles, and ritual practices.[104] In the words of Zedeño and her colleagues, bison hunting became "an activity of industrial proportions" in this part of the Northern Plains. The intense focus on bison hunting and concurrent accumulation of "bison wealth" by some band members spurred more complex social arrangements and ideologies. Plains Indian culture was never static.

The First Peoples Buffalo Jump also is a culturally engineered landscape. Unlike the Two Medicine River Valley, however, many of its component stone features were lost because of agriculture and rural development. Nonetheless, in 2008, as part of the National Historic Landmark study, archaeologist Steve Aaberg and his survey crew identified hundreds of archaeological features within the 1,906-acre state park, including multiple bone middens and processing areas below the cliffs, stone alignments and cairns, camps denoted by stone circles or tipi rings,

At First Peoples, archaeologists inspect rocks built up along the south rim of Taft Hill. Called "trip walls," these stone features apparently created a ledge and eliminated possible escape routes. Their effectiveness is unknown as archaeologists have yet to explore the area below for bison bonebeds. Many drive lanes at First Peoples and other jump sites don't end in bonebeds, indicating that not all jump plans were successful. PHOTOGRAPH COURTESY OF MONTANA STATE PARKS.

and rock art.[105] Several unique, stacked rock walls at the very edge of the escarpment, called "trip walls" by Aaberg, may have disguised the cliff edge, eliminated escape routes, and forced the stampeding bison to run off the cliff edge.

Who exactly "engineered" and used the cultural landscape at First Peoples? The jump lies in the heart of traditional Blackfeet Indian country. The Blackfeet called the Sun River, which was part of their winter hunting grounds, the Natoosi River or Medicine River. As told to Maria Zedeño by a Blackfeet elder, in addition to procuring hides and meat at First Peoples, bands harvested bison fetuses which were ceremonially fed to shamans or priests and important elders. The bison fetuses were also made into offerings to the Sun. During these hunts, Blackfeet hunters used spears—not bows and arrows—to dispatch the first bison that fell below the cliffs. The preponderance of Old Women's (archaeological) culture tools supports this Blackfeet presence. Still, other tribal groups such as the Assiniboine, Salish, or Shoshone may have occasionally visited and used the jump; archaeologists have yet to test or excavate all of the bone middens at Taft Hill. Today, Indian people from many Plains tribes recognize the extreme cultural value of First Peoples, preform ceremonies at the park, and participate in its educational and interpretive programs.

Our knowledge of ancient bison hunting does not derive entirely from archaeology. European and American explorers, traders, missionaries, and Native peoples themselves have left us rich and detailed accounts of bison hunts using drives, impoundments, and horses.[106] One prominent theme in this literature is that bison hunting occurred throughout every season of the year in order to provide fresh meat and augment precious dried food stores. It was not confined to the fall months as preparation for the harsh, relatively immobile winter months to come (this is a Western agrarian ideal, in any case). Still, bison were in prime condition from summer through fall, and many kills did occur during that time. In the winter, some Indian bands camped together, rather than disperse to home territories, in order to take advantage of large bison herds wintering in sheltered basins.

Over millennia, Indian peoples traveled from western Montana, the Columbia Plateau, and northern Great Basin to hunt bison on the Plains. Countless human feet, dogs, horses, and travois poles converted the travel routes into wide, well-beaten "Indian roads." Rock piles next to these ancient roads, and on

Western Montana, Columbia Plateau, and Northern Great Basin Indian groups traveled over well-worn trails and roads to hunt bison on the northwestern plains. The "Qoq'aalx 'Iskit" or "Road to the Buffalo Trail" is one of Montana's best documented Indian trails. The trail-road segment shown here passes over Lewis and Clark Pass (on the Continental Divide) near Lincoln, then descends into the Missouri River foothills and plains south of Great Falls. This scenic pass is named after Meriwether Lewis, who hastily traveled over it in 1806, fearing attacks from Blackfeet war parties. PHOTOGRAPH COURTESY OF SARA SCOTT.

top of mountain passes, served as trail markers and places where offerings of bison skulls, fetishes, tobacco, and sacred items were made to ensure a safe journey—similar to those created and decorated by pilgrims and travelers in the Tibetan Himalayas today. "Stone forts" on the top of some passes were used to scout the territory for enemies. These trails facilitated Native commerce in toolstone, food, ornaments, animal hides, and other products, and were used for horse raiding and warfare.

During the mid-nineteenth and twentieth centuries, miners, homesteaders, transportation engineers, and the U.S. Forest Service co-opted these ancient Indian travel routes, and many are now the locations of recreational trails, country roads, and interstate highways.

The Buffalo Road Trail, or "Qoq'aalx 'Iskit" in the Salish language, is one of Montana's best-documented Indian trails.[107] It passed through the Blackfoot Valley of western Montana and over the Continental Divide near the present-day community of Lincoln. The Kootenai, Nez Perce, Salish, Pend Oreille, Spokane, and other Columbia Plateau tribes traveled this route in the late spring through early fall when the mountain passes were snow-free. Meriwether Lewis and his party of nine men traveled hastily along this old Indian road on their return trip in 1806, lending the famous expedition's name, perhaps unfairly, to Lewis and Clark Pass. Blackfeet war parties (the cause of Meriwether Lewis' haste) traveled far into western Montana and the Columbia Plateau on these same trail networks. Indeed, Hell Gate Canyon just west of Missoula owes its name to ambushes by the Blackfeet and other Indian groups in this narrow and rocky defile. The Shoshone from the Great Basin also crossed over low-lying passes in southwest Montana to access the rich hunting grounds. Historically, they sometimes allied themselves with the Salish for mutual defense against Plains tribes.

Communal bison jumps became a thing of the past once Native peoples acquired horses in the mid-1700s. Still relying on their intimate knowledge of bison behavior, equestrian hunters charged into herds, individually killing many bison. Well-trained horses ran alongside the fleet and agile bison, allowing skilled riders to shoot arrows and bullets and plunge lances into their prey. (The bow was often preferred over a musket or rifle even in the Historic period because it was easier to reload on horseback.) Men and women skinned and quartered dead bison on the spot, then packed them on horses and travois back to camps.

Although the risky and laborious business of communal bison hunting became unnecessary, the industrial scale of bison hunting still prevailed. Bison were intensively hunted by Indians to obtain meat and hides for trade. Finally, the bloody mass slaughter and near extermination of the bison by American hide hunters in the mid- to late-nineteenth century, combined with high bison mortality during the harsh, blizzard-filled winter of 1886-1887, brought an end to bison hunting by Native peoples.[108]

Literally hundreds of bison kill sites are known throughout the Plains. In Montana alone, some 350 bison kill sites are on

Bison jumps became a thing of the past once Native peoples acquired horses in the 1700s. As shown in this painting of a Blackfoot hunter (circa 1890 by an unknown Indian artist), equestrian hunters charged into the herds on well-trained horses, individually killing bison with bows and arrows, lances, and guns. PAINTING COURTESY OF THE BRITISH MUSEUM.

record with state historic preservation authorities. This total includes traps, pounds, and jumps, of which most have not been investigated. Excavation has mostly occurred in northern Montana at sites such as Henry Smith, Bootlegger Trail, and Kremlin. For example, a small visitor center interprets the Wahkpa Chu'gn Bison Jump in Havre, Montana. The Madison Buffalo Jump State Park near the community of Three Forks has interpretive signing and trails. Bison jumps are always impressive places to visit.

On the brink of extinction, bison survived into the early twentieth century in only a few places in Montana—Yellowstone National Park and the National Bison Range in the Flathead Valley near the community of Charlo. Today, herds on Indian reservations and private ranchlands produce meat, hides, and other products for commercial and cultural purposes. Bison management is challenging because, as all field managers agree, bison pretty much go wherever they want to go. Cattle fences do not deter them. Montanans are working together to address several issues: agricultural concerns over the possibility of bison-caused brucellosis infection of cattle herds, tribal bison hunting under federal treaty rights, and the appropriate management of the National Bison Range. This essential cross-cultural dialogue is especially fitting now that this iconic species is an official historical symbol of the United States, as declared under the 2015 National Bison Legacy Act.

Indian rock art provides information about pre-horse Indian warfare that cannot be realized through "dirt archaeology" alone. The small war parties shown in this dramatization are dressed in their finest garb. Taunts and a volley of arrows lead to fierce hand-to-hand combat with spears, bow-spears, maces, clubs, and knives. Warriors who counted coups and other war honors later commemorated their bravery and deeds in rock art galleries in special places like Bear Gulch and Atherton Canyon. Illustration by Eric S. Carlson.

WARRIOR ARTISTS

BEAR GULCH AND ATHERTON CANYON SITES

24FR2 & 3

500 YEARS AGO

Anyone who floats the scenic Smith River in central Montana may see Indian paintings on the surrounding cliffs, including the popular painted "Indian Cave" which determined boaters must scramble up a steep hillside to visit. In fact, human figures, animals, and designs are painted and carved on rock cliffs and boulders throughout Montana. Commonly called rock art, these pictographs (paintings) and petroglyphs (carvings) are an extraordinarily rich source of information about American Indian life.

Until recently, many archaeologists paid little attention to Indian rock art because determining the meaning of the designs and compositions seemed beyond the conventional archaeological inquiry of shovels and trowels. The door was thus opened to amateur interpretations. Red blotches were wooly mammoths; arrows signaled travel routes; horned creatures denoted various animals; and undecipherable designs were simply noodling. Although this naïve legacy persists, rock art research is now serious business. Today we know far more about ancient rock art than we did only 20 years ago. Rather than being indecipher-

Pictographs and petroglyphs are a rich source of information about American Indian cultures in the distant and recent past. Bear Gulch, shown here, and nearby Atherton Canyon contain one of the richest concentrations of rock art in Montana. Extensive rock art galleries along the sandstone cliffs can be viewed by visitors from a well-worn trail. The grassy terrace (top photo, with the tent pitched in the center) contains widespread archeological refuse of ancient Indian camps, some of which may be attributable to warrior artists.

able, the cultural context for rock art is now better understood and, in some cases, specialists can actually "read" rock art narrative compositions. Rock art studies routinely occur throughout Montana, but few are on the scale of the Bear Gulch project.

Bear Gulch is located in the sheltered foothills of the Little Snowy Mountains within the Judith Basin of central Montana. It and nearby Atherton Canyon contain more than 30,000 painted and incised images spanning some 2,500 to 3,000 years. Bear Gulch would be unknown and unstudied without the interest and enthusiasm of the Ahlgren family on whose property the Bear Gulch site is located. The Ahlgrens supported a multi-year rock art research program led by rock art authority Jim Keyser. Published in 2012, the richly illustrated report is an essential read for any serious student of Plains Indian rock art.[109]

Bear Gulch and Atherton Canyon were places of supernatural power for Plains Indian warriors for some 1,000 years, peaking sometime before A.D. 1700 and the arrival of Europeans. Both places are filled with painted and incised figures holding large war shields and many different types of weapons decorated with feather "flags" and streamers. Arranged individually and in groups, they wear a variety of headdresses, masks, face paint, feather bustles, medicine bundles, moccasins, robes, and other regalia. Called shield-bearing warriors, these colorful figures occur in a variety of forms but all exhibit shields, headdresses or hairstyles, regalia, and weaponry. They belong to what specialists call the Ceremonial Rock Art Tradition on the Northwestern Plains.[110] As far we now know, the greatest concentration of Ceremonial Tradition warrior art in Montana occurs in Bear Gulch and Atherton Canyon.

There is a lot to see at Bear Gulch but visitors' eyes are invariably drawn to the elaborate war shields because of their striking designs or shield heraldry. Like the shields carried by the knights of Medieval Europe, Plains Indian shields served as a form of

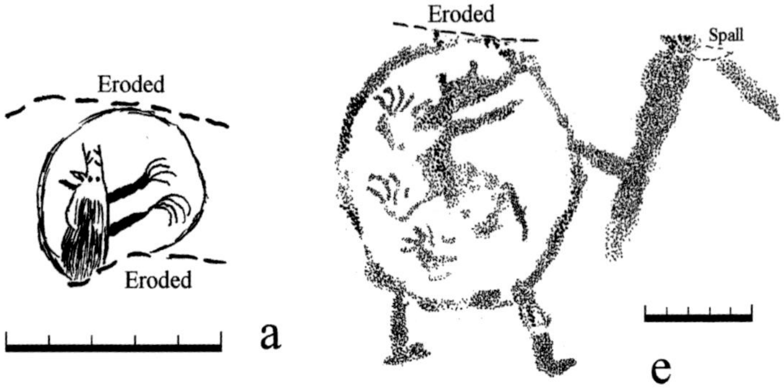

A handful of Bear Gulch shields show grizzly bears charging from their dens or rearing up on their hind legs as though ready to attack. These fearsome "Bear Comes Out" shield images, shown here as tracings, signaled the intimidating power of bears and metaphorically protected the shield owner in combat. FROM KEYSER ET AL. 2012.

recognition, status, and intimidating spiritual power, as well as offering physical protection in combat. Shield designs range from patterned lines, crosses, crescents, and circles to animals (particularly bears and birds) to abstract faces showing eyes and bared teeth. Some are neatly painted or incised while others are less carefully done, presumably reflecting variable artistic skills. For reasons unknown, the shield figures at Bear Gulch and Atherton Canyon are slightly smaller than the average shield figure on the Northwestern Plains, ranging from the size of a quarter coin to the size of a hand.

Bears, identified by teeth and claws on a handful of shields, are called the Bear Comes Out and Standing Bear motifs by rock art specialists. Bear Comes Out shows a grizzly emerging from one side of the shield as if it were charging ferociously from its den. Standing Bear shows a bear rearing up on its hind

The rock art in Bear Gulch and Atherton is overwhelmingly Ceremonial style warrior art. One example out of many hundreds, this Shield-bearing Warrior figure wears a roach-style headdress, face paint, knee pendants and footwear, and carries a large multi-colored shield and decorated lance. Plains Indian war shields provided protection and served as a form of recognition, status, and intimidating spiritual power. PHOTOGRAPH COURTESY OF JIM KEYSER.

legs as though ready to attack. Both of these fearsome shield designs were drawn in similar ways by the Crow, Hidatsa, Sioux, and other tribes, and Bear Gulch shows that these motifs have a history of at least four centuries on the Plains. However, the specific ethnic identity of the artists who drew these fear-inspiring figures at Bear Gulch remains unknown.

In another drawing, nine warriors carry shields with a human arm and hand reaching out from a darkened half of the circular field. The Bear Gulch investigators named this formidable motif "The Hand of God" because it seemed to portray a supernatural being reaching out to both protect the shield owner and to strike down his enemy.

In both cases, the heraldic designs of bears and supernatural beings metaphorically signified intimidating cosmic power and protection for the shield owner in battle. Rock art specialists and tribal people know that shield imagery is derived from the warriors' vision quests and their spirit helpers.

Solitary shield-bearing warriors are common in Bear Gulch and Atherton Canyon, but in more than 40 instances, multiple warriors occur in horizontally oriented rows or phalanxes. Most wear carefully executed shields and a variety of regalia and weapons. In some cases, the phalanxes are drawn over, rubbed, scratched, or modified with new shield figures or other designs. Detailed analyses of the compositions revealed that warriors in the earliest Bear Gulch phalanxes wear their hair in a scalp lock or a crested roach (Mohawk) style, and later warrior phalanxes carry clubs or maces and lances tipped with metal points. Shield figures and compositions evolved artistically over time, reflecting changes in Plains Indian society, including the acquisition of metal trade goods, guns, and, eventually, horses.

Scenes of actual combat are rarely depicted in the warrior phalanx compositions. Instead, these motifs show either war parties heading out or forming up for battle or, perhaps more

Stand-alone shield bearing warriors are common but they occasionally occur in planned compositions of multiple warriors in horizontal rows. Here two of the warriors wear distinctive wolf-hat headdresses, indicated by pointed ears and long snouts. Three warriors hold fearsome spike maces, made of long, wood shafts studded with one or two curved horn spikes. PHOTOGRAPH COURTESY OF MAVIS AND JOHN GREER.

likely, assemblies of warrior societies in camp parades, as documented ethnographically for many Plains tribes. However, 11 combat scenes do occur at Bear Gulch. Most of the scenes are simply drawn, typically showing a warrior's lance touching another shield-bearing warrior figure, or a warrior shooting arrows. It is easy to conclude that it was the warrior's spiritual prowess and accomplishments on display, not his actual deeds in combat—something that comes later in biographic art.

Rock art is an invaluable source of information for archeologists because it provides tangible insights into the lives, customs,

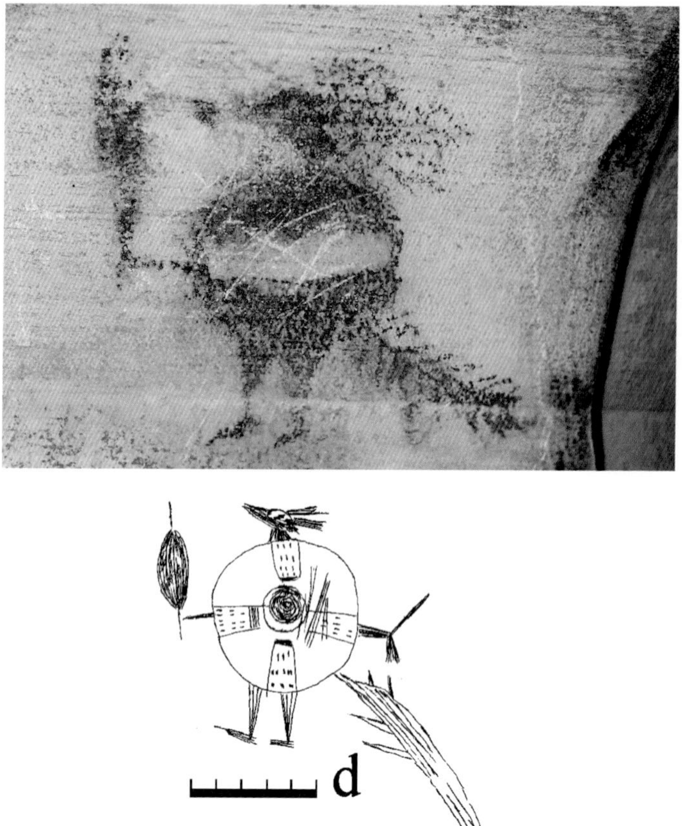

Archaeologists traced and photographed all of the Bear Gulch and Atherton Canyon rock art to obtain precise, scaled images (many images are too faint and worn to be fully seen without careful tracings and computer enhanced photography). This tracing (bottom image) shows an Indian warrior holding an elaborate shield and a spear with flagging decoration. He carries a large (otter, coyote) animal skin medicine bundle. His tribal identity is unknown. A similar pictograph is shown in the top photo. FROM KEYSER ET AL. 2012.

Biographic Tradition rock art frequently depicts raids and warfare after Indians had acquired horses in the early eighteenth century. These images in Turner Rockshelter in the Bull Mountains (central Montana) show three distinct activities. The top one shows horses and riders battling pedestrian enemies; a Blackfeet warrior wearing a bonnet spears a pedestrian warrior (the simple box figure with a small head). In the middle scene, bonneted Blackfeet riders, with bridles and quirts, return from horse raid with the enemy in hot pursuit. The bottom scene shows warriors attacking enemy fortifications (log or rock breastworks). Two warriors are assaulting the smaller fortification, which is occupied by six enemies. These images were drawn by the Blackfeet during the last decades of Blackfeet-Crow warfare (1875-1890). DRAWINGS COURTESY OF JIM KEYSER.

and beliefs of Indian peoples that cannot be realized from "dirt" archaeology alone. While projectile points tell us very little about ancient warfare, Bear Gulch and Atherton Canyon warrior rock art allows us to imagine a Plains Indian battle during the "dog days"—(the long time period before Indians acquired horses and instead used dogs to pull pole sleds or travois.)

Protected by large, colorfully painted war shields, the combatants, perhaps no more than a dozen on each side, would have faced off in irregular skirmish lines. Combat probably began with a rain of arrows from the opposing sides, which may have only rarely penetrated the large hide shields. At last, a warrior, possibly wearing a fearsome wolf hat, taunts his enemies, eventually drawing the sides into fierce hand-to-hand combat. In the ensuing fight at close quarters, several warriors hit their enemies with bow-spears, counting coup—touching, but not killing, an enemy combatant—while another is mortally wounded. Because neither side wins the day, the combatants slip away with their wounded and dead. Not to be forgotten, successful warriors traveled to the sacred canyons near the Little Snowy Mountains to paint their individual war deeds on the canyon walls and pay homage to their spiritual helpers.

Unfortunately, the 900 or more painted and incised Bear Gulch Style shield figures have yet to be linked with a particular Plains Indian group. Elsewhere on the Plains, large crosses and stars are common on Cheyenne shields. Bears occur frequently on Sioux shields, though not exclusively. Wolf hat headdresses and feathered spears have, to date, no counterparts at other rock art sites. However, archaeological sites located along the Missouri River in central Montana date to this same time period and show artifacts assemblages that suggest they are the product of the same people who painted rock art at Bear Gulch.

In addition to the warrior art, other Plains rock art traditions are found in lesser amounts in both Bear Gulch and Atherton canyons. To mention only a few, the Pecked Abstract Tradition shows broad lines, light scratches, polished grooves, and cupules (a small hollowed-out "dimple"). They are in poor shape due to extensive weathering and the addition of later art. The cultural

This is perhaps the best known shield-bearing warrior figure at Bear Gulch. The figure wears headdress feathers and a trailing feather bustle, and prominently carries a white weapon flag. The remarkable pictograph is surrounded by four smaller painted and incised warriors. Sadly, the composition is scratched over with modern graffiti—a common problem at rock art sites throughout Montana. PHOTOGRAPH COURTESY OF JIM KEYSER.

meaning of these motifs is unknown. Pecked art is not common here, which may partly be attributed to the region's geology. Surviving pecked tradition art survives only in regions of the Plains with harder, denser (less erosive) surfaces.

Cliff faces painted with extensive washes of red pigment (ocher) are found at a few places in both canyons. Called the Foothills Abstract Tradition, this widespread Indian rock art style extends along the Rocky Mountains from Alberta, Canada, to Dillon, Montana. In addition to applying red washes, artists drew simple stick figures, animals (bear, bison, lizards, and turtles), geometric designs, splotches, handprints, and finger lines.[111] These figures are often painted over the red wash. Radiocarbon dates of Foothills Abstract pictographs near Helena, Montana, demonstrate that the tradition is at least 1,200 to 1,400 years old.[112] This is obviously a very small, spatially constricted dating sample and other evidence indicates that this tradition may extend further back in time.

What is the purpose and meaning of Foothills Abstract rock art? Archaeologists think that shamans and vision questing supplicants "fixed" their visual images on cliff walls in sacred fasting locales. Many of the designs—finger lines, splotches and blobs, and geometric figures—are similar from site to site. Possibly, these commonly repeated designs are entoptic phenomena or phosphenes—geometric patterns visualized within the human eye while in trances and altered states of consciousness involving fasting and sleep deprivation (tightly close your eyes and patterns of light and designs will appear, even without fasting). Based on neurological studies, some archaeologists believe that these universal images may arise from the common structures of the human brain and nervous system but their meanings varied widely among rock-art-making cultures.[113]

Another unusual aspect of Foothills Abstract rock art is the deliberate human-made scratches and abrasions on top of many painted figures. The incisions are very precise (contained almost exclusively within painted figures) and are clearly not the result of bushes, wild animals, or livestock rubbing against the surface. In a remarkable discovery at the Hellgate pictograph site near Helena, Montana, geochemical analysis of a small stone-engraving tool left in a small crack in the cliff revealed iron pigment on its tip.[114] Archaeologists speculate that this ancient cultural practice either cancelled or captured the images' power by removing the paint for use in magical rites.

Bison, bighorn sheep, moose, antelope, deer, elk, wolves or coyotes, foxes, skunks, rabbits, birds, and reptiles are also drawn in Bear Gulch and Atherton Canyon. Some animal figures occur individually in naturalistic poses while others are parts of larger scenes, showing spears or arrows protruding from their bodies. One popular interpretation is that painted or engraved animals reflect "hunting magic," whereby hunters or shamans, to ensure success, appealed to the sympathies of the targeted animals through painting and ritual.

Plains rock art scholars and tribal people agree that this popular explanation is probably overworked since "hunting" art was surely drawn for many purposes.[115] For example, Early Hunting Tradition art consists entirely of petroglyphs pecked in sandstone cliffs which show detailed scenes of communal animal hunting (deer, elk, mountain sheep, bison, and rabbits). It is the oldest rock art tradition on the Plains. Animals in these composed "hunting" scenes may have been drawn as part of shamanistic practices to invoke the supernatural attributes of particular creatures or even to teach young tribal members the hunting practices and rituals of their band. Still, the Miniature Figure Style at Bear Gulch and Atherton Canyon contains a disproportionate, though small, number of hunting scenes showing hunted, wounded, or inverted (dead) animals. The animals are shot through with spears or arrows. In this case, some kind of ritualized activity involving sympathetic hunting magic may be associated with these figures.

Finally, the unusual Vertical Series Tradition is found in Atherton Canyon and Bear Gulch. It includes simple rectilinear T, H, and + shaped symbols, sometimes reversed or inverted. This poorly understood rock art tradition may have functioned as a rudimentary symbolic writing system or a code that depicts, as rock art expert Larry Loendorf suspects, medicinal or ceremonial plants including sacred tobacco. Specialists disagree about

Shield heraldry offers clues as to cultural affiliation. The design on this well-preserved Bear Gulch shield, with its central cross and flared arms, is called "cross pate" by rock art specialists. Cross pate is common on the Bear Gulch shields, as well as on Cheyenne, Kiowa, and even Pueblo shields. However, further research is necessary to tie the many shield designs and other warrior accoutrements at Bear Gulch and Atherton Canyon to specific Plains Indian groups. Photograph courtesy of Jim Keyser.

the antiquity of this tradition, some placing it in the eighteenth century and later, while others think it may be as old as Foothills Abstract rock art.

Biographic Tradition warrior art succeeded the Ceremonial Tradition on the Plains. Although it is widespread throughout central and eastern Montana, this rock art style is surprisingly scarce in both canyons, for reasons unknown. As its name implies, the Biographic Tradition is best known for its exquisitely detailed depictions of warriors with horses, guns, and other weaponry, frequently illustrated in mortal combat. Dating from the early 1700s to the 1880s, Biographic Tradition art documents, sometimes in great detail, the cultural events in nineteenth century Judith Basin of central Montana and an ancient Indian lifeway and warrior culture undergoing irrevocable change.

Biographic rock art encompasses many distinctive styles whose nuanced differences are mainly of interest to specialists. These styles help to bridge the gap between the earlier Ceremonial Tradition and Biographic Tradition warrior art. In several cases, ethnic identifications can be made. For example, V-neck and hourglass-shaped human figures, some with heart lines and some not, are characteristic of the Blackfoot Style, dating between 500 and 300 years ago when the Blackfeet were a dominant presence on the plains of central Montana.

Despite its emphasis on raiding and combat, Biographic Tradition is not exclusively warrior art. Many rock art compositions include villages, dances, hunts, parades, sex and birth scenes, and all aspects of Euroamerican settlement—wagons, boats, forts, and trains. Some of this art has been attributed to bored sheepherders and cowboys, rather than Indian peoples, particularly when found on complicated rock art panels that span prehistory and history. But recent research has shown that Native peoples drew many of these historic features, sometimes in considerable detail, and placed them among older rock art images.

Rock art specialists can "read" Biographic Tradition art as narratives.[116] Their "Rosetta Stones" are painted bison robes and ledger book drawings on which many of the designs observed in rock art are also drawn. Native peoples used ledger and accounting books obtained from traders, soldiers, and missionaries to portray old battles, hunts, and personal experiences in pencil or crayon and, in some cases, explain their meanings.

From these sources, archeologists have learned that a pattern of C-shaped horse tracks denotes the movement of equestrian warriors in battle. Simply drawn "capture hands" above a warrior figure indicate counting coup. A series of triangular configurations denote a tipi village under attack. A slash mark on a rider's abdomen identifies a combat wound. Put together, a narrative of an Indian battle comes to life.

Rock art can be dated in several ways. First, the superimposition of one figure atop another obviously shows which production technique and style is younger. In Atherton Canyon and Bear Gulch, red crayon, scratched, and charcoal figures are overlain by figures painted with white and red liquid paint. Next, the extent of weathering and erosion gives an indication of relative age, although local geology and environmental conditions must be taken into account. The relatively good shape of most of the Bear Gulch and Atherton Canyon rock art in the harsh central Montana plains, coupled with its placement on highly fractured limestone bedrock, indicates that it cannot be very old. In fact, most of the rock art dates to within the last 1000 years, if not significantly more recent. Finally, stylistic similarities among various rock art images place them in a relative chronological sequence. Clearly, panels with horses, guns, and metal projectile points are more recent than rock art where such features are absent, as in the Ceremonial and Foothills Abstract traditions. This kind of analysis requires careful study of the evolution of many different rock art styles and figures over time and across geographic distance.

Scientists also use instruments to more precisely date rock art. Radiocarbon dating is the most common, but it is very tricky.[117] Since minerals such as hematite are the primary component of aboriginal paint, there must be enough organic content (carbon), such as animal fat or charcoal used in the paint binder, to allow dating. Moreover, samples must be carefully chosen and removed from thickly painted figures—typically those already flaking or exfoliating off the rock face—so as not to damage the image. Special laboratory techniques are then used to purify and extract organic carbon. Insufficient organic content in the paint is the bane of rock art dating.

Luckily, Bear Gulch rock art experts Marvin Rowe and Karen Steelman successfully obtained a handful of radiocarbon dates.[118] A skunk figure in Bear Gulch is 1,560 years old, while a geometric design at another site dates to 900 years ago. A solid black shield-bearing warrior in Atherton Canyon dates to about 650 years ago. Theses radiocarbon dates, spanning the past 1,000 years, are compatible with estimates derived from other rock art dating techniques.

Archaeological testing in the grassy bottom of Bear Gulch could not directly link the rock art with the archaeological deposit below by the chance discovery of exhausted paint crayons, palettes, or related artistic evidence. Nonetheless, the thinly scattered butchered animal bones and few stone tools are probably the widespread refuse of hunting and gathering groups and warrior artists, which accumulated over many centuries. Importantly, the small sample of radiocarbon dates obtained from this archaeological work correlate exactly with the dates obtained from the rock art testing.

The rock art of western Montana contrasts markedly with the warrior art of the Plains. From the Bitterroot Valley to Libby, most of the known rock art belongs to Columbia Plateau artistic traditions.[119] Here, common motifs comprising animals, human stick figures, geometric figures, rays, and tally marks were painted on the faces of nearly inaccessible ledges and overhangs in craggy mountain and lakeshore cliffs. Usually drawn with red pigment, this rock art does not involve complex scenes or narratives like the Plains rock art, although hunting scenes occasionally portray mountain sheep, deer, elk, hunters, dogs, and nets or timber surrounds. This particular rock art style may indeed be "hunting magic" intended to control or placate the animals

Cliff walls were portals into the supernatural world. Foothills Abstract rock, common along the Rocky Mountain foothills from Alberta, Canada, to Dillon, Montana, is characterized by red paint (hematite, ochre) washes with overlying geometric designs, finger lines, animals, and simple human stick figures. This rock art probably commemorated Indian vision questing experiences and shamanic ceremonies. PHOTOGRAPH COURTESY OF MAVIS AND JOHN GREER.

before or after the hunt, or it may simply document the events in some special way.

Ethnographies and oral histories report that vision questing was a common practice among Columbia Plateau men and women, and the majority of western Montana rock art records such vision quests. Many examples show where male or female supplicants "fixed" a pictograph image of their guardian spirit, usually at secluded fasting spots. The resulting images, their meanings, and their locations were known only to the owner,

Western Montana rock art is more similar to Columbia Plateau imagery than the warrior art of the Northwestern Plains. Common images in western Montana include animals, stick figures, geometric figures, and tally marks painted in isolated places in rocky cliffs. Some compositions with animals may depict hunting scenes. The majority of the rock art records vision quests, whereby male and female supplicants "fixed" a pictograph image of their vision and guardian spirit at secluded fasting places. As shown here, tally marks are thought to mark the length of time that the supplicant spent seeking guidance or visions. PHOTOGRAPH COPYRIGHT BY DAVID MINICK.

who might return to this special place during his or her lifetime to call on the guardian spirit to pray, fulfill vows, and solicit guidance and instruction.

Located near the community of Grass Range, Bear Gulch can be easily visited. For a small fee, the Ahlgren family offers guided hikes, informed by their own deep personal interest and knowledge gained from the professional investigations of the remarkable Bear Gulch and Atherton Canyon sites.

Centuries ago, Hagan village was a busy place. As depicted here, Hagan villagers lived in sturdy earth lodges near the Yellowstone River. Here they put dried corn, beans, and squash, grown on the Yellowstone River floodplain, in deep, below-ground cache pits to protect their precious food stores from deer mice and vermin. (Later, non-native Norway rats had little trouble gnawing their way into such cache pits, with dire consequences for Middle Missouri villagers.) Hunters brought game to camp from the surrounding plains (bison) and the nearby Yellowstone River breaks (deer, antelope). A large burial mound (with flying crows and buzzards above) is shown in the distance at the edge of the village. Illustration by Eric S. Carlson

FRONTIER FARMERS

HAGAN VILLAGE SITE

24DW1

400 YEARS AGO

Long before the arrival of Europeans, Montana's Indian peoples had adapted to the Montana plains in different ways. Some were full-time bison hunters who resided year-round on the windswept plains and in the Rocky Mountain valleys and foothills. Others were part-time agriculturalists who seasonally journeyed onto the plains to obtain bison meat and hides, and then returned to their well-protected villages on the lower Missouri River and its tributaries. In rare instances, some villagers migrated onto the Plains *en masse* to live full time.

The Hagan site is one of those rare places. It lies on a high bluff above the north bank of the Yellowstone River, about five miles upstream from the community of Glendive in eastern Montana. The flat bluff drops abruptly to the river bottom on the east and is bounded on the north and west by a small arroyo. Today it overlooks a wide expanse of lush Yellowstone River bottom, prairie grasslands, and dissected badlands across the river. The land, which is owned by the Hagen family (WPA excavators misspelled their name, and the misspelling has stuck in the literature), is carpeted with native grasses and cultivated fields. This ancient place is protected by virtue of its location on private farmlands as well as its inclusion in the National Register of Historic Places and its designation as a National Historic Landmark.

The Hagan site investigations closely mesh with the WPA's Pictograph Cave project during the Great Depression of the 1930s.[120] Glendive rancher and amateur archaeologist Oscar Lewis first discovered the Hagan site and conducted minor testing there in 1936 and 1937 with a National Youth Administration crew (an early arm of the WPA). His probes yielded stone artifacts, bison scapula hoes, pottery sherds, and squash or pumpkin seeds. These promising results prompted Melville Sayre, then director of the Montana Statewide Survey, to secure WPA funding for more extensive work. Upon receiving permission from landowner Thomas Hagen, the dig commenced in 1938 under the direction of Lewis, who was soon called away to supervise the Pictograph Cave project.

The dense grassy sod covering the Hagan site offered few clues as to what might lie underneath. One oddity was a low, flat-topped, circular mound at the north end of the site. With the mound as one focus, the WPA grid system divided the large site into 10-foot squares, just like at Pictograph Cave. Artifacts were found in a layer of sod and sand one foot below the surface. The WPA crew discovered the remains of an ancient earth lodge, a burial mound, multiple food storage or cache pits, and hundreds of artifacts.

When fully exposed, the house ruin proved to be a circular depression measuring about 16 feet in diameter. Its clay floor was hard-packed and blackened from heavy use. Twelve evenly spaced postholes, some 18 inches deep, surrounded the depression. These postholes and four interior postholes were packed with bison bone to stabilize vertical posts. People entered the

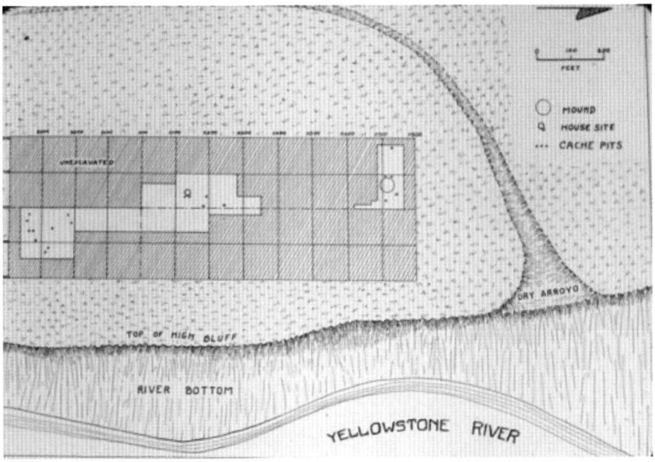

WPA crews excavated the Hagan village site on the Yellowstone River near Glendive in the late 1930s. As seen in the historic WPA photograph, digging occurred adjacent to the Yellowstone River, where earth lodges, a burial mound, food storage pits, and hundreds of artifacts were discovered. The Yellowstone River breaks can be seen in the distance. A map of the excavation is also shown. Hagan is a designated National Historic Landmark. PHOTOGRAPH COURTESY OF THE MONTANA HISTORICAL SOCIETY RESEARCH CENTER-PHOTOGRAPH ARCHIVES, HELENA, MONTANA.

Agricultural villages are exceedingly rare in Montana. Montana State University archaeologists conducted limited excavations at Hagan in 2001 to determine, once and for all, if the Hagan villagers grew corn. Because there is little to distinguish Hagan from the surrounding landscape or indicate the location of WPA excavation pits some 70 years later, the MSU crew used magnetometers and dug test pits, as shown here, to find archaeological features, particularly storage pits that did, indeed, contain evidence of corn agriculture. PHOTOGRAPH BY LESLIE B. DAVIS.

lodge from the east via a covered doorway, as evidenced by hard-packed earth and two more postholes. The lodge was once roofed with timber rafters, branches, and earth. An ash-filled fire pit lay near the lodge center. All told, the structure appeared to be a less elaborate version of a typical Plains Indian earth lodge built historically by the Mandan, Hidatsa, and other Middle Missouri River villagers in North and South Dakota.

The WPA crew excavated 20 bell-shaped storage pits located outside of the lodge. Measuring about three feet deep and wide,

The MSU crew excavated two deep, aboriginal storage pits from which they extracted artifacts, new radiocarbon dates, and evidence of corn agriculture. The two storage pits excavated by MSU were about 3- to 4-feet deep, but earlier WPA crews dug others that were as much as 6-feet deep, resembling the deep storage pits in Middle Missouri villages to the east. PHOTOGRAPH BY LESLIE B. DAVIS finger marks were still visible on some of the pits' mud plaster walls. Other pits were as much as six feet deep and looked more like those found in Middle Missouri agricultural villages. During the life of the village, the pits contained stores of dried squash, pumpkin, and corn. When emptied, they served as convenient trash dumps for fire ash and charcoal, pieces of broken animal bone, pottery sherds, stone tool fragments, and chipping debris.

The unique circular mound was laid out on a nearly level part of the site. Measuring about 45 feet in diameter, it was built up by a two-foot-thick layer of mixed clay, gravel, and sand which had been deliberately placed there by the site's inhabitants (it is definitely not a geological or farming feature). There were no signs of postholes, storage pits, or other features on top of the mound. Instead, the mound contained human skull and bone fragments, pottery sherds, and artifacts identical to those found throughout the site. The WPA investigators concluded this was a burial mound on which pole scaffolds were once placed to hold human bodies—an established funerary practice among Northern Plains Indian tribes. Once the bodies decomposed on the scaffolds, the disarticulated skeletons were assembled and buried within the mound. WPA consulting forensic expert Richard Snodgrass concluded that the remains of 23 to 40 or more individuals lay buried inside the mound.[121]

When WPA excavations ceased, the Hagan site artifacts were transported to laboratories in Lewistown and Eastern Normal School in Billings (now City College, Montana State University-Billings). Based on field notes and his own artifact analysis, William Mulloy published the final project report in 1942. In it, he documented a rich material culture of stone tools, mauls, grinding stones, abraders, tablets, beads, pipes, and pendants. Organic artifacts comprised bone awls, wrenches, knife handles, scrapers, fishhooks, dice, beads, decorated bracelets, paint applicator, scapula digging tools, river mussel and Pacific Coast dentalia shell beads and, possibly, snow goggles. To say the least, Hagan village was the scene of much industry and must have been a lively place. Discounting the presence of squash seeds, Mulloy thought that agriculture was just "suggested" by the scapula hoes. (Technically speaking, Plains Indian farmers practiced "horticulture," which means growing plants with hand tools, while "agriculture" involves animals, mechanized equipment, or irrigation.)

There things sat until 2001, when the indefatigable Les Davis of the Montana State University-Museum of the Rockies in Bozeman and his colleagues conducted limited testing to determine, once and for all, if the Hagan villagers grew corn (maize) along the Yellowstone River.[122] He questioned the received wisdom that, at Hagan's longitude, the frost-free growing season was too short to reliably support corn agriculture. His team struggled to find the original WPA excavation area but they subsequently conducted a magnetometer survey to locate buried features. Eventually, they struck upon two deep cache pits, from which they extracted artifacts, plant evidence, and new radiocarbon dates.

As at Pictograph Cave, WPA excavations at Hagan occurred before the advent of radiocarbon dating. That Hagan was related in some way to ancient and historic Middle Missouri River agricultural village cultures in North and South Dakota was never in question. WPA consulting ceramics expert James Griffin, an eminent Eastern Woodlands archaeologist at the University of Michigan, told Mulloy that the Hagan pottery closely resembled ceramics made by the Mandan Indians. From this evidence, Mulloy inferred that Mountain Crow Indians, who had separated from the Hidatsa (the Mandan's close neighbors) sometime in the distant past, inhabited the Hagan site.

In the 1970s, archaeologists dated several wood samples from the WPA collection. These first assays and the ceramic styles led them to conclude that Hagan was occupied from about 1675 to 1700 A.D. The 2001 MSU dates from one of the cache pits pushed the occupation back another 200 years. This earlier age supported an analysis by Middle Missouri ceramic experts, who surmised that the Hagan pottery closely resembled ware from archaeological sites in the Knife-Heart River region of North Dakota, dating from 1400 and 1524 A.D.[123] So it now seems that Indian farmers inhabited Hagan sometime between 600 and 350 years ago.

Agricultural villages typically yield pottery cooking and storage vessels, and Hagan is no different. WPA excavators unearthed nearly 30,000 sherds from which they were able to partly restore 14 vessels. The MSU team found more sherds comprising at least two vessels. The Hagan potters made globular-shaped jars with well-defined shoulders, decorated collars and rims, and slightly flattened bottoms. Using the paddle and anvil method, potters worked and shaped the clay by patting the exterior with a paddle while supporting the interior with an anvil or stone. The pottery was then fired in an open hearth, giving it a dark grey to brown buff hue. It was not fancily painted like the ancient Indian pottery of the American Southwest. But collared vessels were richly decorated with stamped and incised lines, hatches, and other designs. The interiors of many sherds are heavily blackened with the residues of soups and stews. Some ceramics in the Hagan collection are atypical of the Middle Missouri region and reflect ceramic input and trade with pottery-using nomadic groups living north and west of Hagan in present-day Montana and Canada.[124]

It might come as a surprise that the nomadic Indian peoples of Montana once used ceramic cooking ware and water vessels. After all, pottery is both time-consuming to make and easily broken. Nonetheless, it is not only found in the few rich, semi-sedentary villages like Hagan but also in nomadic camps and

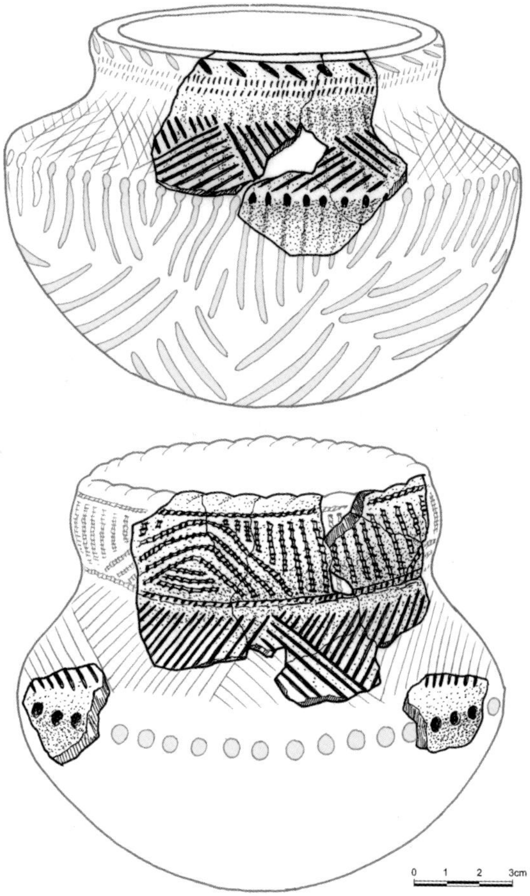

Agricultural villages like Hagan typically yield abundant pottery. William Mulloy's lab workers patiently restored fourteen vessels and parts of many others, as shown here. The unpainted, collared jars and bowls were richly decorated with incised lines, hatch marks, and other carved designs. Hagan villagers used ceramic pots to store water and cook soups and stews. Illustration by Eric S. Carlson based on Mulloy 1942.

animal procurement sites across the plains and interior Rockies. Some vessels were stored at repeatedly used camps (for example, under rock ledges) while other pots were carried from place to place. Ceramics first appear in the archaeological record of nomadic Plains Indian groups about 1,500 years ago (called Besant and Avonlea by archaeologists). Some Montana pottery is related to ceramic traditions in the Middle Missouri region of the Dakotas, while others resemble wares from the Saskatchewan Basin of Canada and the northern Great Basin of Idaho and Utah. This wild mix of pottery styles reflects the sharing of ever-evolving ceramic ideas through centuries of band migrations, travel, trade, and cultural interactions, including the exchange of women potters through marriage and bride capture, as was commonly practiced among Plains Indian groups.

Hagan hunters killed a variety of wild game but, predictably, bison predominated. The WPA crew recovered the remains of 341 bison. Faunal analysis by Jack Fisher of MSU revealed that the bison were killed some distance away on the surrounding plains and only select parts of the carcasses were taken to the village. Whitetail or mule deer were also taken from the Yellowstone River breaks. Mammal bones were smashed open with heavy stone mauls to obtain nutritious marrow. The recovered canid bones are no doubt from domestic dogs (*Canis familiaris*), not wolves, since packs of dogs were familiar sights in Indian villages, as attested by Lewis and Clark and other early explorers. Hagan people hunted turkey, bald eagle, and crow for food and to acquire bones for beads and tools, and feathers for headdresses, ornaments, and medicine bundles. The villagers also harvested channel catfish with bone hooks and possibly willow weirs or traps in the Yellowstone River, along with lesser amounts of bass and minnows or chub.

Mulloy could not say much about the plant remains in the 20 or so cache pits due to the WPA crew's poor recovery techniques and the state of floral analysis at the time. The MSU team excavated and carefully analyzed the contents of two cache pits for plant macrofossils, pollen, and other plant residue. Pollen specialist Linda Scott Cummings retrieved squash or pumpkin pollen from cache pit 1, along with grass, pine, sage, and herbaceous plant pollen.[125] The presence of grasses, also confirmed by phytoliths, probably indicates its use as pit lining. The charred wood is the residue of fuel wood that washed or was tossed into pits when they were abandoned. *Et voila!* Cache pit 2 yielded corn pollen. So, we now know with certainty that the Hagan villagers grew corn and squash or pumpkins and stored their vegetable produce in deep, grass-lined pits, exactly like days gone by in their Middle Missouri River villages.

Ancient Native American civilizations first arose in Mesoamerica some 3,200 years ago. Influenced by the flow of goods and ideologies from these faraway cosmopolitan cultures, the Native peoples of the Eastern Woodlands and Lower Mississippi Valley had also developed into complex societies by 2,000 B.P.[126] With an agricultural foundation, these Indigenous Woodland societies grew into sophisticated chiefdoms and confederacies. They had hereditary leaders living in capital towns, earthen temples and burial mounds managed by religious specialists, craftspeople and traders, and outlying agricultural hamlets that fed them all. The elaborate trade systems of Hopewell, Mississippian, and other so-called "Mound Builder" cultures extended in all directions, creating a vast and vibrant Native economy stretching from the eastern seaboard, to the Gulf coast, and to the Rocky Mountains. Raiding and warfare among competing chiefdoms led to the construction of defensive fortifications of walls, ditches, and dry moats. The best-known ancient city in America is Cahokia Mounds State Park in southern Illinois, located directly across the Mississippi River from modern St Louis.[127]

A less elaborate version of this new cultural pattern eventually percolated northward into the middle reaches of the Missouri River and westward deep into its tributary river valleys in what archaeologists call the Plains Woodland and, later, Middle Missouri traditions. Thus, an agricultural way of life began some 700 years ago in the Knife-Heart River region of North Dakota.[128] Here, farmers cultivated corn, squash, beans, and sunflowers. Gardens were tilled with bison scapula hoes in rich alluvial soils along the river bottoms. At the geographic limits of reliable agriculture, farmers were at the mercy of drought, hail, wildfire, plant diseases, grasshoppers, and early frosts. Sealed, underground cache pits kept carefully stacked piles of corn, beans, and squash reasonably safe from mice and other varmints. Wild and domesticated plants and meat were cooked in pottery vessels inside and outside of substantial earth lodges. Food stores tempted neighboring villagers and nomadic raiders, especially during times of drought, crop failure, and famine. Earth lodge villages, with dry moats and palisades, were strategically placed on high bluffs above the Missouri River and its tributaries to defend against raids.

The inhabitants of Hagan brought this Middle Missouri agricultural lifestyle to the grassy bluff above the Yellowstone River. Although the WPA crew excavated only one earth lodge, Oscar Lewis's field notes indicate that several others are present under the prairie sod—something that was also suggested by the MSU magnetometer survey. The pumpkin-squash seeds, corn pollen, and scapula hoes all show that agriculture was practiced here. The diverse ceramics, lithic materials, and other artifacts demonstrate that the Hagan villagers interacted with other friendly groups and did not feel the need to defend their village from attack with fortifications—as far as we can tell. They died and were buried here, as the mound and its burials attest.

Archaeologists call the Hagan phenomenon a "site unit intrusion"—a fancy way of saying the migration of peoples to a new area where they assumed a new life with their cultural identity, economy, and traditions largely intact. On the Plains, the Hagan lifestyle contrasts with other Indian groups who gave up many aspects of their former agricultural lifeways to pursue nomadic, bison-hunting economies. Few agricultural sites like Hagan exist so far west on the Plains, leading many archaeologists to speculate that mass population movements were spurred by specific cultural circumstances such as band tension, drought and starvation, or pandemic disease.

Eastern Woodland and Mississippian chiefdoms and confederacies began to disintegrate about 500 years ago due to internal political stress, warfare, the cooling climate of the Little Ice Age, and first arrival of Europeans. The Hernando de Soto Expedition of 1539 to 1543 A.D. in the southeastern United States introduced the first of many pandemic European diseases—cholera, measles, scarlet fever, and smallpox—that eventually decimated Native populations, first in the Eastern United States and then across the entire American continent. To escape these horrible diseases, Indians from small villages and from larger communities often fled into untouched regions and into other Indian territories.

The Middle Missouri villagers of the Dakotas were eventually affected by these same events, having first contracted these deadly diseases in the Native trade centers from visiting European explorers and later by European and American travelers and traders coming up the Missouri River. These non-Indian travelers also carried aboard their keel boats another foreign pest, the brown Norway rat, which invaded Middle Missouri Indian villages and caused catastrophic devastation of Indian food stores and crops—bringing starvation and more cultural turmoil. As historian Elizabeth Finn poignantly documents, the history of the Mandan and Hidatsa during the eighteenth and nineteenth centuries largely concerns the joining of peoples in an ever-decreasing number of shrinking earth-lodge villages as they struggled to maintain their old ways of life.[129]

In contrast to their Middle Missouri relatives, the exact fate of the Hagan villagers is speculative. Why did they leave? Where did they go? The traditional interpretation first proposed by William Mulloy in 1942, and reworked in various guises by other Plains archaeologists, is that the Hagan people became the Mountain Crow. According to tribal oral tradition, the Mountain Crow separated from their Awatixa Hidatsa relatives,

The Hagan site is associated with ancestral Crow people who migrated from their Middle Missouri farming villages in search of sacred tobacco, which they eventually found growing in the Bighorn Mountains. Tobacco is documented in this Crow rock art. The figure on the left is a buffalo spirit. The flat lines above the figure's head represent tobacco. On the second buffalo spirit figure's headdress, the seed is shown by the equilateral cross and the plant with branches or leaves are shown along its course. The rock art exactly matches historic photographs of Crow Indians wearing tobacco headdresses. PHOTOGRAPH COURTESY OF LARRY LOENDORF.

villagers who lived along the Missouri River in North Dakota. Mountain Crow bands then took a circuitous route through the West in search of the sacred tobacco (*Nicotiana multivalus*). They eventually found it growing in the Bighorn Mountains of Montana and Wyoming and settled there. Hagan on the Yellowstone River was but one rather substantial stop on their far-flung journey.

The Crow place name for Hagan is *Xoo'xashe Alatshiile Awooshisee,* or the "place where corn was planted but died."[130] According to Crow traditions, another village at the mouth of Rosebud Creek and the Yellowstone River was abandoned because farmers were only successful in growing tobacco there, not food. Ancestral Crow presence across the region is signaled archaeologically by Crow pottery, wood structures, and rock art depictions, including images of sacred tobacco ceremonies. Depictions of tobacco plants, seedpods, and ceremonies, and archaeological evidence (tobacco pollen) in southeastern Montana can be tied directly to the Crow Sacred Tobacco Society, according to rock art authority Larry Loendorf.[131]

Other archaeologists are skeptical. Ceramic expert Ann Johnson, for example, suggests that the Hagan people possibly moved back to their Middle Missouri villages, spurred by deteriorating Little Ice Age conditions and the great difficulties that it wrought on corn agriculture. She points out that "Crow pottery" actually is a hodge-podge of different ceramic types.[132] The feasibility of traveling hither and yon by Hagan villagers/turned Mountain Crow peoples in a relatively short amount of time is also questionable. The paucity of villages like Hagan gives these ideas credence, although several other large, relatively unexplored ceramic-bearing sites like Hagen are located on the Yellowstone River and the Bell Fourche River in Wyoming and they might tell a different story. While the Crow-Hidatsa surely figures in here somewhere, at this juncture, archaeologists are reluctant to firmly assign an ethnic identity to the Hagan villagers, although contemporary Crow people are not so hesitant.

In closing, one should pause to appreciate the many fruits and vegetables domesticated by the Indigenous peoples of the Americas which grace our dining room tables today: avocado, cocoa, corn, beans, peanut, peppers, potatoes, pumpkin, squashes, tomato, and sunflower, to name only the best known. As Hagan attests, neither the Plains nor Rocky Mountains fell outside the sphere of highly significant agricultural and cultural innovations originating in Central America and then spreading into the Eastern Woodlands and Lower Mississippi Valley of North America.

Had the ancient chiefdoms and confederations of the East Coast, Southeast, Midwest, and Middle Missouri survived the ecological changes of the Little Ice Age without European interference, diseases, and genocide, the Indigenous and European histories of North America would be very different. Densely populated and sophisticated urban centers could well have spread out deep onto the Plains and westward towards the Rockies, with ever more elaborate Indian towns, cities, trade centers, and travel networks. We will never know. Our modern conception of "wilderness," however, partly hinges on this chance of history, for the first European settlers of eastern North America did not, in fact, look upon "untrammeled nature" as later romanced by writers, painters, and naïve ecologists, but upon the abandoned and overgrown agriculture fields of America's first farmers and urbanites.

Wickiup Cave once sheltered a small, extended family band of Sheep Eater or Mountain Shoshone during the nineteenth century. As depicted here, a husband and wife skin several mountain sheep. Other animal skins are drying on the long support pole extending from the conical lodge. Women and children tend a cooking fire. The Sheep Eater's hunting and pack dogs poke around camp, looking for meat and hide scraps. Illustration by Eric S. Carlson.

MOUNTAINEERS

WICKIUP CAVE
24BE601

200 YEARS AGO

The picturesque basin and range topography of southwest Montana looks a lot like the neighboring northern Great Basin of Idaho and Utah. In the distant past, small bands of Great Basin Shoshone hunter-gatherers traveled north into the sage-covered mountain valleys of present-day Idaho, Montana, and Wyoming. When and why this migration occurred is a matter of scholarly debate. (Archaeologists call it the "Numic expansion" for the language spoken by migrating Shoshone and linguistically related peoples.)[133] Some experts conservatively place their arrival in the Central Rockies by 1,000 years ago, while others believe that their presence here is far older, beginning as early as 4,000 years ago if not well before that. But a single "Shoshones on the march" scenario is unlikely because the evidence suggests that there were multiple treks by Shoshone bands into the mountain-plains region. Whenever the Shoshone took up residence, they followed their old Great Basin ways. Small bands carried an effective technology of durable and perishable clothing, equipment, weapons, and shelter, all finely tuned to the requirements of basin and mountain living.

Early western travelers and, later, anthropologists came to

identify the scattered Shoshone bands by their principle food sources, so that these Indian people were known as "salmon eaters," "ground hog eaters," "mountain sheep eaters," and so forth. Shoshone bands that acquired horses and pursued a bison economy were called "buffalo eaters." In reality, these names were misleading because all Shoshone bands ate a diversity of foods and band membership was fluid, which is the way of many hunter-gatherers. Anthropologists lumped these widely dispersed Indian bands into the Western (Great Basin), Eastern (Wyoming), and Northern Shoshone (Idaho, Montana). The Sheep Eaters or Mountain Shoshone (the terms are used interchangeably here) of southwest Montana, the focus of this chapter, are Northern Shoshone.

Wickiup Cave is located in a large, north-facing limestone cave above Big Sheep Creek in the Tendoy Mountains of southwest Montana.[134] Concealed by tall Douglas fir, the cave provides a sweeping vista of the adjacent mountains and the valley bottom below. Inside the cave a family of Sheep Eater Shoshone built a conical timbered lodge, which is more commonly known as a wickiup. Despite the cave's secluded location, artifact collectors pillaged the lodge in the 1960s, removing an untold number of stone, wood, ceramic, and metal artifacts. Following up on a tip, a University of Montana field crew, including the author, documented and mapped the site in 1974.

Although the lodge inside the cave is protected from weather, it is a marvel that is has survived so intact. A thick pole, some 23 feet long, braced against several rocks and the back wall of the cave, supports the structure. Two other poles rest in the crotch of this main support pole, forming a solid tripod foundation. Another 15 poles and then sticks and boughs were added. Rocks piled up around the base of the lodge held down hide covers and provided protection from the bitter winter winds sweeping up Big Sheep Creek canyon. A wide gap between the upright poles

Sheep Eater or Mountain Shoshone built many conical timber lodges or wickiups in southwest Montana and the Greater Yellowstone area. These Shoshone pole lodges were covered with sticks, brush, and hides. One of the best documented lodges is Wickiup Cave, shown here, which is located inside a large limestone cave in the Tendoy Mountains near Lima. PHOTOGRAPH COURTESY OF THE BLM-DILLON FIELD OFFICE.

suggests that people entered the lodge from the east. The lodge's interior is badly dug up so there is no longer evidence of an interior fire hearth. But the abundant burned sticks and charcoal are clear evidence of warming and cooking fires.

Site pilfering was so thorough that there was little left for University of Montana archaeologists to recover. Fortunately, I was able to track down several artifact collections. One relic collector related that a variety of tools and refuse was discovered inside and outside of the old lodge. Another revealed that his collection came from beneath a "bed" made from rock, pine boughs, and grass. Combined, the known collections include obsidian and chert arrowheads (one still hafted onto a wood shaft); stone knives, scrapers and a drill; wood arrow shaft fragments; tanned bison hide scrap and hair; bone awls; pottery sherds; and a metal nail, pendant, and possibly a rifle part. My informants stated that other, no longer locatable, artifacts were taken from the cave, including a rifle (or just the barrel). This surviving material culture points to an extended family of Sheep Eater or Mountain Shoshone who inhabited the Tendoy Range early in the nineteenth century.

Besides Wickiup Cave, more than 90 wood conical lodges still survive in Idaho, Montana, Wyoming, and the Dakotas. (This small number must pale in comparison to what once existed.)[135] The few lodges dated by tree ring studies are about 150 years old, which is consistent with the historic glass and metal artifacts found inside them. Many Indian groups built temporary wood structures for hunting and war expeditions as well as for sweating, healing, mourning, and other social, religious, and medicinal purposes. However, based on ethnography and archaeology, archeologists can reasonably attribute some of the more durably built lodges in the mountains of this tri-state region as being longer term domiciles for small, widely dispersed Sheep Eater family bands.

Hunting and fishing off-reservation in the early twentieth century, Chief Tendoy's sons and their families used the Pass Creek conical lodges, shown here, in the Medicine Lodge Valley in the late 1800s and early 1900s. The Shoshone gifted beaded leather gloves and other items to surrounding ranching families. The now dilapidated Pass Creek lodges have not been excavated but their cultural deposits may contain the same kinds of artifacts as found at Wickiup Cave.

As their name implies, Sheep Eaters hunted bighorn sheep (*Ovis canadensis*), sometimes constructing timber enclosures or traps. One trap, called the LaMarche site, is located high above the Big Hole River in the Pioneer Mountains west of the community of Melrose.[136] It is composed of converging timber fences leading uphill to an earth-filled timber ramp and a four-sided pole catch-pen placed just below the crest of a narrow, forested ridge. To operate the trap, hunters and dogs gently pushed the sheep up the grassy, south-facing slope (likely mountain sheep bedding grounds) toward the ridge. Small hideouts in the drive-line walls may have concealed the hunt leader or a shaman who helped orchestrate the operation from their vantages and perhaps even coaxed the sheep by thumping on wood to imitate fighting rams.[137] Bighorn sheep skulls placed in the crotch of a nearby tree at traps in Wyoming sites may have served a practical (marking the traps' locations) or ritual purpose (we don't know), but none have yet been found at LaMarche. By taking advantage of "follow the leader" sheep behavior, hunters, at the last minute, spooked and funneled the sheep into the timber-concealed ramp and catch-pen, whose tall, inward leaning poles prevented leaping and escape.

Fiber nets may have then been used to ensnare the panicked sheep and make their final dispatch easier, much as modern biologists do today to quiet thrashing bighorn sheep during tagging operations. Several such nets, dating to around A.D. 700, have been discovered in the mountains of Wyoming. Hunters likely used wood clubs to finish off the sheep, as suggested by several clubs found at a Wyoming sheep kill site.[138] In fact, no arrowheads, knives, or other artifacts have been found at LaMarche, but then no subsurface testing has been done here. At other sheep traps in Wyoming, butchered carcasses were carried to back to nearby camps but archaeologists have yet to find a butchering area or campsite in the vicinity of the LaMarche trap.

Today, it is difficult to imagine that enough mountain sheep once roamed the mountains of southwestern Montana and the Greater Yellowstone area to sustain Sheep Eater families for any significant period of time, let alone many other Indian bands. However, we know that the once abundant mountain sheep populations in Montana were decimated in the late nineteenth and twentieth centuries by diseases contracted from modern domestic sheep herds and remain in low numbers today, for the same reason.

Whether Sheep Eater bands came to reside in this mountainous region as the last representatives of a long-lived cultural

Mountain Shoshone bands hunted bighorn sheep for meat, hides, bone, horn, and other products. Sheep were hunted individually or driven into wood enclosures and dispatched. At the LaMarche Game Trap in the mountains near Melrose, sheep were gently driven up this grassy slope (top photo) between log drive lanes, over a narrow forested ridge, and into the dirt ramp and pole enclosure shown in the bottom photograph. Hunters dispatched the sheep trapped inside the lodgepole enclosure with clubs or arrows.

tradition or came to these mountains as refugees from the onslaught of Euroamerican immigrants is a topic of debate.[139] The historical accounts of Sheep Eaters by American explorers, trappers, and U.S. government officials are not particularly helpful, for they typically describe these seemingly reclusive peoples as impoverished, wretched, and primitive. This prejudice was hardly reserved for just the Sheep Eaters. Shoshone bands without horses in the Great Basin were called "diggers" and compared poorly to their materially richer equestrian, bison-hunting relations and other Indian groups. Moreover, these observations were colored by the cultural turmoil of the nineteenth century, during which settlers, miners, ranchers, and livestock fanned out through Shoshone country, despoiling ancient plant gathering areas, fishing streams, and hunting grounds. Domestic pigs, for example, extensively rooted up camas—a major Indian food source. A small, mobile but primarily foot-dwelling people had little chance against these odds, and many Shoshone bands were by then impoverished.

Nonetheless, archaeological evidence at places like Mummy Cave in northwestern Wyoming document a Sheep Eater presence in the Rocky Mountain region for quite a long time. In more recent times, mountain man Osborne Russell encountered a band of about 20 Sheep Eaters in 1835, whom he described as skilled hunters, bow-makers, and excellent furriers well adapted to mountain living. Thirty hunting and pack dogs accompanied the group.[140] As if referencing Wickiup Cave, explorer Alexander Ross recounted that the "mountain Snakes . . . [live] in the small recesses of the mountains and are to be found in small bands, or single wigwams among the caverns and rocks."[141]

Surprisingly, the nomadic Northern Shoshone, including the reclusive Mountain Shoshone bands, are one of the few Intermountain Indian groups whose ethnic identity can now be

Mountain sheep are a popular rock art motif in southwestern Montana, but none can be positively associated with the Sheep Eater Shoshone. Once abundant, mountain sheep populations were decimated by diseases contracted from domestic sheep herds in the late nineteenth century and early twentieth centuries, and population numbers remain low even today.

reasonably inferred from the region's largely homogenous archaeological record. In addition to conical timber lodges and sheep traps, a constellation of traits identifies their presence. Foremost are distinctive carved soapstone (steatite) pots and flat-bottomed ceramic jars that look like flowerpots. Called Intermountain Ware, the thick-walled pottery, often made of local crushed granite, was coiled or hand-molded. These ceramics are found in a dozen or so Shoshone sites in southwest Montana, usually as sherds since the poorly fired ware was easily broken.[142] External charring and carbonaceous residue indicates these ves-

Pottery sherds were among the stone, bone, organic, and metal artifacts removed by collectors from Wickiup Cave. Called Intermountain Ware, the pottery (painstakingly reconstructed here from sherds in another Shoshone camp) is typically shaped like a tall flowerpot. Laboratory analysis of the residues inside the ceramic pots and similarly shaped steatite (soapstone) vessels show that Shoshone used the vessels to cook stews of meat, wild onions, and various fresh, dried, or ground roots. PHOTOGRAPH (LEFT) BY LESLIE B. DAVIS; DRAWING (RIGHT) FROM BUTLER 1983.

sels were placed directly on cooking fires to make stews of meat, wild onions, and various fresh, dried, or ground roots.

The Sheep Eaters were also famous for their composite bows made of split bighorn sheep horns with sinew backing. Sheep Eater bowyers first softened elk or mountain sheep horn by soaking and heating it. Once sufficiently pliable, strips of horn were cut from the horn core with sharp stone tools. The lin-

Bighorn sheep were an important food source for Sheep Eater Shoshone bands living in mountains and valleys of southwestern Montana and the Greater Yellowstone area. Shoshone bands harvested sheep with an ingenious array of talus-slope hunting blinds, wood drive lanes, and pole corrals or traps. Well-trained dogs helped drive sheep toward these structures where hunters were lying in wait. A variety of domestic implements—spoons, bowls—were made from the massive horns, as well as powerful bows. PHOTOGRAPH BY CHRISTOPHER CAUBLE.

ear horn staves were straightened, shaped, and smoothed. Two staves of equivalent lengths were spliced together with horn glue and sinew, and the entire bow was backed with multiple layers of glued sinew, giving it strength and flexibility. A twisted sinew bow string was then attached to cut notches or slight bends at the ends of the bow. By this long and tedious production process, Sheep Eaters built 3-foot long bows with 60- to 70-pound draw weights (experiments suggest). These short, powerful bows were aimed and fired in a single motion. One such bow, found in a cave in the Gros Ventre Mountains of Wyoming, radiocarbon dated to A.D. 1737, which is within the timeframe when Sheep Eaters inhabited the Greater Yellowstone area and southwest Montana.[143] Sheep Eater hunters also made longer, single piece bows made of various wood species.

As the few widely scattered Sheep Eater groups kept to their mountain lifeways, other Shoshone bands obtained horses around 1730 A.D. from their close linguistic relatives, the Comanche, and other groups, who traded and stole horses from Spanish settlements and traded them northward. The Eastern Shoshone in Wyoming and the Lemhi (Northern) Shoshone in Idaho and Montana took up the horse and thence the buffalo chase and were soon an equestrian power on the Montana plains. Sometimes allied with the Salish and Crow, the equestrian Shoshone (or "Snakes") hunted bison in mountain valleys and foothills as well as on the Plains. But their military prowess did not last once competing Assiniboine, Blackfeet, Sioux, and other northern groups obtained horses and guns from American and British traders by the mid-18th century.

Perhaps the best-known Shoshone individual is Sacajawea, the young Indian woman who accompanied Lewis and Clark and the Corps of Discovery on their remarkable travels through the Pacific Northwest in 1804-1806. Once held captive by the agricultural Hidatsa, Sacajawea's vital role as an interpreter and guide, the expedition's search for the Shoshone and horses, and Sacajawea's reunion with her Lemhi Shoshone brother Cameahwait at Horse Prairie in southwest Montana and Idaho are three of the most compelling narratives of the entire expedition.[144] Sacajawea discovered her long-lost relatives in the farthest corner of southwest Montana only because, by the time of the famous journey, the Lemhi had been forced back into their familiar Rocky Mountain haunts by well-armed, equestrian Plains tribes.

By the mid-nineteenth century, American miners and settlers pouring into Northern Shoshone territory caused conflict. The mining community of Bannack, on the banks of Grasshopper Creek about 25 miles from Dillon, was a thriving but violent Gold-Rush community in the early 1860s. Tiovanduah, or "Snag" as the settlers knew him, was friendly to Mormon settlers in the Lemhi Valley. Tiovanduah occasionally camped with his band in the sagebrush flats west of Bannack (called Yankee Flats today). Drunken hooligans shot into the tipi of a Shoshone elder who had earlier protested the treatment of an Indian women married to a miner, killing him and several children (there are several contradictory accounts of this event).[145] While bathing in Grasshopper Creek, Tiovanduah was then gunned down in cold blood by the outlaw Buck Stinson. Only Lemhi Shoshone leader Tendoy's diplomacy prevented retaliation by angry Shoshone warriors. Vigilantes hanged Stinson in 1864 for other alleged homicides but not for Tiovanduah's death. Archaeological investigation of Indian camps near Bannack would no doubt shed light on this tumultuous period in Northern Shoshone culture. Unfortunately, the extensive earth disturbance from historic dredge mining in Grasshopper Creek largely precludes such research.

In 1875 the Lemhi and Sheep Eater bands in Idaho and Montana were consolidated on the Lemhi Reservation on the Salmon River in east-central Idaho. (Sheep Eaters of Yellowstone National Park joined their bison-hunting relations on the Wind River Reservation in Wyoming, as well as at Fort Hall.) Life was bleak for the Shoshone peoples on the Lemhi Reservation.[146] Government annuities were perpetually scarce, and agriculture was difficult in the narrow mountain valley with limited arable land. Given these conditions, reservation agents allowed the Lemhi people to leave the reservation to hunt bison in central Montana. On several occasions, Chief Tendoy visited the Territorial Governor of Montana,

B. F. Potts, in Virginia City to complain about reservation conditions, to little apparent effect.

Tendoy became a mediator of friendly White-Indian relations throughout his lifetime. En route to camps in various mountain valleys and hunting grounds to the east, Shoshone people befriended ranchers, farmers, railroad workers, and town people in southwestern Montana communities. Hunting and fishing off-reservation in the early twentieth century, Tendoy's sons and their families used the Pass Creek conical lodges on ranchlands in the Medicine Lodge Valley.[147] In return, the Shoshone gifted beaded leather gloves and other items to the ranching families. The now dilapidated Pass Creek lodges have not been excavated but their cultural deposits may contain the same kinds of artifacts as found at Wickiup Cave.

The Lemhi Reservation closed in 1907, causing interactions among the Shoshone and Whites in southwest Montana to all but cease. Northern Shoshone bands were consolidated on the Wind River Indian Reservation in Wyoming and the Fort Hall Indian Reservation in southern Idaho, where tribal headquarters are located today. The Shoshone-Bannock tribe maintains an active cultural resource program and, as is only fitting, remains closely involved in the management of public lands and cultural resources in southwestern Montana.

The Big Sheep Creek Wickiup Cave is listed on the National Register of Historic Places. Because of its fragility and vulnerability, the BLM does not encourage public visitation. However, Shoshone students visit the cave as part of federal and tribal education programs. This is one way modern Shoshone youths stay connected with the rigorous mountain and basin lifeways of their ancestors.

Chief Tendoy's band frequently visited their southwestern Montana haunts following their placement on the Lemhi Reservation in east-central Idaho. This photograph taken by E. Allen on July 5, 1904, at Selway Park north of Dillon, Montana, and published as a postcard shows Tendoy and his son Parmby. Beaverhead County Museum Archives, BCM 172.10. Photograph courtesy of the Beaverhead County Museum, Dillon.

This dramatization of Buffalo Calf Road Woman's rescue of Comes in Sight is based on a colored drawing in the Ledger Book of Spotted Wolf-Yellow Nose. The original drawing shows the Northern Cheyenne brother and sister in their finest battle dress, including her elk teeth-covered dress and his long feathered war bonnet. Illustration by Eric S. Carlson.

RIFLES AND COUPS

BATTLE OF THE ROSEBUD SITE 24BH2461

1876 A.D.

The acquisition of war honors and personal glory, rather than killing the enemy, was a crucial goal of Plains Indian warfare. Warriors gained prestige by "counting coup" (hitting an enemy with a coup stick or a weapon or by a hand slap), capturing enemy weapons, and performing other daring feats of individual bravery.[148] Experienced leaders and military societies like the Cheyenne Crazy Dogs and the Sioux Kit Foxes organized and led war parties, but warriors were largely on their own once the fight began. Indian warfare depended on opportunity, surprise, and individual prowess above any military strategy. When a battle reached a stalemate, warriors retreated to fight another day. Shaped feathers, ornaments, and designs painted on warriors' bodies, regalia, and ponies signified successful war exploits and coups.

The origin of the Plains Indian war complex and honors ranking system is unknown. Some scholars believe it developed in the Midwest sometime in deep prehistory (recall the warring Mississippian chiefdoms and palisaded Middle Missouri villages mentioned in the Hagan site chapter). The skirmish lines of shield-bearing warriors shown in Bear Gulch and other Plains rock art sites suggest it was in place 1,000 years ago, but it may be far older. As depicted in Biographic style rock art, and later dramatized by Charlie Russell, Frederic Remington, and other Western artists, warfare became more freewheeling and deadly once Indian bands acquired horses and guns. The capture of horses and other deeds involving horses were simply added to the war honors system.[149]

Long before the arrival of Europeans, raiding and warfare created bitter enemies and friendly, though interchangeable, alliances and coalitions among Plains and Intermountain Indian bands and tribes. For example, by the early fur trade period in the eighteenth century, Crow, Salish, and Shoshone bands were commonly allied against the Blackfeet, Gros Ventre, Assiniboine, and Sioux in what historian Theodore Binema called the "northern and southern alliances."[150] These ages-old alliances played out in the U.S. military and Indian battles to come.

In the early 1800s in the West, Indian people from many tribes assisted the first explorers, trappers, missionaries, and settlers in their frontier travels and enterprises. Indian bands participated in the fur trade, which brought guns, horses, metal, wool blankets, and other commodities into their Native economies. However, the relentless westward press of miners and settlers soon evolved into hostilities and bloodshed. By the mid-1800s, Indian animosities became increasingly directed at the encroaching Europeans and Americans, although intertribal warfare and horse raiding never ceased. At first, to calm the growing storm, the U.S. Government and Indian tribes negotiated treaties. The Fort Laramie treaty of 1851 defined the territories of the Crow, Cheyenne, Sioux, Assiniboine, and other Plains groups while, in turn, allowing construction of roads and military posts for the safe passage of American settlers through tribal land.

Native peoples were misled about the true nature of the treaties, and the federal government violated the treaties by failing to provide promised rations, annuities, and security. Further, the government could not and would not slow the steady westward flow of immigrants and miners into the western goldfields. Red Cloud's War of 1866-1868 and the subsequent Fort Laramie Treaty of 1868 temporarily halted American travel along the Bozeman Trail by granting a vast amount of land to the Sioux. But the land granted to the Sioux was in the heart of Crow country, and the tribes were steadfast enemies. Tensions soon boiled over again, starting the Great Sioux War of 1876-1877. The two most significant battles of the Great Sioux War occurred on the Little Bighorn and at Rosebud Creek. Much has been written about the Battle of the Little Bighorn (Custer's Last Stand), but militarily, the lesser-known Battle of the Rosebud is just as important.

Rosebud Battlefield State Park lies next to the vast Crow Reservation in south-central Montana. The state park encompasses some 3,052 acres purchased from rancher Elmer "Slim" Kobold in 1972. By choosing not to lease his land for coal development, Kobold saved a small piece of the battlefield. In fact, the expansive battlefield, which historic preservationists regard as a largely intact "cultural landscape," covers another 7,948 acres of private ranch and agricultural land. Today, the Rosebud Battlefield's historical significance is recognized both by its listing on the National Register of Historic Places and its National Historic Landmark status. The battlefield's sweeping prairie and butte landscape looks much as it did some 140 years ago with the exception of a small parking area, outbuildings, trails, fences, and interpretive signs.

Prior to its acquisition by the state of Montana, metal detector enthusiasts combed the Rosebud Battlefield for shell casings, weapons, and other U.S. military and Indian artifacts. Outstanding among these collectors, Jesse Vaughn, a Colorado attorney and Indian war buff, extensively worked the battlefield during the latter half of the 1950s, eventually publishing an in-

Two major battles of the Great Sioux War of 1876 were fought in southeastern Montana. General Custer's defeat at the Battle of the Little Bighorn is best known. The preceding, and lesser known, Battle of the Rosebud is now partly protected in Rosebud Battlefield State Park. From the parking area on Rosebud Creek, visitors can look north into grassy terrain where some of the fiercest fighting occurred. COURTESY OF TRAVEL MONTANA.

teresting book on the subject.[151] Steve Aaberg completed the first professional survey of the park and identified dozens of sites relating primarily to the area's archaeology rather than the 1876 battle.[152] In fact, a 3,000-year-old bison jump also lies within park boundaries, and the small sandstone cliff comprising the jump is covered with shield-bearing warrior rock art. The extraordinary density of archaeological sites throughout the pine parklands region of southeast Montana, and within the Rosebud battlefield itself, is testimony to the fact that the Rosebud area was not a neutral battleground. Rather, it was the ages-old homeland and hunting territory of many Plains Indian tribes.

In 2007, expanding coal development prompted the Montana Preservation Alliance to develop a management plan for the park.[153] In 2011 and 2012, the University of Montana and Montana State Parks collaborated in surveys in select areas of the state park, leading to a master's thesis by Tom Milter.[154] Further survey was completed in 2013 and in 2015. In total, archaeologists surveyed about 500 acres or roughly six percent of the entire battlefield—a small but telling sample.

Battlefield archaeology requires metal detectors. The University of Montana crews used metal detectors to sweep along transect lines set in key areas. One crew poked pin flags in the ground wherever their detectors beeped. If a second metal de-

Metal detectors are an important part of battlefield archaeology. Here, University of Montana field crews use metal detectors on the hotly contested Royall's Ridge to find Indian and U.S. military ammunition and other artifacts. Rosebud Creek, where the fight first began, and Van Vliet Ridge, controlled by General Crook's troops, are seen in the background. Photograph courtesy of Kelly Dixon.

tector verified the discovery, another crew excavated the flagged spot with hand trowels. The metal artifacts—mostly bullets and casings—were typically buried in one to six inches of grassy sod. Students carefully measured the strike (horizontal orientation) and dip (vertical orientation) since these give an indication of the direction and trajectory of bullets. Because a stake-and-string grid system was unrealistic over such a large scale, the transect lines and artifacts were mapped with handheld Global Positioning Systems (GPS) instruments.

Predictably, the field crews picked up considerable non-battle "white noise" related to modern use of the property for farming and ranching (nails, fence staples, motor parts, and the occasional pop can). The total number of actual battlefield artifacts included 191 cartridge cases, 51 bullets, a buckle, a carabineer hook, a chinstrap, and a rifle barrel. As all fans of police shows know, spent cartridges and bullets leave distinctive marks or signatures that allow experts to identify the types of weapons. To unwrap the forensic riddle of the Rosebud, Milter and Douglas Scott, a battlefield archaeology authority, went to work. However, because their analyses are meaningful only when placed within context of the battle itself, the fierce fighting of June 17, 1876, must be examined.

Continual violations of the Fort Laramie treaties by the Federal Government and White immigration were the root causes of the Great Sioux War of 1876-1877. Retaliatory harassment and killing of White settlers and military personnel by off-reservation Lakota Sioux and Northern Cheyenne bands made President Ulysses S. Grant's resolve to either bring the Native bands to the reserves or force a fight. An earlier campaign in March of 1876 under General George Crook fell short with the attack on Old Bear's neutral Cheyenne village near Broadus, Montana. Called the Battle of Powder River, Crook believed he was attacking Sioux leader Crazy Horse's camp. Federal troops fired

Archaeologists estimate that some 10,000 rounds of ammunition were fired by federal troops and Indian warriors over the course of the one-day battle. The location and type of expended cartridges and bullets at Rosebud Battlefield enabled archaeologists to study battlefield positions and tactics. This expended bullet (top) and shell casing (bottom) are from a 45.70 carbine used by federal troops. PHOTOGRAPH COURTESY OF TOM MILTER.

upon Cheyenne men, women, and children; set on fire most of their worldly possessions and food stores; and ran off their horse herds—all sadly reminiscent (though with less Indian mortality) of the Sand Creek Massacre and Battle of Washita River in Colorado and Oklahoma, respectively, in the decade before.

This time, a three-pronged campaign was drawn up, with Colonel John Gibbon coming east from Fort Ellis near Bozeman (Montana), General Alfred Terry traveling west from Fort Abraham Lincoln (North Dakota), and General Crook moving north from Fort Fetterman (Wyoming). The plan was to surround and subdue roving bands somewhere between the Little Bighorn and Powder rivers, preferably by striking sleeping Indian villages—by then a proven U.S. military tactic. But the 1876 military campaign was doomed from the start. Despite careful planning, the Army's strategy failed to anticipate the massing of restless Cheyenne and Lakota Sioux warriors whose reservations had yet to receive treaty-promised rations and provisions. Nor did the commanders realize the number of angry, revenge-minded warriors who had joined the Lakota in the aftermath of Crook's destruction of Old Bear's peaceful camp. Finally, the far-flung plan simply did not allow for effective field communications or coordination in the vast and very hostile Indian country.

Crook and 1,300 cavalry and infantry troops accompanied by a long supply train of wagons and ambulances headed north from Fort Fetterman, Wyoming, for a second time in late May of 1876. Crook anticipated adding much-desired Crow and Shoshone scouts and warriors to his column as well as a detachment of miners from the Montana goldfields. Unbeknownst to Crook, the Cheyenne and Lakota closely observed the army's northward progress, eventually firing into his camp on the night of June 9. The camp was then moved to Goose Creek in northern Wyoming, where Crow and Shoshone warriors led by Chiefs Plenty Coup and Washakie, finally arrived to assist the U.S. Army. Crook's troops celebrated the arrival of these Indian warriors, who, as part of the Southern Alliance, were ancient enemies of the Sioux and Cheyenne. They reported that the Lakota (led by Crazy Horse) were camped somewhere on Rosebud Creek.

By early June, an immense combined force of Sioux under Sitting Bull and Crazy Horse, Assiniboine warriors, and Arapaho warriors had come together at the confluence of the Yellowstone River and Rosebud Creek. Moving and camping together as security against U.S. military attack, this large group traveled south through the Rosebud Valley, eventually stopping at the confluence of Rosebud and Greenleaf creeks. Their village is said to have stretched for two miles. Here, they encountered large bison herds, enabling hunters to feed the large, mobile camp.

Upon learning from their "wolves" or scouts that a large number of U.S. Army troops was on the move, Northern Cheyenne bands under Spotted Wolf, Black Bird, Two Moons and other experienced leaders traveled east from the Tongue River, eventually arriving at Reno Creek near present-day Busby, Montana. Other Cheyenne bands camped a few miles north on Trail Creek. Little Hawk's scouts reported that Crook would likely march up Rosebud Creek. At the behest of their military societies, Cheyenne warriors halted to paint, dress, and purify themselves for battle. Experienced warriors advised younger fighters about tactics and encouraged success in counting coups. In all, as dawn broke on the day of the battle, a large, formidable, and motivated Plains Indian military force was massed north and east of Crook's unaware troops.

Given new intelligence of an Indian village on Rosebud Creek, the now-anxious General Crook decided to take the battle to the Sioux. He stripped his column to a bare-bones military strike force by mounting the infantry on mules and providing only four days of rations and 100 rounds of ammunition to each trooper. Medical wagons and supplies were held in reserve at Goose Creek, some 30 miles away from the eventual battlefield. Deep in Indian country, Crook's troops were in high spirits, anticipating a definitive victory. The command soon came upon a large herd of bison, which prompted a round of loud rifle fire from the Crow and Shoshone hunters in Crook's contingent. Crook's Indian scouts also ran into a Sioux or Cheyenne bison hunting party whose warriors, after exchanging insults with their enemies, hurried back to their village to warn of the on-coming blue coats. By that point, all the Army's hope for a surprise attack on an unaware Indian village was lost, if it ever had been a reality.

Crow leader Plenty Coups also discovered two dead military horses (but not their riders), likely from Gibbon's command who had probably carried warnings of the strong build-up of Lakota and Cheyenne warriors to the west and north. Paying little heed to this scouting report, Crook's command swung west and stopped on the banks of Rosebud Creek on June 17 to rest the fatigued troops, boil coffee, and graze the horses and mules. Gunfire erupted at about 8:00 a.m.

Crow and Shoshone scouts fired first on Lakota and Cheyenne warriors rapidly coming down Trail and Reno creeks from the north and northwest. Further east, Lakota and Cheyenne warriors under Little Hawk charged down a drainage called The Gap. The Gap is a narrow passage between two slopes to the west and a sandstone cliff to the east (also the site of the centuries-old Kobold bison jump). Strong resistance by the Crow and Shoshone scouts and Captain George M. Randall's skirmish line on Rosebud Creek bought Crook enough time to deploy his surprised command. Calvary troops quickly secured the advantageous southern bluffs above Rosebud Creek (Van Vliet Ridge,

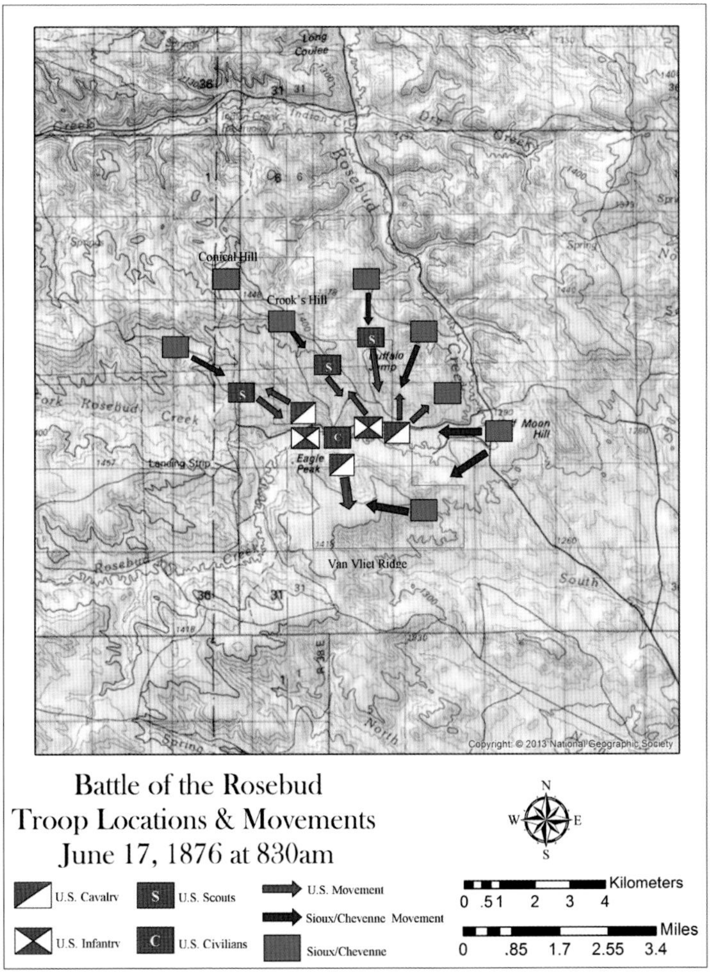

This schematic shows Indian and federal troop positions at the beginning of the Battle of the Rosebud. Lakota and Cheyenne warriors attacked General George Crook's troops from the north and east, forcing his troops to take up positions on Conical Hill, Crook's Hill, and Van Vliet Ridge. Despite repeated, day-long attacks by Indian warriors, and a near disaster on Royall's Ridge, federal troops could not be dislodged, resulting in a stalemate, retreat, and the Battle of Little Bighorn one week later.
(From Merritt, Milter and Dixon 2014).

where small stone fortifications or breastworks are still visible) and the high hill and ridgeline to the north, now called Crook's Hill. During this initial phase of fighting in The Gap, Buffalo Calf Road Woman fearlessly rode a galloping horse to rescue her Cheyenne warrior brother Comes-in-Sight, whose horse had been shot from under him. From this heroic act we owe the Northern Cheyenne name for the battle, "Where the Girl Saved Her Brother."[155]

Drama then unfolded to the west, where Colonel William B. Royall's cavalry troops first resisted a strong flanking maneuver by a mass of warriors and then attempted to sweep the enemy off a prominent ridgeline. Royall soon found parts of his command on the ridgeline stretched thin and too far away from reinforcements one mile east on Crook's Hill. This left his command vulnerable to a counter-attack, to which Cheyenne warriors enthusiastically obliged. With casualties mounting, fierce fighting ensued as Royall's troops slowly retreated down the rocky ridge.

A mid-morning lull in the battle convinced an optimistic Crook to split his command, ordering Captain Anson Mill's cavalry to pursue their original military goal of attacking Sioux Indian villages to the west. Perceiving Mill's troop sudden movement as a sign of retreat, coupled with Royall's predicament on the ridge, the Lakota led furious but unsuccessful charges on the western flanks. The firepower of Crow and Shoshone warriors and the strong military fire coming from Crook's Hill enabled Royall's troop to hold their lines and eventually join Crook's main forces, but not without suffering dozens of wounded and dead.

In late morning, and still with a fierce fight still on his hands, Crook rethought his dire situation and consolidated his command. He ordered Mill's cavalry to give up their pursuit of the Indian village and turn back. With Mill's sudden return to Crook's Hill, warriors ready for a potentially fatal attack of

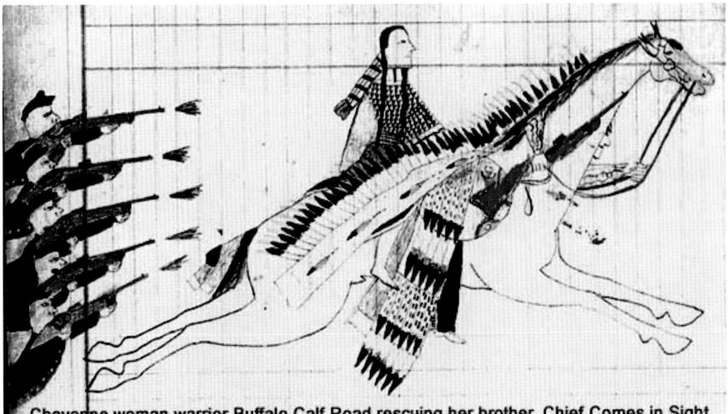

Cheyenne woman warrior Buffalo Calf Road rescuing her brother, Chief Comes in Sight, at the Battle of the Rosebud, from the Spotted Wolf / Yellow Nose Ledger Book

The Northern Cheyenne name for the Rosebud Battle is "Where the Girl Saved Her Brother." South of Crook's Hill, Buffalo Calf Road Woman heroically raced through The Gap (top photo) on her horse to save her brother, Comes in Sight, with federal troops and tribal enemies in hot pursuit. The scene was drawn in the Spotted Wolf/Yellow Nose Ledger Book (bottom). To the right of the survey archaeologist in the photo is the ancient Kobold Bison Jump, attesting to the ancient use of this area by Native peoples. PHOTOGRAPH COURTESY OF MONTANA STATE PARKS.

Miners, packers, and scouts attached to General Crook's command took up positions at the northwest end of Crook's Hill in a place now called Packers' Rocks. Hiding behind sandstone boulders and fortifications made by stacking rocks, as shown here, this civilian contingent fired on Sioux and Cheyenne positions to the north on Conical Hill. The stacked-rock fortifications are some of the surviving, but fragile, archaeological features of the Battle of the Rosebud. From Merritt, Milter and Dixon 2014.

Crook's Hill from the north paused and then retreated. At that point, the battle dwindled to a stalemate. The Lakota and Cheyenne began withdrawing from the field because they were tired and hungry, and not in any sense defeated. Crook started off in pursuit only to be warned by his Crow scouts that the Lakota were no doubt laying an ambush. The next day, Crook's tattered command returned to their bivouac on Goose Creek and then traveled to Camp Cloud Peak near present day Sheridan, Wyoming, to resupply. Crook's withdrawal left Colonel Gibbon and General Terry to find the roving Lakota and Cheyenne bands—and led to the fates of Colonel George Custer and his troops at the Battle of the Little Bighorn on June 25.

Crazy Horse, Wooden Leg, and other Indian participants in the battle gave detailed accounts of the fierce one-day fight at Rosebud Creek. Indian warriors were dressed in their best regalia and fighting gear, fully aware of the on-coming soldiers. Wooden Leg recounted that Indians led numerous charges and retreats, as did the federal troops and their Indian scouts, and that the fighting continued into late afternoon.[156] The battle saw many acts of individual bravery and old-style bravado. Cheyenne warrior Limpy, who was wounded on his left side and had his horse killed, kept fighting. Jack Red Cloud, a Sioux, had his horse shot out from under him. He was pursued on foot and taunted by three Crow riders, who were only driven away when Sioux reinforcements arrived. Once Crook's troops departed, Cheyenne and Sioux returned to collect whatever the military had left behind—ammunition, crackers, bacon, gloves, hats, and other gear.

Some 1,500 Native warriors and 1,300 U.S. Army troops fired an estimated 10,000 rounds of ammunition in the one-day battle. These expended cartridge casings and bullets lend themselves to ballistic analyses—once you find them. From their analysis, Milter and Scott learned that Cheyenne and Sioux warriors and Shoshone scouts used a diversity of firearms, ranging from Winchester and Spencer repeating rifles to muzzleloaders to long-bore Sharps rifles of various calibers. These well-used firearms were no doubt obtained in a variety of ways—through trade, raiding, and warfare. Survey crews found little evidence of the bows and arrows, lances, and axes reportedly used in the fight, though some battlefield artifacts are probably mixed with archaeological materials collected by Steve Aaberg. In contrast to this array of Indian arms, U.S. Army troops primarily used Model 1873 Springfield rifles and carbines as well as Colt .45 revolvers. In all, the ammunition artifacts represented 61 individual firearms, with 44 attributed to Cheyenne and Sioux warriors and the remainder to U.S. troops. (The weapons used by the detachment of miners cloud the picture a small bit.)

Using this basic distinction in Indian and U.S. Army weaponry, archaeologists Milter and Scott plotted and analyzed the expended bullets and casings to track Indian and army movements across the battlefield and determine if their distributions matched battlefield accounts. Their results fit the historical narrative with several enlightening exceptions. Although their role was dismissed by some of the event's military participants and by newspaper reporters accompanying the Army, the Shoshone and Crow warriors fought fiercely in all phases of the battle. As one example, a Crow or Shoshone scout armed with a .50/70 Sharps rifle can be tracked from the defense of Royall's Ridge to fighting on Crook's Hill, about a half-mile away. Many Sioux/Cheyenne cartridges were found within 100 yards of Crook's main camp, suggesting that warriors came much closer to overcoming the panicked troopers than previously thought.

Historical accounts suggest that it took time for Crook's soldiers to saddle their horses and mules and remount during the initial attack. But the lack of bullet casings along the picket line at Rosebud Creek demonstrates that this was done quickly enough to escape the onslaught of Cheyenne and Sioux warriors. Unspent .45/70 rifle rounds on Royall's Ridge suggest that U.S. troops, many green to combat, started out in battle formation but panicked, leaving precious ammunition behind, and dissolved into smaller detachments over the course of the day, leading to fierce fighting and a near military disaster on Royall's Ridge.

The Rosebud battle was a departure from previous fights. As events unfolded, Lakota and other Sioux, Cheyenne, Assiniboine, and Arapaho bands assembled into a disciplined fighting force and formidable "light cavalry." They abandoned their traditional "hit and run" tactics with its focus on acquiring individual warrior honors. Instead, they formed sweeping mass charges with the aim of annihilating the enemy. Indeed, the U.S. military and its Crow and Shoshone allies were surprised by the ferocity of the attacks. Had this strategy succeeded, Crook's column might have met the same fate that Custer and his troops met a week later.

In the aftermath of the Rosebud and Little Bighorn battles, the Lakota, Cheyenne, Assiniboine, and Arapaho bands and warriors quickly dispersed south to the Bighorn Mountains and elsewhere, hoping to find respite from the U.S. military retaliation that was sure to follow.

Today, archaeological study of Indian-U.S. military battlefields in Montana is in its infancy. Some 20 battles were fought between 1865 and 1887—a number that does not include skirmishes with trappers, miners, and settlers. Nor does it account for the infinite number of skirmishes and battles between competing Indian bands. Such studies may seem unnecessary given the abundance of battlefield literature. However, most historical accounts inevitably slant toward the U.S. military's side, not the Indians' side. Thus, archaeological study helps to "ground truth" how military battles unfolded, correcting inconsisten-

Indian participants offered their own accounts of the Great Sioux War of 1876. In this historic photo, Northern Cheyenne leader Two Moons (on left) recounts the Rosebud battle with interpreter Rowland and author O. D. Wheeler 25 years after the fight (1901). The "big bend" of Rosebud Creek is visible beyond them. Through this river valley and others, Lakota and Cheyenne warriors attacked General Crook's troops bivouacked about mile to the west (to photo left) on upper Rosebud Creek. PHOTOGRAPH COURTESY OF THE MONTANA HISTORICAL SOCIETY RESEARCH CENTER-PHOTOGRAPH ARCHIVES, HELENA, MONTANA

cies and biases in the written records. Of course, more accurate information benefits the many visitors to Rosebud Battlefield. Less widely appreciated, the U.S. Army Command and General Staff College uses the Rosebud Battlefield to educate military officers in "irregular warfare," where the landscape strongly dictates outcomes.

The transition to reservation life was not an easy one for Native peoples. As illustrated here, many Crow families continued their traditional plains and mountains lifestyle, only returning periodically to Absaroka Agency for annuities and supplies. Persistent American encroachment on Crow tribal lands, disease, depletion of bison herds, and Blackfeet horse raiding eventually led to Crow settlement on reservation lands. Illustration by Eric S. Carlson.

LINES DRAWN IN THE EARTH

ABSAROKA AGENCY SITE
24ST89

1875 TO 1884 A.D.

The current geographic locations and sizes of Montana's Indian reservations give a very misleading impression of the lands once held by these Indian peoples. Treaties established between individual Indian nations and the U.S. Government, as ratified by the U.S. Congress, initially established tribal territories and, later, reservation boundaries. The Fort Laramie treaties of 1851 established the tribal lands of the Arapaho, Arikara, Assiniboine, Cheyenne, Crow, Gros Ventre, Mandan, and Sioux nations. At Council Grove near Missoula, Indian Commissioner Isaac Stevens negotiated the Hellgate Treaty of 1855 with the Kootenai, Pend d'Oreilles, and Salish, establishing what would become the Flathead Indian Reservation. That same year, the Blackfeet and other tribes negotiated lands with the Federal Government in the Lame Bull Treaty. In southeastern Montana, the Fort Laramie Treaty of 1868 defined the Crow Reservation as the area south and east of the Yellowstone River and east to the divide between the Bighorn River and Rosebud Creek.

In 1871, the U.S. Congress stopped making treaties with Indian tribes, and existing tribal territories and Indian reservations began to be incrementally reduced in size by a succession of Congressional actions and presidential executive orders to accommodate ever-expanding American interests—homesteading, agriculture, ranching, mining, logging, railroad construction, and settlement. Furthermore, Congress passed the Dawes Act of 1887, which divided communal reservation lands into individual family allotments.[157] Reservation allotments not claimed by individual Indians were deemed "surplus lands" and opened to non-Indian settlement. That is why many Montana Indian reservations today have a checkerboard pattern of tribal and private lands within the reservation. Tribal governments fell into disarray as million acres of original treaty lands passed out of Native ownership. The Indian Reorganization Act of 1934 ended the Dawes Act, initiating a revival of Indian governance and control of reservation lands, but a huge amount of treaty land and its resources had already been lost.

Throughout this time period, the ultimate goal of the U.S. Government was to assimilate Indian peoples into American culture so that they would accept their status as American citizens. Government officials paid little attention to the Constitutional provisions and treaty clauses that regarded Indigenous peoples as sovereign nations, a distinction definitely understood by tribal leaders. Thus, the long process of cultural assimilation began on Indian reservations under the dark cloud of vastly different cultural beliefs and agendas.

Indian peoples resisted assimilation, a process already undermined by government ineptitude, lack of annuities, and conflicting federal directives. Individual allotments of land to tribal members were often too small for viable agriculture or ranching operations, making the transition from nomadism to ranching and farming that much harder.

The U.S. Government initially established Indian Agencies

to cultivate formal relationships with Native American groups from whom it had acquired new aboriginal lands. As various treaties and agreements were developed with tribes, Indian Agents evolved into resolving conflicts between Indians and settlers; distributing government annuities; assisting in the settlement of Indians on reservations; and generally working to assimilate Indian peoples into the American mainstream.

Reports of Indian agents and biographies of tribal leaders shed light on this time period. Reservation period archaeology, through rarely done, also adds to our knowledge by providing information that is minimally covered or entirely left out of written records. Recent archaeological work at Absaroka Agency helps explain how Crow (Apsáalooke) people integrated the old with the new in a landscape defined by geopolitical reservation boundaries rather than by their ages-old hunting and gathering territories.

Absaroka Agency (also called Second Crow Agency) lies adjacent to State Highway 78 about three miles south of the community of Absarokee in southeastern Montana, some 40 miles west of the present Crow Reservation. The agency once sat on lands between East Rosebud Creek and Butcher Creek. The old agency is within the shadow of the stunning Beartooth Mountains, which rise up about 15 miles to the southwest. Today, much of the old agency lies on private farmland, which has been plowed, irrigated, and hayed for more than a century.

As summarized from the work of project historian Joan Brownell,[158] Crow Territory was established in 1851 under the Fort Laramie Treaty. The first Crow Agency was created in 1868 under a second treaty that defined the reservation boundaries. Fort Parker, the first Crow agency, was built in 1869 on Mission Creek in the Yellowstone Valley near present-day Livingston. In 1875, the Federal Government authorized funding for a new Crow Indian agency located further to the east. The

George DeForest's oil painting is the only surviving depiction of Absaroka Agency. The painting looks to the southwest, with Butcher Creek in the foreground, and shows the east wing of the agency compound, including "warerooms," an "issue room" (where annuity issuance records were likely kept), and office and bedroom. The sutler's store or trading post and the agent's quarters (the prominent two-story structure) are on the painting's right. The main gate on the north side of the compound was located between the Sutler's store and agent's quarters. Courtesy of the Annin Collection, Museum of the Beartooths, Columbus, MT.

Indian Agent's stated rationale for the move was to secure better agriculture land, separate the tribe from the illicit whiskey trade on the Yellowstone River, and move Crow people away from the unhealthy "cannon" winds sweeping down the river valley. But an underlying government motive was for the Crow to cede or relinquish the western part of their reservation into federal ownership. In fact, the federal government began negotiations with the Crow about land cessions soon after the first agency at Fort Parker was established. The western reservation lands were finally ceded in 1882.

Construction of Absarokee Agency on East Rosebud Creek began in June of 1875. Dexter Clapp, the first in a string of Indian Agents, supervised the work with an initial Congressional allocation of $15,000. Sioux attacks on timber camps and supply trains briefly delayed progress. Despite the constant Sioux threat, workers completed the compound on schedule and Crow bands began arriving there after the fall hunt. The timely arrival of annuities in Nelson Story's supply train facilitated the convergence of Crow bands on the Absaroka Agency.

Agent Clapp eventually resigned his post following charges of defrauding the government in collusion with rations-vendor Nelson Story. Clapp's replacement did not last long on the job either, so Reverend George Frost took over in July of 1877. He quickly took stock of the compound's condition and requested white wash, adobe, cement, and other supplies to spruce up the place. Frost's careful inspections resulted in a fine drawing of the compound. Agent Augustus Keller later replaced Frost and proved to be more competent than his predecessors. Significantly, he proposed building "cheap and plain" Indian housing, using income derived from selling hay, as a way to induce the still far-flung Crow to settle down, farm, and ranch. Eventually, a dozen houses at the agency belonged to prominent Crow chiefs Iron Bull, Bear In-The Water, and others. The Absaroka Agency gradually became economically important to the Crow because the government, having failed to teach farming, at least continued to distribute needed supplies and annuities in the compound. Still, many tribal members preferred to live away from agency in their old mountains and plains haunts for much of the year.

In December of 1881, Henry Armstrong, a member of the

Wyandotte Tribe of Kansas, took over for Keller. He was greatly dismayed by the overall lack of farming progress, although many families actually grew vegetable gardens and put up hay to feed their livestock. Armstrong was a staunch proponent of two seemingly contradictory goals: allotting lands to individual families and immediately directing them to farm and raise cattle, or removing the Crow to a new agency in the Bighorn Valley. In the later, he succeeded. In 1884, buffeted by vanishing bison herds; scarlet fever and measles epidemics; drought; equine diseases; incessant Blackfeet raids of Crow pony herds (Crow wealth); continued American encroachment on reservation lands; and inconsistent, if not inept, agency management, the Crow began the move to the new reservation. A long wagon and pony train, led by Armstrong, arrived at the new Crow Agency just south of present-day Hardin in early April of 1884.

Because the old agency lies adjacent to a state highway today, proposals to reconstruct the two-lane rural road spurred various cultural resource studies sponsored by the Montana Department of Transportation. Although initial archaeological work suggested the old agency's plowed-over cultural deposits might not have much potential, more intensive work in 2006 by archaeologist Steve Aaberg proved otherwise.[159] The Crow people reinforced Aaberg's assessment, telling the transportation department that the old ruins represented an important transitional period in their long history. All parties, including the Montana State Historic Preservation office, agreed that the old agency was eligible for listing in the National Register of Historic Places and thus qualified for protection and preservation.[160]

The archaeological project's successful outcome rested largely on the discovery of a detailed map of Absaroka Agency drawn by Indian Agent George Frost in 1878. (Montana DOT historian Jon Axline found the map in the Montana Historical Society archives.) Using the Frost map as a guide, the research

Reservation period archaeology, through rarely done, sheds light on a difficult transitional period among Montana's Native Americans. A proposal to widen a highway triggered archaeological work at the Absaroka Agency site on the Crow Reservation. Here archaeologists screen soil from the cultural deposit in the agency compound, now buried in a hayfield. PHOTOGRAPH COURTESY OF THE MONTANA DEPARTMENT OF TRANSPORTATION

team completed a geomagnetic survey to detect anomalies in the soil representing architectural and other features (a magnetometer measures the magnetic signal of artifacts buried in the ground). As the magnetometer work progressed along an extensive grid, magnetic gradient data were downloaded on a laptop computer and portrayed in colored relief maps. With some scaling, a transparency of Frost's scaled map laid atop the magnetometer maps identified overlaps. To everyone's excitement, a rectangular cluster of magnetic anomalies matched

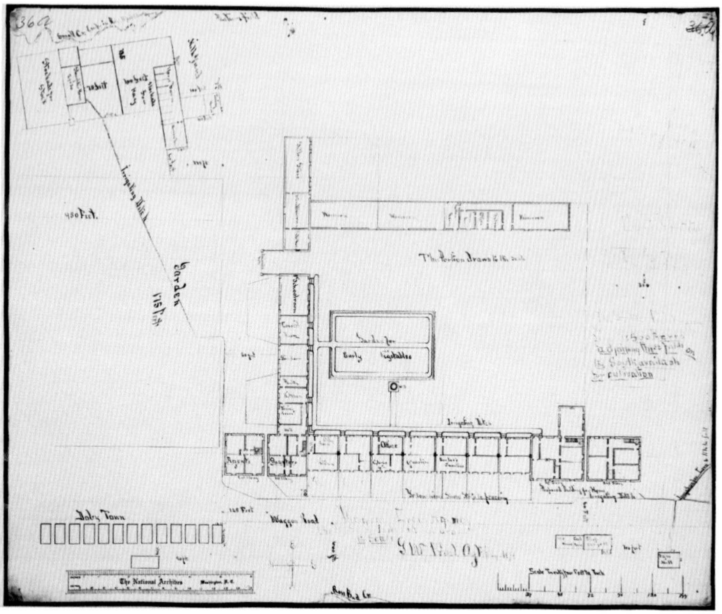

Archaeologists were lucky to have Agent George Frost's 1878 plan map of the Absaroka Agency, shown here, to guide their research. On the lower right is Doby Town, where Crow Indian leaders and their families lived. A transparency of Frost's scaled map laid atop the archaeologist's geomagnetic survey maps identified anomalies matching the compound's architectural and other features where excavation would be productive and informative. PHOTOGRAPH COURTESY OF THE MONTANA HISTORICAL SOCIETY RESEARCH CENTER-PHOTOGRAPH ARCHIVES, HELENA, MONTANA.

the main compound shown on the map. Testing work then focused on overlapping anomalies.

According to Agent Frost's map and the new archaeology, Absaroka Agency contained a main stockade or compound, located 600 feet east of East Rosebud Creek. Inside were connected adobe structures, a parade ground, and a vegetable garden. The compound was entered through a stockade gate on the north wall to which a council room, dining and sitting rooms, kitchen, pantry, storeroom, and the agent's quarters were attached. Buildings on the east and west walls incorporated various quarters, offices, and storage rooms. The civilian merchant's ("sutler") store, which sold provisions to the army post, is located just outside the northeastern corner of the compound. Nearby stood an icehouse, coalhouse, shop, and sawmill. A ditch brought water inside the compound.

Another warren of buildings and features lay adjacent to Butcher Creek, including a barn and tack room, livestock and hay stockades, milk yard, slaughterhouse, fenced pasture, and vegetable fields. Of particular interest here, the Frost map shows a row of 13 buildings near the agent's quarters and compound, which aligned directly with Highway 78. Called "Doby Town," these structures are the adobe-brick cabins first built for agency employees and their Crow wives and later occupied primarily by Indian leaders, according to Agent Armstrong.

Aaberg's crew excavated a variety of test pits across the old agency site, revealing old ditches, wall remnants, trash dumps, latrines, and a hand-stacked stone well. The crew also found the ruins of the agent's house, blacksmith shop, and sawmill site. Within these different structural features they recovered a wide range of historic artifacts including square nails, window glass and porcelain ornament fragments, buttons, buckles, and eyelets, glass and metal trade beads, cut plug tobacco tags, a clay pipe fragment, cartridge casings, boot and shoe fragments, and many pieces of lead, iron, charcoal, coal, and bone. The MDOT project artifact collection no doubt pales in comparison to what still must exist in the highway right-of-way and hayfield, because Aaberg's crew excavated less than one percent of the site!

Shedding archaeological light on Crow culture during this transitional period was a key project goal. Correspondence by

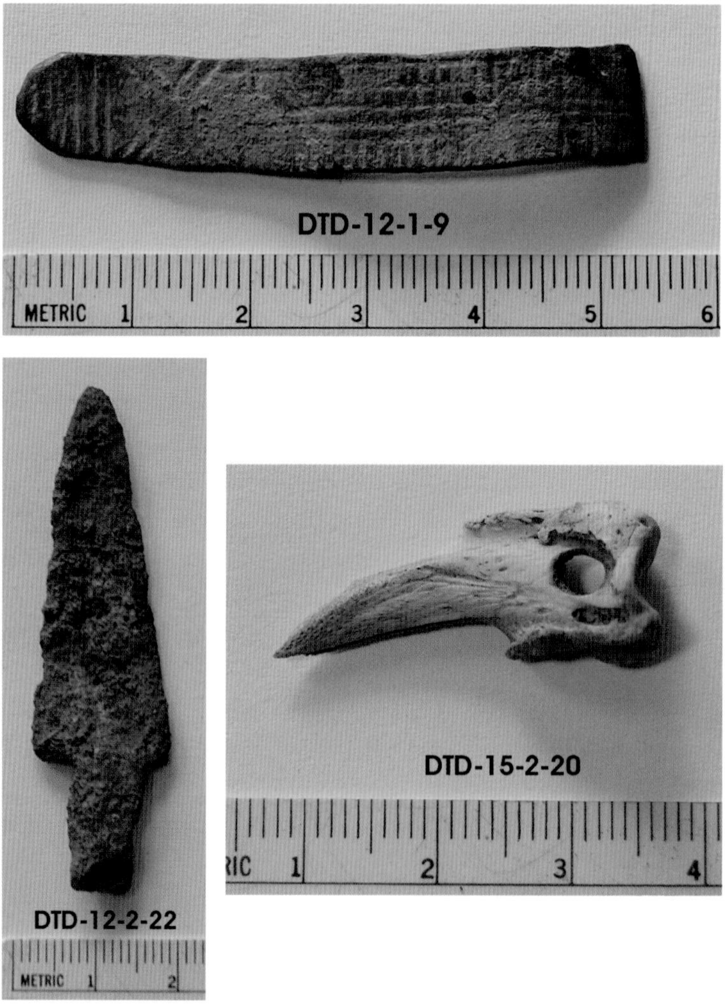

A variety of Crow artifacts discovered by archaeologists in Doby Town near the agency compound include part of a metal bracelet (top), a metal arrowhead (left) and a perforated badger claw that was part of a necklace (right). These and other artifacts contrast with those left by agency staff in the old compound. PHOTOGRAPH COURTESY OF STEVE AABERG.

Agent Frost states that about 20 Indian families used the cabins in Doby Town. What is the archaeological evidence? First, the faunal record from Doby Town contrasts significantly with the rest of the site, reflecting the different but changing diets of Crow peoples. Nearly twice as many animal species are represented in the Doby Town assemblage compared to what was found in the agency compound trash dump. It is difficult to differentiate between domestic and wild species in some cases—for example, bison and cows or grouse and chicken. Nonetheless, the residents of the main compound dined on beef, bison, elk, deer, and chicken while the inhabitants of Doby Town had a more diverse "Native" menu including bear, antelope, turtle, grouse (probably), duck, and cutthroat trout.

More telling, bones in Doby Town were heavily fractured to obtain bone marrow and grease, whereas in the main compound such "green fractures" are rare and bones there are usually sawn. Several hide-scraping tools made of bottle glass, a metal knife, and a hand-forged axe head also indicate "old style" animal butchering by the Crow. Archaeologists also recovered a small "Insikim" or buffalo-shaped stone made of fossil baculite in one of the Crow cabins. Such sacred items were put into medicine bundles and pouches. An abundance of wild plum and chokecherry pits revealed the importance of traditional plant foods.

Other telltale Indian evidence from Doby Town included fragments of a catlinite pipe bowl fragment; bone, brass, glass, and shell beads; metal tinklers or jingles used to decorate hide clothing; an iron bracelet; and the faunal remains of a golden eagle wing fan used in Crow ceremonies and festivities. Aaberg's team wondered if the presence of military buttons, a cavalry shoe, a belt buckle, and cartridge casings also indicated a military presence in Doby Town. This question is unresolved, but Aaberg points to the fact that Crow scouts and police were also issued uniforms and arms similar to those worn and used by U.S. Army troops. Many of the artifacts are Civil War-era surplus that was sent to Indian Reservations across the American West. However, the Crow modified many of these items to suit their own culture purposes.

The Absaroka Agency operated for less than 10 years. Major Fellowes Pease, who married a Crow woman, reportedly purchased the buildings and gave them to his daughter Lavina, who selected the old agency site as her allotment. In late December of 1891, a fire destroyed most of the buildings and locals salvaged the surviving structural materials, although picturesque adobe wall ruins remained there until the early 1920s. Lavina later received a homestead patent and ranched there until 1914, after which the property was sold to several families and finally to the Ostrum family, the current owners. Used today for agricultural production, the "Old Crow Agency" would only survive as a vague memory without the MDOT's vigilance and Aaberg's efforts.

At the new agency on the Little Bighorn, the Mountain Crow assimilated with the River Crow. Chief Plenty Coups, the renowned leader of the Mountain Crow, never moved to Crow Agency, preferring his old home near the Pryor Mountains, which today is Chief Plenty Coups State Park.[161] Plenty Coups became a formidable spokesperson for the Crow tribe and fought hard and successfully to prevent Congressional dissolution of the Crow tribe and its lands.[162] In this effort, Plenty Coups and other Crow leaders were more successful than other tribes at protecting their people and their lands. Nonetheless, from the original Crow territory of 38 million acres identified in the Fort Laramie Treaty of 1851, by 1904 Crow lands were reduced through treaties and Congressional actions to the reservation's present size of 2.3 million acres.[163]

As on all Montana Indian reservations, Crow people cautiously adapted in their own way to an alien "American" culture

Chief Plenty Coups (top photo), the renowned leader of the Crow, never moved to any of the three Crow agencies, preferring his old home (bottom photo) near the Pryor Mountains. Today, Chief Plenty Coup State Park is a peaceful and poignant place to visit. TOP: MONTANA HISTORICAL SOCIETY RESEARCH CENTER-PHOTOGRAPH ARCHIVES, HELENA, MONTANA. BOTTOM: COURTESY OF MONTANA STATE PARKS.

Absaroka Agency operated for nearly a decade before agency headquarters were transferred to present-day Hardin, Montana. Plenty Coups, Iron Bull (shown in the center of this 1881 photograph) and other leaders encouraged far-flung Crow bands to come to the agency for rations and annuities, and to take up ranching and farming. Crow people tenaciously hung on to their traditional self-reliant ways of life as a cultural imperative and survival strategy, resulting in a strong and vibrant culture today. Courtesy of Montana Historical Society Research Center Photographic Archives, Haynes Foundation Collection.

in the face of constantly changing U.S. government policies, incompetence, and reservation hardships. Acceptance only happened when the once-immense bison herds were depleted, or nearly so, and the pressures of White settlement were inevitable and overwhelming. The Crow then took up farming and ranching, led by the example and encouragement of tribal leaders like Plenty Coups. They hung on to their traditional self-reliant ways of life as a cultural imperative and survival strategy in the late nineteenth and early twentieth centuries. The tenacity of the Crow during the early reservation period has resulted in a strong and effective twenty-first century tribal government and culturally vibrant reservation life.

Today, Montana is home to seven Indian reservations. The Northern Cheyenne (*Tsistsistas* and *So'taa'eo'o*) occupy a reservation just east of the Crow Reservation in southeastern Montana.[164] The Fort Belknap Reservation in north-central Montana, established in 1888, accommodates the Gros Ventre or White Clay People (*A-a-nimin*) and Assiniboine (*Nakoda*) bands. Other Assiniboine bands inhabit the Fort Peck Reservation located in the far northeastern corner of Montana. Established in 1871, the reserve is also home to the Sisseton, Teton Hunkpapa, Wahpeton, and Yanktonai (*Lakota, Dakota*) Sioux.[165]

The Algonquian-speaking Southern Piegan (*Aaamsskáápipikani*) reside on the Blackfeet Reservation in northwest Montana. Formed in the mid-1850s, their reservation was substantially reduced in size with the formation of the Flathead Forest Reserve, the creation of Glacier National Park, and by successive federal executive orders at the turn of the nineteenth century.[166] The Rocky Boy Reservation was also created in this region in 1916 to accommodate landless Chippewa or Ojibwa (*Anishanabe*) and Cree (*ne hiy awak*) who had migrated west. The Little Shell Tribe of Chippewa Indians, which includes the *Métis* of mixed blood Cree, Irish, and Scots ancestry, is not yet federally

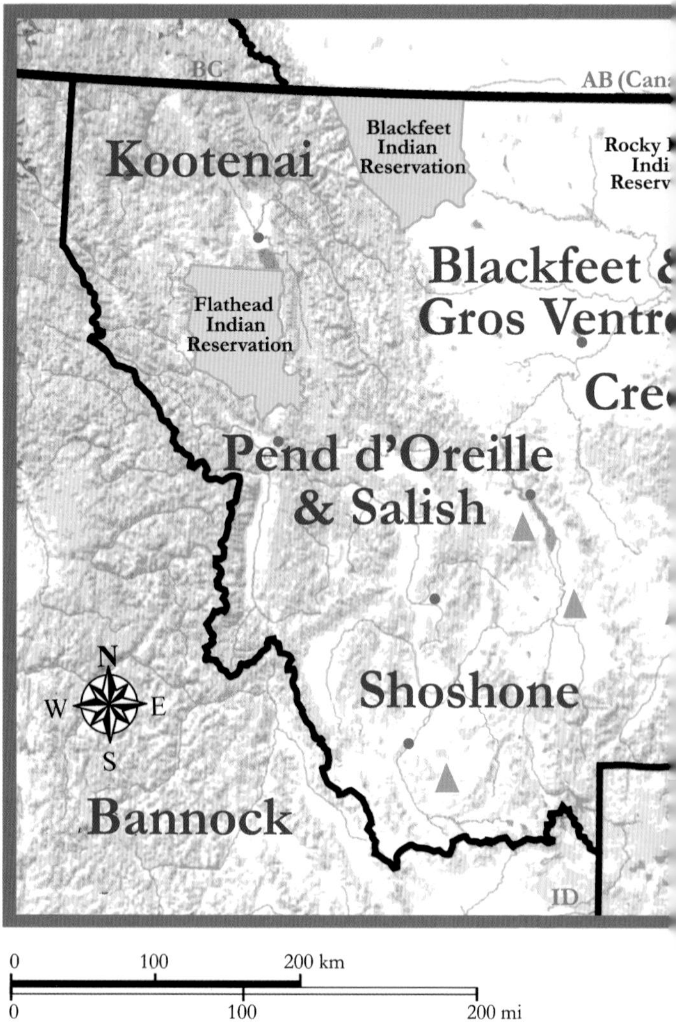

Seven Indian reservations are located in Montana. The state-recognized Little Shell Band of Chippewa Indians do not have their own reservation at this time. Reservations are shared by diversity of once

independent Plains and Intermountain Indian tribes. Their boundaries do not reflect the once vast aboriginal territories of Montana's First Peoples. Illustration by Eric S. Carlson recognized and is thus without its own reservation.[167] The tribe is officially recognized by the state of Montana.

Established in 1855, the Flathead Reservation in western Montana is the home of the Kootenai (*Ktunaxa*), Pend d'Oreille (Upper Kalispel, *Qlispé*), and Salish (Flathead, *Sqelio*) peoples.[168] The Pend d'Oreille and Salish, both Salishan speakers, are linked linguistically to coastal peoples. When they arrived in Montana is unknown, though Salish bands resided on the Plains in the distant past. Historically, the Salish inhabited the mountain valleys of southwestern Montana until they were moved to the Flathead Reservation, reluctantly in the case of Chief Charlo, whose band only came to the reservation in 1891 accompanied by military troops. The Kootenai speak a separate language from the Salish.[169] Their linguistic isolation, oral tradition, and the archaeological record indicate their long presence in western Montana and the adjacent plains.

Not all Indian tribes who once lived within Montana's borders occupy reservations here today. The Northern Shoshone (*Newe*) people now live on reservations in Idaho and Wyoming. Various lines of evidence also suggest that the ancestral Kiowa (*Kai-i-gwu*) once lived here, first migrating north into the Plains and Rocky Mountain regions, then moving eastward to the Black Hills in the 1400s, and finally, on horses, onto the southern High Plains in the early 1700s. However, the homogenous material culture of Plains and Intermountain Indian hunter-gatherers makes it very difficult to identify all of the groups who once lived or passed through the state in the distant past.[170]

The study of historic sites like Absaroka Agency and Rosebud Battlefield brings us into the realm of historical archaeology, where historical records define or influence archaeological inquiry. To date, Montana researchers have paid relatively little attention to historic period Indian sites. This research, whenever it is done—as at Absaroka Agency—will shed new light on this complicated and perhaps "lost" period in our state's history. Recently, Montana State University-Bozeman and the BLM archaeologists, in collaboration with the Crow tribe, created an educational curriculum about Absaroka Agency for fourth and fifth graders. In any event, Montana transportation department engineers shifted the highway alignment to prevent further harm to the old agency and its rich and informative archaeological deposit.

Modern Indian peoples maintain deep ancestral ties to Montana's diverse landscapes, including many of its most scenic places like the Sweet Grass Hills, Rocky Mountain Front, and the Pryor Mountains. These lands, once part of vast aboriginal territories, contain abundant culturally interconnected archaeological sites, place names, and sacred sites. They are still visited and used by tribal people for cultural, educational, and spiritual purposes. Such places can be designated "traditional cultural properties" under the National Historic Preservation Act. Illustration by Eric S. Carlson.

CONNECTING PAST AND PRESENT

The goal of historic preservation is not just to save archaeological sites for future scientific research and education. In the United States, modern Indian communities retain deep ancestral ties to both archaeological sites and the landscapes in which they are found. Recognizing this fact, in 1992 the National Park Service began designating these kinds of places *traditional cultural properties* (TCP) as part of its National Register of Historic Places program. By definition, traditional cultural properties are cultural resources that are both rooted in a community's history and important for maintaining its continuing cultural identity and beliefs, customs, and practices.[171] In practical terms, this means that contemporary tribal (or any ethnic group) ties to cultural resources are recognized in the federal historic preservation process, and these values can be considered in project planning, along with archaeological, historical, and architectural ones. The National Park Service now officially lists a small number of traditional cultural properties in Montana. Below are three noteworthy examples.

KOOTENAI FALLS

Breathtaking Kootenai Falls between the communities of Libby and Troy in far northwestern Montana is a culturally significant place to Kootenai people. Situated in the heart of the tribe's

Spectacular Kootenai Falls lies between Libby and Troy in northwestern Montana. Used by the Kutenai Indians for thousands of years, archaeological sites lie hidden on the riverbanks surrounding the falls. Today, Kootenai people perpetuate their traditional cultural knowledge and practices at the falls area, which is now designated a Traditional Cultural Property. iStock/mjphototacoma

ancestral territory, the cascading falls and its surrounding forested riverbanks are considered to be a deeply sacred. Because Kootenai Falls is a consecrated or holy site, tribal members seek visions and revelations here to assist and guide them through life. Tribal place names and oral histories associated with this place are used to educate Kootenai youth in the ways of their ancestors and perpetuate traditional cultural knowledge. Tribal ceremonies happen regularly at the falls, as well as age-old subsistence practices—gathering food and medicinal plants, cedar bark collecting, and fishing for bull and cutthroat trout.

Rock piles, red pictographs, old camps, and other archaeological sites lie hidden in the dense vegetation on both banks of the river, although a state highway, railroad tracks, and a county park disturb the south shore. Access to the less disturbed north shore is via a swinging wooden footbridge above the falls. Sadly, vandals have pilfered some of the archaeological sites at the falls but the U.S. Forest Service has been able to recover some of the invaluable artifacts. (They are now safely housed at the Peoples Center in Pablo.)

A portage trail perched precariously on a talus slope above the roaring falls enabled Kootenais to carry their "sturgeon-nosed" cedar canoes around the rushing torrent.[172] In 1808, explorer David Thompson's fur trapping brigade portaged their canoes and supplies across this same precipitous section of trail, which was part of an extensive network of Indian trails and roads connecting the Columbia Plateau with the interior Rocky Mountains and Northern Plains. For Indians and non-Indians alike, Kootenai Falls is a powerful and awe-inspiring place.

Luckily, Kootenai Falls has fared better than have other culturally important places in Montana. In 1987, the Federal Energy Regulatory Commission (FERC) denied an application to build a run-of-river dam across Kootenai Falls because it would impair the Kootenai's ability to practice their religion.[173] The Falls area had not yet been designated a TCP (the concept is part of the 1992 amendments to the National Historic Preservation Act) so FERC based its legal decision on the 2nd Amendment of the U.S. Constitution and the American Indian Religious Freedom Act of 1978.

Still, at the time of the Federal Energy Regulatory Commission decision against the run-of-river dam of Kootenai Falls, a significant portion of the Kootenai River basin, where Kootenai people have lived since time immemorial, already lay within the flood pool of Lake Koocanusa, which extends 48 miles to the U.S.-Canada border and another 42 miles into British Columbia. A significant chunk of traditional Kootenai territory has been grievously impacted by hydropower facilities, roads, timber harvest, powerlines, urban sprawl, and other intrusions, and the consequent loss of Kootenai Indian cultural sites is enormous.

Chicago Peak, another Kootenai Traditional Cultural Property, is associated with the cultural and spiritual practices of the Kootenai people dating back to their creation. Located in the Cabinet Mountains, Chicago Peak could be affected by a gold mine. PHOTOGRAPH COURTESY OF BARA, THE UNIVERSITY OF ARIZONA.

CHICAGO PEAK

A traditional cultural property of equivalent value to the Kootenai people lies further west in the Cabinet Mountain Wilderness Area overlooking the Clark Fork River and Noxon Reservoir. Called Chicago Peak, this mountain landscape is associated with the cultural and spiritual practices of the Kootenai people dating back to their creation. According to Montana Kootenai elder

Francis Auld, Chicago Peak is sacred and associated with many stories that have been passed orally from generation to generation. This relatively untouched place enables contemporary Kootenai people to connect with their history free of human intrusion or modern disturbances. Old trails, archaeological sites, and other isolated places associated with this prominent mountain peak are used today for vision questing and religious rites.

Chicago Peak is threatened by a proposal to build an underground mine. The Kootenai tribe strongly objects to this project, stating that they don't want one of their most significant holy sites to end up as a "hollowed out" mountain. This project is now being reviewed in federal court because of environmental and tribal traditional cultural property concerns.

BADGER-TWO MEDICINE

The Badger-Two Medicine area along the highly scenic Rocky Mountain Front is probably the best-known traditional cultural property in Montana. This 130,000-acre area encompasses a remote and rugged part of the Continental Divide and national forest lands near Glacier National Park, the Bob Marshall Wilderness Area, and the Blackfeet Indian Reservation. Covered by an 1896 treaty, the Blackfeet call this vast highland landscape (including Glacier and Waterton Lakes national parks) and its many mountain peaks the "Backbone of the World."

The Badger-Two Medicine area is significant for its cultural and spiritual uses by ancestral and contemporary Blackfeet people. Fasting and vision questing occur on ledges in its rocky cliffs and on top of mountain peaks. Wooden pegs that attached the chests of Blackfeet supplicants to leather tethers on Sun Dance poles are retired here. Water from certain springs is collected to bless newborn babies. With the demise of bison herds at the turn of the nineteenth century, Blackfeet people turned

Badger-Two Medicine, Montana's best known Traditional Cultural Property, is located on the Rocky Mountain Front near East Glacier. Blackfeet people have used this remote area since time immemorial for spiritual purposes and to sustain their cultural traditions. Natural gas leasing and development in Badger-Two Medicine has led to years of cultural resource analyses and litigation. PHOTOGRAPH COURTESY OF BARA, THE UNIVERSITY OF ARIZONA.

to elk hunting in the Badger-Two Medicine to sustain age-old cultural traditions and sacred knowledge. Many archaeological sites are present within this Traditional Cultural Property, including historic Blackfeet elk hunting camps replete with stoves, fire hearths, and animal carcass hanging racks.

Political turmoil surrounds the Badger-Two Medicine because it is the scene of natural gas and oil well leasing along the Rocky Mountain Front. In the early 1980s, the Blackfeet pressed the U.S. Forest Service and Department of Interior-BLM not to allow exploratory drilling in the Badger-Two Medicine due to its extreme spiritual value and cultural sensitivity. Nonetheless, leases were issued, sparking 30 years of archaeological and ethnographic studies, historic preservation consultation, and litigation. The Secretary of the Interior cancelled the remaining Badger-Two Medicine leases in recognition of the area's traditional cultural property designation and its spiritual connection to the Blackfeet.[174] The drilling leases were recently (September 2018) reinstated under a federal court ruling. Further legal maneuvering is sure to follow, leaving the ultimate fate of Badger-Two Medicine TCP unknown.

Today, Montana historic preservation officials, federal agencies, preservation groups, and Indian tribes are responsible for identifying and designating TCPs. Many of the state's most scenic and popular recreation areas on public lands, like the Sweet Grass Hills, Smith River Canyon, and the Pryor Mountains, contain an abundance of culturally interconnected archaeological sites, place names, and sacred sites within already designated or potential TCPs.

In broader perspective, the state's mountains and plains regions accommodated the diverse lifeways and economic pursuits of Indians, and later, Euromerican peoples for millennia. As one consequence, successive cultural groups have each left a unique cultural "footprint" on the land, creating multiple layers of personal and community attachment, meaning, memory, and history. Anthropologists call these places "storied landscapes."

Today, storied landscapes are identified, designated and protected in several ways. In addition to TCPs, archaeological and historic sites linked by site type, an event, or a historical theme may be grouped into larger National Register "districts." The most significant of these National Register districts may rise to the level of a National Historic Landmark (NHL). Four NHLs are described in this book: First Peoples

Buffalo Jump, Hagan Village, Pictograph Cave, and Rosebud Battlefield. Whatever their official designation, identifying and protecting cultural landscapes is an important historic preservation goal in Montana.

Superimposition of images is relatively common at Montana rock art sites. In this example from Bear Gulch, the shield-bearing warrior (top) was drawn first. Later, the V-neck human figure (center) was incised onto the shield-bearing warrior, resulting in the composite image (bottom). Such changes show that rock art compositions were dynamic, not static. Whether it is discerning successive layers of rock art or excavating layers of soil in an ancient campsite, archaeologists, and their tribal and other collaborators, still have much to learn and understand about Montana's deep, Indigenous human past.

THE WAY FORWARD

The past 50 years have witnessed an explosion in our knowledge of Montana's American Indian past and history, spurred in large measure by the crucial passage of state and federal antiquities laws. Cultural resource management programs are now an integral part of federal, state, and tribal governments, and agency and tribal leaders routinely consider cultural resource values in their land use decisions and actions. Montanans have more access to archaeological information than ever before and can even participate in university and agency projects.[175] Federal, state and tribal museums and interpretive facilities like First Peoples Buffalo Jump and Pictograph Cave state parks; state and federal trailhead and roadside interpretive signs, trails, and routes; and educational programs provide innumerable opportunities to learn about archaeological sites and Indian peoples. Heritage tourism is a substantial contributor to Montana's economy.

Naturally, much work remains to be done. Foremost, hundreds of archaeological sites scattered across Montana require proper identification, evaluation, and protection. Many regions of Montana are still archaeologically little known. Relatively few archaeological investigations have taken place in western Montana with the important exception of work along the Kootenai River in the 1960s-1980s.[176] This is partly because few projects requiring salvage excavations (data recovery) have occurred in this part of the state, as compared to the federally mandated archaeological work in the coal lands and oil fields of central and eastern Montana.

Someday, perhaps, American Indian and non-Indian archaeologists will collaborate in this necessary research, in their own time and way, which will lead to a fuller understanding of cultural relationships among western Montana, Columbia Plateau, and Plains Indian peoples in the near and distant past. Similarly, archaeologists would do well to consider the role of the adjacent Great Basin and Columbia Plateau in southwest Montana prehistory, for it is still viewed largely through the lens of the northwestern Plains. For that matter, future archaeological discoveries (pre-Clovis sites), field and lab methods (aerial drones, DNA analysis) and ideas will surely correct or alter current interpretations of Montana's ancient Indigenous past, including many of those presented in this book.

Admittedly, archaeological data can be technical and dry. Thankfully, educators, tribal cultural specialists, and archaeologists are translating "archaeology-speak" into popular vernacular, readable prose, and culturally sensitive interpretive media and school curricula.[177] In fact, archaeology has mostly been written—this book is no exception—from a "western science" point of view. Future archaeological syntheses will substantially benefit by the inclusion of tribal knowledge, perspectives, and interpretations.

Agriculture, mining, logging, urban and rural sprawl, and other human activities daily threaten archaeological sites across the state. Relic collecting and digging is not entirely a thing of the past, and archaeological sites are still defaced and looted, sometimes motivated by commercial interests in the artifacts. Catastrophic wildfire, severe flooding, drought-caused erosion, and other natural events, now amplified by anthropogenic global warming, all pose threats to cultural resources.[178]

Thus, a significant number of archaeological sites are in

Perennial, high-elevation ice patches on the Beartooth Plateau and elsewhere are now melting due to global warming, exposing once ice-encased Indian artifacts such as the wood dart shaft shown here. Archaeologists are gaining new insights into the use of high elevation environments by Native peoples but the rapid rate of melting in the Anthropocene precludes timely discovery and recovery of freshly exposed artifacts. PHOTOGRAPH COURTESY OF CRAIG LEE.

jeopardy or are in danger of disappearing altogether. Montana citizens must encourage state, federal, and tribal officials, local governments, and preservation groups to be vigilant in the protection and preservation of our archaeological resources, for once they are gone they can never be replaced.

Finally, the arbitrary dividing line between Montana's recent history and its archaeological past needs blurring. With so much new information at our fingertips, the state's archaeological history is more knowable than ever before, and the history of American Indian hunter-gatherers is as integral to a holistic and complete understanding of Montana's history as British explorers, Irish miners, or Norwegian homesteaders.

Ultimately, we *Homo sapiens* all share an ancient and common hunter-gatherer ancestry. During the Late Pleistocene and Holocene our paths diverged, leading to the remarkable ethnic, linguistic, and cultural diversity of humankind around the world today. And so it came to be that, in this place we now call Montana, the Anzick Clovis child, the Spiro pithouse builders, the First Peoples bison hunters, the Bear Gulch warrior artists, the elusive Sheep Eaters, the brave Buffalo Calf Road Woman, and the other Indigenous peoples described in this book became Montana's first pioneers and residents, beginning millennia ago.

ENDNOTES

1 The American Antiquities Act of 1906 is the first cultural resource protection law in the United States, but it did not lead to a broad federal historic preservation program. This happened some sixty years later with the passage the National Historic Preservation Act of 1966.

2 Montana's Indian tribes and nations each have distinct Indigenous names. In this book, the terms American Indian, Native American, Native peoples, Indigenous peoples, and First Americans are used interchangeably to collectively describe Montana's ethnically diverse First Peoples.

3 Nancy Capace, *Encyclopedia of Montana.* (Santa Barbara, California: Somerset Publishers, Inc., 2000)

4 Nevin M. Fenneman, *Physiography of Western United States.* (New York: McGraw-Hill Book Company, 1931).

5 Brian Fagan, *The Complete Ice Age: How Climate Change Shaped the World* (London: Thames & Hudson Ltd., 2009). Doug Macdougall, *Frozen Earth: The Once and Future Story of Ice Ages* (Berkeley: University of California Press, 2004).

6 COHMAP Members, "Climate Change of the Last 18,000 Years: Observations and Models," Science 241 (1988): 1043-1052.

7 These mega-beasts are wonderfully illustrated in Ian M. Lange, *Ice Age Mammals of North America: A Guide to the Big, the Hairy, and the Bizarre* (Missoula, Montana: Mountain Press Publishing Company, 2002).

8 David D. Alt, *Glacial Lake Missoula and Its Humongous Floods.* (Missoula, Montana: Mountain Press Publishing Company, 2001).

9 The concept of Holocene "stability" is elegantly explained in Dianne Dumanoski, *The End of the Long Summer: Why We Must Remake Our Civilization to Survive on a Volatile Earth.* (New York: Crown Publishers, 2009).

10 Brian Fagan, *The Great Warming: Climate Change and the Rise and Fall of Civilizations* (New York: Bloomsbury Press, 2009).

11 Brian M. Fagan, ed., *The Little Ice Age: How Climate Made History 1300-1850* (New York: Basic Books, 2000). Sam White, *A Cold Welcome: The Little Ice Age and Europe's Encounter with North America* (Cambridge: Harvard University Press, 2017).

12 Brian Kahn, "We Just Breached the 410 PPM Threshold for CO2," *Scientific American* April 2017. Elizabeth Kolbert, *The Sixth Extinction: An Unnatural History* (New York: Picador, 2014).

13 Gordon R. Wiley and Jeremy Sabloff, *A History of American Archaeology* (New York: W.H. Freeman Co., 1993), 42-87.

14 David Hurst Thomas, *Archaeology* (New York: Holt, Rinehart and Winston, 1979) p. 30.

15 See Roger C. Echo-Hawk, "Ancient History in the New World: Oral Traditions and the Archaeological Record of Deep Time." *American Antiquity* 65, no. 1 (2000): 541-570.

16 R.E. Taylor, "Radiocarbon Dating," In: *Chronometric Dating in Archaeology*, R.E. Taylor and Martin J. Aitkens, ed. (New York: Plenum Press, 1997), 65-96.

17 Two classic introductory texts about flintknapping are: Don Crabtree, *An introduction to flintknapping.* Occasional Papers of the Idaho State University No. 28, Pocatello, Idaho. John C. Whittaker, *Flintknapping: Making and Understanding Stone Tools* (Austin: University of Texas Press, 1994).

18 Errett Callahan, *The Basics of Biface Knapping in the Eastern Fluted Point Tradition: A Manual for Flintknappers and Lithic Analysts* (Lynchburg: Piltdown Productions, 1996).

19 Robert L. Kelly, *The Lifeways of Hunter-Gatherers: The Foraging Spectrum.* 2nd Edition. (Cambridge: Cambridge University Press, 2013), 166-174.

20 Larry A. Lahren, *The Meyers-Hindman Site: An Exploratory Study of Human Occupation Patterns in the Upper Yellowstone Valley from 7000 B.C. to A.D. 1200.* (Anthropological Researches International, Livingston, Montana, 1976). Earl H. Swanson Jr., *Birch Creek: Human Ecology of the Cool Desert of the Northern Rocky Mountains 9,000 B.C. – A.D. 1850.* (Pocatello: The Idaho State University Press, 1972); Wilfred M. Husted and Robert Edgar, *The Archaeology of Mummy Cave, Wyoming: An Introduction to Shoshonean Prehistory.* (Lincoln: Midwest Archaeological Center and Southeast Archaeological Center Special Report No. 4. National Park Service Technical Report Series No. 9., 2002).

21 William Mulloy, *A Preliminary Historical Outline for the Northwestern Plains* (Laramie: University of Wyoming Publications 22, 1958).

22 Brian O. K. Reeves, *Cultural Change on the Northwestern Plains: 1000 B.C. – A.D. 1000,* (Edmonton: Archaeological Survey of Alberta Occasional Paper No. 29, 1983). Marcel Kornfeld, George C. Frison and Mary Lou Larson, *Prehistoric Hunter-Gatherers of the High Plains and Rockies.* (Walnut Creek: Left Coast Press Inc., 2010). Douglas H. MacDonald, *Montana Before History 11,000 years of Hunter-Gatherers in the Rockies and Plains.* (Missoula: Mountain Press Publishing Company, 2012).

23 Eugene E. Harris, *Ancestors in our Geonomes The New Science of Human Evolution.* (New York: Oxford University Press, 2015)

24 Steve Olson, *Mapping Human History Genes, Race and Our Common Origins.* (New York: Houghton Mifflin Company, 2002), 11-54.

25 The fascinating but ever-controversial story of the Pleistocene colonization of the Americas is described in: J. M Adovasio and Jake Peddler, *The First Americans: In Pursuit of Archaeology's Greatest Mystery* (New York: Random House Inc., 2016). Brian Fagan, *The Great Journey: The Peopling of Ancient America* (Gainesville: University of Florida Press, 2004). David J. Meltzer, *First Peoples in a New World: Colonizing Ice Age America* (Berkeley: University of California Press, 2009).

26 Ben A. Potter et al., "Early colonization of Beringia and Northern North America: Chronology, routes, and adaptive strategies," *Quaternary International* (2017), http://dxc.doi.org/10.1016/j.quiant.2017.02.034.

27 Ewen Callaway, "Plant and Animal DNA suggests first Americans took the coastal route." Nature 536, no. 138 (11 August 2016), doi:10.1038/536138a; Jon M. Erlandson and Todd J. Braje, "From Asia to the Americas by boat? Paleogeography, paleoecology, and stemmed points of the northwest Pacific." *Quaternary International* 239, no. 1-2 (2011): 28-37.

28 Jorie Clark, Jerry X. Mitrovica and Jay Alder, "Coastal Paleogeography of the California-Oregon-Washington and Bering Sea continental shelves during the latest Pleistocene and Holocene: implications for the archaeological record," *Journal of Archaeological Science* 52 (2014): 12-23.

29 Duncan McLaren et al. "Terminal Pleistocene epoch human footprints from the Pacific coast of Canada." *PloS One* 13 (3): e0193522; doi: 10.1371/journal.pone.0193522, 2018.

30 David Reich, *Who We Are and How We Got Here: Ancient DNA and the New Science of the Human Past.* (New York: Pantheon Books, 2018), 176-181.

31 Dennis J. Stanford and Bruce A. Bradley, *Across the Atlantic Ice: The Origin of America's Clovis Culture* (Berkeley: University of California Press, 2012).

32 Michael I. Bird, Damien O'Grady and Sean Ulm, "Humans, water and the colonization of Australia." *Proceedings of the National Academy of Sciences* 113, no. 41 (2016): 11477-11482.

33 Steven R. Holen et al., "A 130,000-year-old archaeological site in southern California, USA." *Nature* 544 (2017): 479-483.

34 Anthony T. Bouldurian and John L. Cotter, *Clovis Revisited: New Perspectives on Paleoindian Adaptations from Blackwater Draw, New Mexico* (Philadelphia: University of Pennsylvania Museum of Archaeology and Anthropology, 1999).

35 Thomas D. Dillehay et al., "Monte Verde: Seaweed, Food, Medicine, and the Peopling of South America." *Science* 320 (2008): 784-786.

36 J.M. Adovasio and David Peddler, *Strangers in a New Land: What Archaeology Reveals about the First Americans.* (Buffalo, New York: Firefly Books, 2016).

37 Michael B. Collins and Bruce A. Bradley, "Evidence for Pre-Clovis Occupation at the Gault Site (41BL323), Central Texas." *Current Research in the Pleistocene* 25 (2008): 70-72.

38 Thomas M. Gilbert et al., "DNA from Pre-Clovis Human Coprolites in Oregon, North America." *Science* 320 (2008): 786-89.

39 Christopher L. Hill and Leslie B. Davis, "Stratigraphy, ams radiocarbon age, and stable isotope biogeochemistry of the Lindsay mammoth, eastern Montana. *Current Research in the Pleistocene* 15 (1998): 109-112. Except possibly at Lindsay, no mammoth remains in Montana are definitely associated with humans, see Christopher L. Hill, "Stratigraphic and geochronologic contexts of mammoths (*Mammuthus*) and other Pleistocene fauna, Upper Missouri River Basin (northern Great Plains and Rocky Mountains), U.S.A." *Quaternary International* 142-143 (2006) 87-106.

40 Dee C. Taylor, "The Wilsall excavations: An Exercise in Frustration," *Montana Academy of Science Proceedings* 29:147-150.

41 The Anzick human skeletal remains are described in Douglas W. Owsley and D.R. Hunt, "Clovis and Early Archaic Period Crania from the Anzick Site (24PA506), Park County, Montana." *Plains Anthropologist* 46 (2001): 115-124.

42 Thomas Y. Canby, "The Search for the First Americans." *National Geographic Magazine*: 156 (1979): 330-363.

43 Morton Rasmussen et al., "The genome of a Late Pleistocene human from a Clovis burial site in western Montana," *Nature* 506 (2014), 225-229.

44 Geneticist Bryan Sykes popularized the concept of MtDNA inheritance in *The Seven Daughters of Eve: The Science That Reveals Our Genetic Ancestry*. (New York: W.W. Norton & Company, 2002).

45 Thomas W. J. Stafford, "Accelerator C-14 dating of human fossil skeletons: Assessing accuracy and results on New World specimens." In. *Method and Theory for Investigating the Peopling of the Americas.* (Corvallis, Oregon: Oregon State University, 1994), 45-55; Edited by Robson Bonnichsen and D.G. Steele. Juliet E. Morrow and Stuart J. Fiedel, "New Radiocarbon Dates for the Anzick Clovis Burial," In *Paleoindian Archaeology: a hemispheric perspective*. Edited by J. E. Morrow and C. G. Gnecco, (Gainesville: University of Florida Press, 2006), 123-138.

46 The discrepancy between the bone rods and Anzick-1 child radiocarbon dates has led some archaeologists to speculate that they are separate cultural events. See Ruthann Knudson, "We are All One: Anzick Child Reburied." *Mammoth Trumpet* 3, no. 2 (2015): 11-14. See also Morrow and Fiedel, ibid: 131-133.

47 J. Scott Jones, "The Anzick site: Analysis of a Clovis Assemblage" (Master's thesis, Oregon State University, 1997).

48 Juliet E. Morrow and Stuart J. Fiedel: ibid, 129. Bone and antler can be difficult to differentiate in archaeological specimens and are often referred to as "osseous" tools. At Anzick, the osseous rods have been identified as elk antler.

49 Larry A. Lahren and Robson Bonnichsen, "Bone foreshafts from a Clovis burial in southwestern Montana," *Science* 186 (1974): 147-150.

50 Philip J. Wilke, Jeffry. J. Flenniken and Terry L. Ozbun, "Clovis Technology at the Anzick Site, Montana." *Journal of California and Great Basin Anthropology* 13 (1991): 242-247.

51 R. Lee Lyman and Michael J. O'Brien, "A Mechanical and Functional Study of Bone Rods from the Richey-Roberts Clovis Cache, Washington, U.S.A," *Journal of Archaeological Science* 25 (1998): 887-906.

52 Ben Potter et al., "New insights into Eastern Beringian mortuary behavior: A terminal Pleistocene double infant burial at Upward Sun River," *PNAS* 111 (2014): 17060-17065.

53 Gary Haynes, *The Early Settlement of North America, The Clovis Era* (Cambridge: Cambridge University Press, 2002).

54 The seminal work on Clovis mammoth hunting is by George C. Frison and Lawrence C. Todd, *The Colby Mammoth Site: Taphonomy and Archaeology of a Clovis Kill in Northern Wyoming* (Albuquerque: University of New Mexico Press, 1986).

55 Pleistocene extinctions are concisely explained in Shepard Kretch III, *The Ecological Indian Myth and History* (New York: W. W. Norton & Company, 1999, 29-43.

56 Paul L. Koch and Anthony D. Barnosky, "Late Quaternary Extinctions: State of the Debate," *Annual Review of Ecology, Evolution and Systematics* 37 (2006): 215-250.

57 Brian M. Fagan, *Cro-Magnon: How the Ice Age Gave Birth to the First Modern Humans* (New York: Bloomsbury Press, 2010), 165-168. R. Lee Lyman, "North American Paleoindian Eyed Bone Needles: Morphometrics, Sewing, and Site Structure." *American Antiquity* 80 (2015): 146-160.

58 George C. Frison, *The Mill Iron Site* (Albuquerque: University of New Mexico Press, 1986).

59 Michael R. Waters and Thomas W. Stafford, Jr., "Redating the Mill Iron Site, Montana: A reexamination of Goshen Chronology," *American Antiquity* 79, no. 3 (2014): 541-548.

60 George C. Frison, *Survival by Hunting: Prehistoric Human Predators and Animal Prey* (Berkeley: University of California Press, 2004).

61 Gordon R. Willey and Jeremy A. Sabloff, *A History of American Archaeology*, ibid: 126-127.

62 Marcel Kornfeld, George C. Frison and Mary Lou Larson, *Prehistoric Hunter-Gatherers of the High Plains and Rockies.* (Walnut Creek: Left Coast Press Inc., 2010).

63 P. Skoglund et al., "Ancient Wolf Genome Reveals an Early Divergence of Domestic Dog Ancestors and Admixture into High-Latitude Breeds," *Current Biology* 24 (2015):1515-1519. Ed Yong, "A New Origin Story for Dogs" in *The Atlantic*, July 2, 2016.

64 Leslie B. Davis et al., "Montane Paleoindian Occupations in the Ruby Valley, Southwestern Montana: The Barton Gulch Occupations." *Current Research in the Pleistocene* 6 (1989): 7-9. "Paleoarchaic Foragers of the Middle Rockies: The Barton Gulch Occupations," ed. Leslie B. Davis, unpublished 2013 MS, 57-97, copy in author's collection.

65 Stephen Armstrong, "Alder Complex Kitchens: Experimental Replication of Paleoindian Cooking Facilities." *Archaeology in Montana* 34, no. 2 (1993): 1-66.

66 Alston V. Thoms, "The fire stones carry: Ethnographic and archaeological expectations for hot-rock cookery in Western North America," *Journal of Anthropological Archaeology* 27 (2008): 443-460.

67 Stephen A. Aaberg, "Alder Complex Plant Macrofossils," in "Paleoarchaic Foragers of the Middle Rockies: The Barton Gulch Occupations," ed. Leslie B. Davis, unpublished 2013 MS, 57-97, copy in author's collection.

68 Glen Fredlund: "Alder Gulch Pollen and Phytoliths," in "Paleoarchaic Foragers of the Middle Rockies: The Barton Gulch Occupations", ed. Leslie B. Davis, unpublished 2013 MS., 98-108, copy in author's collection.

69 For example, see Francis Densmore, *How Indians Use Wild Plants for Food, Medicine & Crafts* (New York: Dover Publications, 1974). Jeff Hart, *Montana Native Plants and Early Peoples* (Helena: Montana Historical Society Press, 1976).

70 Sunday A. Walker-Kuntz, E. R. Hajic, and Lynelle A. Peterson, "The Spiro Site (24CB1332): A Middle Plains Archaic Housepit Site," *Archaeology in Montana* 47(2) (2006): 1-56.

71 Julian H. Steward, *Culture Element Distributions: XXIII Northern and Gosiute Shoshone. Anthropological Records* 8:3 (Berkeley: University of California Press, 1943), 267-268.

72 The idea of communal rabbit drives by Spiro people finds archaeological support in a recent Wyoming housepit site study by Ronald J. Rood, "Archaic communal jackrabbit hunting in central Wyoming: Faunal remains from the Dick Myal Housepit site, 48FR6256," *Plains Anthropologist* 63, no. 247 (2018): 260-278.

73 Mary Lou Larson and Julie E. Francis, *Changing Perspectives of the Archaic on the Northwestern Plains and Rocky Mountains* (Vermillion: The University of South Dakota Press, 1997).

74 Lynn L. Harrell, Ted Hoefer II and Scott T. McKern, "Archaic House Pits in the Wyoming Basin." In: *Changing Perspectives of the Archaic on the Northwestern Plains and Rocky Mountains* (Vermillion: The University of South Dakota Press, 1997), 334-367.

75 A comprehensive, though now dated, treatment of Montana (and other) tipi rings is Leslie B. Davis, ed., "From Microcosm to Macrocosm: Advances in Tipi Ring Investigation and Interpretation," *Plains Anthropologist* Memoir 19 (1983).

76 See Reginald and Glady's Laubin, *The Indian Tipi: it's history, construction and use.* 2nd edition, (Norman, University of Oklahoma 1989).

77 Stuart Conner, "1982 Archaeology of the Crow Indian Vision Quest," *Archaeology in Montana* 23, no. 3 (1982): 85-128.

78 John H. Brumley, *Medicine Wheels on the Northern Plains: A Summary and Appraisal.* Archaeological Survey of Alberta Manuscript Series No.12, Edmonton, Alberta, 1988.

79 David Schwab, Stuart W. Conner and Ann M. Johnson, "Depression Era Archaeology in Montana," *Archaeology in Montan*a 37, no. 1 (1996): 1-42.

80 Walter T. Vanaman, "The Diggers at Pictograph Cave," *Archaeology in Montana* 32, no. 1 (1991): 67-74.

81 William Mulloy, *A Preliminary Historical Outline for the Northwestern Plains* (Laramie: University of Wyoming Publications 22, 1958).

82 Sara A. Scott, "The Ties that Bind: Contexts for Prehistoric Trade and Travel," (PhD dissertation, University of Montana, 2014), 130-171.

83 Joseph Anthony Baker, "Cultural Ecology and Paleoethnobotany at the Pictograph Cave Site," (Master's thesis, University of Montana, 1989).

84 Sara A. Scott, Carl M. Davis and J. M. Adovasio, "Radiocarbon analyses of four perishable artifacts from Ghost and Pictograph caves, Montana," *Plains Anthropologist* 59, no. 229 (2014): 70-95.

85 David Charles Schwab, "A Spatial Analysis of the Ghost Cave (24YL2) Archaeological Assemblage," (Master's thesis, University of Montana, 1981).

86 Lynn B. Fredlund, "Distribution and Characteristics of Avonlea South of the Yellowstone River, Montana," *Avonlea Yesterday and Today: Archaeology and Prehistory,* ed. Leslie B. Davis, (Saskatoon: Saskatchewan Archaeological Society, 1988): 171-182. Carl M. Davis, James D. Keyser and Cynthia D. Craven. "Coyote House: Prehistoric Butte Top Occupation in the Pine Parklands." *Archaeology in Montana* 35, no. 2 (1994): 5-57.

87 See William C. Meadows, "New Data on Kiowa Prohistoric Origins." *Ethnohistory* 63, no. 3 (2014): 541-570.

88 Julie E. Francis and Lawrence L. Loendorf, *Ancient Visions Petrogylphs and Pictographs of the Wind River and Bighorn Country, Wyoming and Montana* (Salt Lake City: University of Utah Press, 2002), 134, Table 1.

89 Ibid: 164-166.

90 Timothy P. McCleary, *Crow Indian Rock Art: Indigenous Perspectives and Interpretations.* (Abdingdon, Routledge, 2016).

91 Two influential gender works (of my generation) are Francis Dalhberg, editor, *Woman the Gatherer* (New Haven: Yale University Press, 1983); Joan M. Gero and Margaret W. Conkey, *Engendering Archaeology: Women and Prehistory* (Hoboken, New Jersey: Wiley-Blackwell, 1991).

92 Leslie B. Davis, "Investigations of the Schmitt Chert Mine (24BW559) and Natural Environs, Southwestern Montana (1972-1981). "Fact Sheet and Working Interpretations, Montana State University (1981). "Quarriers of Stone" *Montana Outdoors* July/August 1987, Montana Fish, Wildlife and Parks.

93 Montana's ancient toolstone quarries are described in academic literature; one brief exception is Mark Baumler's "Assault on Basalt: The Cashman Quarry Site," *Montana: The Magazine of Western History* 56, no. 2 (2008): 72-74.

94 M. Steven Schackley, "Introduction to X-Ray Florescence Analysis in Archaeology" In: *X-Ray Florescence Spectrometry (XRF) in Geoarchaeology,* ed. M. Steven Schackley (New York: Springer-Verlag, 2011), 7-44.

95 Richard E. Hughes, "The sources of Hopewell obsidian: Forty years after Griffin." In: *Recreating Hopewell,* ed. D. K. Charles and J. E. Buikstra, (Gainesville: University of Florida Press: Gainesville, 2006), 361-375.

96 Steven Rinella, *American Buffalo: In Search of a Lost Icon* (New York: Spiegel & Grau, 2008).

97 Leslie B. Davis, "Twentieth Century Commercial Mining of Northern Plains Bison Kills," In Bison Procurement and Utilization: A Symposium. *Plains Anthropologist Memoir* 14, no. 23-82 Pt. 2 (1978): 254-286.

98 Maynard Shumate, "The Taft Hill bison jump," *Archaeology in Montana* 8(4) (1967): 12-34.

99 John J. Fisher Jr. and Tom E. Roll, "First Peoples Buffalo Jump: Research Results and Interpretation." In *Pisskan: Interpreting First Peoples Bison Kills at Heritage Parks* (Salt Lake City: University of Utah Press, 2016), 87-110.

100 John W. Fisher Jr. and Tom E. Roll, "Ecological Relationships Between Bison and Native Americans During Late Prehistory and the Early Historic Period." In *International Symposium on Bison Ecology and Management in North America,* ed., Lynn R. Irby and James E. Knight, (Bozeman: Montana State University, 1998), 283-302.

101 A seminal treatment of Plains Indian bison hunting is by Jack W. Brink's *Imagining Head-Smashed-In: Aboriginal Buffalo Hunting on the Northern Plains* (Edmonton: Athabasca University Press, 2008).

102 See Shepard Kretch III, *The Ecological Indian Myth and History* (New York: W. W. Norton & Company, 1999) pp. 131-136.

103 Maria Nieves Zedeño, Jesse M. Ballenger and John R. Murray. "Landscape Engineering and Organizational Complexity among Late Prehistoric Bison Hunters of the Northwestern Plains," *Current Anthropology* 55, no. 11 (2013): 23-58.

104 Russell Lawrence Barsh and Chantelle Marlor, "Driving Bison and Blackfoot Science," *Human Ecology* 31, no. 4 (2003): 571-593.

105 Stephen A. Aaberg, "First Peoples Buffalo Jump, Ulm Pishkun (24CA1012) National Register of Historic Places Nomination." 2015. On file Montana State Historic Preservation Office, Helena.

106 Eleanor Verbicky-Todd, "Communal Bison Hunting Among the Plains Indians." *Archaeological Survey of Alberta, Edmonton Occasional Paper* No. 24. 1984.

107 William E. Farr, "Going to buffalo: Indian hunting migrations across the rocky mountains: part 1, making meat and taking robes," *Montana: The Magazine of Western History* (2002) 53(4): 2-21; Sara A. Scott, "Indian Forts and Religious Icons: The Buffalo Road (Qoq'allx "Iskit) Trail Before and After the Lewis and Clark Expedition," *International Journal of Historic Archaeology* 19 (2015): 384-415.

108 Andrew C. Isenberg, *The Destruction of the Bison* (Cambridge: Cambridge University Press, 2000).

109 James D. Keyser et al., *Fraternity of War: Plains Indian Rock Art at Bear Gulch and Atherton Canyon, Montana*. (Portland: Oregon Archaeological Society Press, 2012).

110 James D. Keyser and Michael A. Klassen, *Plains Indian Rock Art* (Seattle: University of Washington Press, 2001) 191-221.

111 Mavis A. Loscheider Greer, "Archaeological Analysis of Rock Art Sites in the Smith River Drainage of Central Montana," (PhD dissertation, University of Missouri-Columbia, 1995).

112 Sara A. Scott et al., "Direct AMS Dates from Four Late Prehistoric Period Rock Art Sites in West-Central Montana," *Plains Anthropologist* 50, no. 3 (2005): 57-71.

113 J. David Lewis-Williams, "Brainstorming Images: Neuropsychology and Rock Art Research. In *Handbook of Rock Art Research*, David S. Whitley, ed. (Walnut Creek: AltaMira Press, 2001), 332-357.

114 Sara A. Scott et al., "The Hellgate Pictographs: shamanism and ritual in west-central Montana." *Archaeology in Montana* 41, no. 1 (1995): 31-52.

115 Linea Sundstrom, "Archaic Hunting Practices Depicted in a Northwestern Plains Rock Art Style," *Plains Anthropologist* 34, no. 124 (1989): 149-169.

116 For example, James D. Keyser, *The Five Crows Ledger: Biographic Warrior Art of the Flathead Indians* (Salt Lake City: University of Utah Press, 2000).

117 Marvin W. Rowe, "Dating by AMS Radiocarbon Analysis" in *Handbook of Rock Art Research*, ed. David S. Whitley (Walnut Creek: Altamira Press, 2001), 139-166.

118 James D. Keyser et al., "Dating the Bear Gulch and Atherton Canyon Rock Art Sites, Central Montana," *Archaeology in Montana* 52, no. 1 (2011): 7-36.

119 James D. Keyser, *Indian Rock Art of the Columbia Plateau (Seattle: University of Washington Press, 1992).*

120 William T. Mulloy, *The Hagen Site: A Prehistoric Village on the Lower Yellowstone.* 1942, University of Montana Publication in Social Sciences No. 1, University of Montana, Missoula

121 Richard Snodgrass, "The Human Skeletal Remains" In: William T. Mulloy, *The Hagen Site: A Prehistoric Village on the Lower Yellowstone.* ibid: Appendix, 92-98.

122 Leslie B. Davis, ed., "Maize Gardening on the High Plains: The Hagen Earthlodge Village Revisited." Unpublished MS, 2014, copy in author's collection.

123 Stanley A. Ahler and Anthony W. Swenson, "KNRI and Upper Knife-Heart Region Pottery Analysis," In *The Phase I Archaeological Research Program for the Knife River Indian Village National Historic Site.* Thomas D. Theissen, ed., Occasional Studies in Anthropology No. 27, (Lincoln: National Park Service Midwest Archaeological Center, 1993), 1-171.

124 Jeff W. Kinney, "The Hagen Site, 24DW1: A Review of Historical Data and a Reassessment of Its Ceramic Assemblage and Position in Northern Plains Prehistory," (Master's thesis, University of Montana-Missoula, 1996).

125 Linda Scott Cummings, Kathryn Puseman, and Laura Ruggeiro, "Pollen, Phytoliths, and Macrofossil Remains," in "Maize Gardening on the High Plains: The Hagen Earthlodge Village Revisited," Leslie B. Davis, ed., unpublished 2014 MS, copy in author's collection.

126 Brian M. Fagan, *Ancient North America: The Archaeology of a Continent.* (London: Thames and Hudson Ltd., 1991), 369-384; Charles

C. Mann, *1491 New Revelations of the Americas Before Columbus*, (New York: Alfred A. Knopf, 2005), 243-279.

127 Tim R. Pauketat, *Cahokia: Ancient America's Great City of the Mississippi*. (New York: Viking-Penguin Books, 2010).

128 Stanley A. Ahler and Marvin Kay, *Plains Village Archaeology: Bison Hunting Farmers in the Central and Northern Plains* (Salt Lake City: University of Utah Press, 2007). Mark D. Mitchell, *Crafting History on the Northern Plains: A Political Economy of the Heart River Region, 1400-1750* (Tucson: University of Arizona Press, 2013).

129 Elizabeth A. Fenn, *Encounters at the Heart of the World: A History of the Mandan People* (New York: Hill and Wang, 2014).

130 Timothy P. McCleary, *Crow Indian Rock Art: Indigenous Perspectives and Interpretations*. (New York: Routledge, 2016).

131 Julie E. Francis and Lawrence L. Loendorf, *Ancient Visions Petrogylphs and Pictographs of the Wind River and Bighorn Country, Wyoming and Montana* (Salt Lake City: University of Utah Press, 2002), 171-172.

132 Ann M. Johnson, "Problem of Crow Pottery," *Archaeology in Montana* 20 (3) (1979): 17-29. Judson Byrd Finley and Maureen P. Boyle, "The frequency and typology of ceramic sites in western Wyoming," *Plains Anthropologist* 59, no. 229 (2014): 38-57.

133 David B. Madsen and David Rhode, ed., *Across the West Human Population Movement and the Expansion of the Numa* (Salt Lake City: University of Utah Press, 1994).

134 Carl M. Davis, "Wickiup Cave," *Plains Anthropologist* 20, no. 70 (1975): 297-305.

135 Carl M. Davis, "Not in Warfare Alone: Conical timber lodges in the Central Rocky Mountains and Northwestern Plains," *Plains Anthropologist* 60, no. 233 (2015): 40-71.

136 James D. Keyser, "The LaMarche Game Trap: An Early Historic Game Trap in Southwestern Montana," *Plains Anthropologist* 19, no. 65 (1974): 173-179.

137 Julian H. Steward, *Culture Element Distributions: XXIII Anthropological Records* 8:3 (Berkeley: University of California Press, 1943) pp. 267.

138 George C. Frison, *Survival by Hunting: Prehistoric Human Predators and Animal Prey* (Berkeley: University of California Press, 2004), 161.

139 The most comprehensive account of Sheep Eaters is by Lawrence L. Loendorf and Nancy Medaris Stone, *Mountain Spirit The Sheep Eater Indians of Yellowstone* (Salt Lake City: University of Utah Press, 2006).

140 Osborne Russell, *Journal of a Trapper (1834-1843)*. ed., Aubrey L. Haines, (Lincoln: University of Nebraska Press, 1955), 26.

141 Alexander Ross, *The Fur Hunters of the Far West*, ed., Kenneth Spaulding, (Norman: University of Oklahoma Press, 1956), 6.

142 Carl M. Davis, Leslie B. Davis and Ann M. Johnson, "The Late Pre-contact Intermountain Tradition and the Historic Sheep Eater Shoshone", unpublished 2009 MS, in author's collection.

143 Lawrence L. Loendorf and Nancy Medaris Stone, *Mountain Spirit The Sheep Eater Indians of Yellowstone*. Ibid: 112-128.

144 Gary E. Moulton, ed., *The Definitive Journals of the Lewis & Clark Expedition, Through the Rockies to the Cascades*, vol. 5, (Lincoln: University of Nebraska Press, 1987), 7-132.

145 David L. Crowder, *Tendoy Chief of the Lembis*. (Caldwell, Idaho: The Caxton Printers, Ltd., 1969), 45.

146 Brigham D. Madsen, *The Lemhi: Sacajawea's People* (Caldwell, Idaho: The Caxton Printers, Ltd., 1979), 122-161. John W. Mann, *The Lemhi Shoshone and the Salmon River Country*. (Lincoln: University of Nebraska Press, 2004).

147 Carl M. Davis and Sara A. Scott, "The Pass Creek Wickiups: Northern Shoshone Hunting Lodges in Southwest Montana," *Plains Anthropologist* 32, no. 115 (1987): 87-92.

148 Anthony McGinnis, *Counting coup and cutting horses* (Lincoln: University of Nebraska Press, 1990).

149 Frank Raymond Secoy, *Changing Military Patterns of the Great Plains Indians* (Lincoln: University of Nebraska Press, 1992).

150 Theodore Binnema, *A Common & Contested Ground: A Human and Environmental History of the Northwestern Plains* (Norman: University of Oklahoma Press, 2001).

151 Jesse W. Vaughn, *With Crook at Rosebud* (Mechanicsburg: Stackpole Books, 1956).

152 Neil C. Mangum, *Battle of the Rosebud: Prelude to the Little Bighorn* (El Segundo, California: Upton and Sons, 1987).

153 *A Historic Preservation Plan for the Rosebud Battlefield, located in Bighorn County, Montana*. Montana Preservation Alliance, Helena, 2007. Montana Department of Fish, Wildlife & Parks, Helena.

154 Christopher Merritt, *Rosebud Battlefield State Park: Summary Report of 2011 Investigations*. University of Montana-Missoula, 2011. Montana Department of Fish, Wildlife & Parks, Helena. Thomas Andrew Milter, "History and Archaeology of the Rosebud Battlefield, June 17, 1876" (Master's thesis, University of Montana-Missoula, 2013). Douglas D. Scott, *Analysis of Ammunition Components from the Rosebud Battlefield and Battle Butte Sites*. Conner Consulting, Grand Junction Colorado, 2013. Montana Department of Fish, Wildlife & Parks, Helena.

155 Buffalo Calf Road Woman's hard and courageous life is fictionalized in Rosemary Agonito and Joseph Agonito, *Buffalo Calf Road Woman: The Story of a Warrior at the Little Bighorn* (Helena, Montana: Twodot, 2006).

156 Thomas B. Marquis, *Wooden Leg: A Warrior Who Fought Custer* (Lincoln: Bison Books, University of Nebraska Press, 2003).

157 D. S. Otis, *The Dawes Act and the Allotment of Indian Lands* (Norman: University of Oklahoma Press, 1973).

158 Joan L. Brownell, *Absaroka Agency History: Second Crow Agency 1875-1884*. 2014. On file Montana Department of Transportation, Helena.

159 Stephen A. Aaberg et al., *Absaroka Agency (24ST0089) Evaluation Investigations, Stillwater County, Montana.* Aaberg Cultural Resource Consulting Service, 2008. On file Montana Department of Transportation, Helena.

160 Steve Platt and Alan Woodmansey. "Unearthing Crow Tribal History" *Public Roads* July/August 2012: 16-19.

161 Timothy McCleary, Thomas Carter, and Edward Chappell, *Tipis and Square Houses: The Chief Plenty Coups Homestead and the Building of the Crow Reservation in central Montana, 1884-1910*. (Helena, Montana: Montana Department of Fish, Wildlife and Parks, 2005).

162 Frank B. Linderman, *Plenty-coups: Chief of the Crows* (Lincoln: University of Nebraska Press, 1930).

163 Frederick E. Hoxie, *Parading Through History: The Making of the Crow Nation in America, 1805-1935* (New York: Cambridge University Press, 1995).

164 George Bird Grinnell, *The Cheyenne Indians: Their History and Ways of Life*, 2 volumes (New Haven: Yale University Press, 1924). See also Montana State Parks, *Indian Tribes of Montana Yesterday and Today* (Helena: Montana State Parks, 2012).

165 Joseph R. McGeshick, *The History of the Assiniboine and Sioux Tribes of the Fort Peck Indian Reservation, Montana, 1800-2000* (Helena: Montana Historical Society Press, 2008).

166 John C. Ewers, *The Blackfeet: Raiders on the Northwest Plains* (Norman: University of Oklahoma Press, 1983).

167 Nicholas C. P. Voorman, "*This Whole Country was… 'One Robe'": The Little Shell Tribe's America* (Helena, Mont.: Drumlummon Institute and Little Shell Tribe of Chippewa Indians of Montana, 2013).

168 John Fahey, *The Flathead Indians* (Norman: University of Oklahoma Press, 1974).

169 Harry Holbert Turney-High, *Ethnography of the Kootenai* 1948, American Anthropological Association, Menasha. Sally Thompson et al., *People Before the Park: The Kootenai and Blackfeet Before Glacier National Park* (Helena: Montana Historical Society Press, 2015).

170 One comprehensive attempt to link prehistory and history is by Karl H. Schlesier, editor, *Plains Indians, A.D. 500-1500, The Archaeological Past of Historic Groups* (Norman: University of Oklahoma Press, 1994).

171 Patricia L. Parker and Thomas F. King, "Guidelines for Evaluating and Documenting Traditional Cultural Properties," *National Register Bulletin 38,* Department of the Interior, National Park Service, Washington D.C. Revised 1998.

172 Carl M. Davis and Edrie Vinson, "The Kootenai Falls Portage Trail" *Archaeology in Montana* 21, no. 3 (1980): 129-148.

173 *The Native American Rights Fund Legal Review,* "Kootenai Religious site saved", Spring 1987, 1-2.

174 Rob Chaney, "US cancels drilling leases in the sacred Badger-Two Medicine area." *The Missoulian*, November 16, 2017; Karl Puckett, "Two more leases in Badger-Two Medicine cancelled," *The Great Falls Tribune*, January 12, 2017.

175 Two highly popular volunteer and educational programs in Montana are the U.S. Forest Service's *Passport in Time* and Montana State University-Bureau of Land Management's *Project Archaeology.*

176 Tom E. Roll, ed. "Kootenai Canyon Archaeology: The 1979 LAURD Project Final Mitigation Report," (Bozeman: Montana State University, 1982); Alston V. Thoms and Greg C. Burtchard, ed., *Prehistoric Land Use in the Northern Rocky Mountains: A Perspective from the Middle Kootenai River*. (Pullman: Washington State University Center for Northwest Archaeology, 1987).

177 For example, "Ancient Teachings: A Curriculum for Montana Archaeology and Prehistory," www.mhs.mtgov/Shpo/Archaeology/Ancient

178 Carl M. Davis, "Effects of Climate Change on Cultural Resources in the Northern Rockies." In *Climate Change and Northern Rocky Mountain Ecosystems.* Advances in Global Climate Research 63, pp. 209-219, eds. Jessica E. Halofsky and David L. Peterson, 2017, Springer International Publishing, Cham, Switzerland.

GLOSSARY

ALTITHERMAL – A warm period dating between 9,000 and 5,000 years ago, also called the Holocene Climatic Optimum.

AMERICAN INDIAN – A general term for any of the Indigenous peoples of Central, North, and South America.

ANTHROPOCENE – According to some scientists, the current geological epoch in which humankind has dominant influence on climate and the environment through human-caused (anthropogenic) global warming.

ANTHROPOLOGY – The scientific study of human societies and cultures past and present, and how they developed.

ANNUITY – Monetary payments and goods given to Indian Tribes under the terms and conditions of treaties with the United States Government.

ARCHAEOLOGY – The scientific study of past human life through the recovery of artifacts, ruins, and other physical evidence.

ARCHAIC – In this book, the ancestors and relatives of anatomically modern beings or *Homo sapiens*.

ARROWHEAD – A small stone, bone, or metal point affixed to a feathered arrow shaft and propelled with a bow. Used from 1,500 years ago into the historic period.

ARTIFACT – Any object made by a human being which is of archaeological or historical interest.

ASSIMILATION – The effort by the United States government in the 19th and early 20th centuries to transform American Indian culture into European-American culture.

ATLATL – A slender, hand-held rod or board, made of wood or bone, used to propel a light spear with an attached stone or bone dart. Also called a spear-thrower.

BAND – The simplest form of human society consisting of an extended family or several extended families. In North America, Indian bands formed larger tribes.

BERINGIA – A landmass connecting North America (Alaska) with Asia (Siberia) during Pleistocene glacial periods when massive continental glaciers caused sea levels to drop. Also called the Bering Strait land bridge, it currently lies under the Bering Sea.

BIFACE – A prehistoric stone implement flaked on both surfaces.

BUFFALO JUMP – A cliff or precipice over which Indians stampeded bison en masse to obtain meat, organs, gut, hides, bone, sinew, and other products.

CACHE PIT – A sealed underground pit used by Indian peoples to store food and supplies, and later dried corn, beans and squash among Plains Indian farming cultures.

CHIEFDOM – A form of political organization where political power and leadership is vested in kinship-related elites in contrast to more egalitarian tribes and bands.

CHRONOLOGY – The ordering of past material culture into a meaningful time sequence.

CLIMATE – Weather patterns prevailing in a region or area over a long period of time (decades, centuries, millennia). The difference between climate and weather is time.

CLOVIS – The first widespread Paleoindian "culture" in the Americas, dated to about 13,500 to 12,800 years ago and best known by its distinctive, basally thinned (partly fluted) projectile point.

CONCHOIDAL FRACTURE – A physical property of fine-grained rock allowing it to fracture with smooth, curved surfaces when struck with a blow.

CONICAL TIMBER LODGE - A type of Indian housing made of vertical poles, sticks, brush, hides, and mats. The term is used interchangeably with wickiup in the Intermountain West.

CORDILLERAN ICE SHEET – The massive continental ice sheet covering western Canada, parts of Alaska, northern Washington, and the Idaho Panhandle during Pleistocene glacial periods.

COPROLITES – Ancient human or animal feces.

COUP – Winning prestige in combat by slapping or hitting the enemy with a hand, coup stick, or weapon. Part of the Plains Indian war honors system.

CULTURAL PATRIMONY – Artifacts and objects having continuing cultural, traditional, or historical importance to the heritage of an ethnic group.

CULTURAL RESOURCE – A general term for archaeological and historic sites.

CULTURAL RESOURCE MANAGEMENT – The practice or vocation of managing cultural resources, as required by state and federal antiquities laws. Abbreviated as CRM.

DART POINT – Stone implements of various shapes affixed to a light, feathered shaft that was propelled from an atlatl (throwing board) and used during most of the Holocene.

DAWES ACT OF 1887 – A Congressional act that divided American Indian land into individual allotments for tribal members to encourage assimilation and subsistence farming. Surplus (unallocated) lands were opened to non-Indian settlement.

DIGGING STICK – An implement comprised of a fire-hardened, pointed stick with an attached horn handle used to dig edible dig roots and tubers like bitterroot and camas.

DEBITAGE – Stone "waste flakes" and other lithic debris resulting from flintknapping and tool production. The term is borrowed from European Upper Paleolithic archaeology.

DNA – Deoxyribonucleic acid, self-replicating molecules within chromosomes that carry all the necessary genetic information to create and sustain organic life.

DRIVE LANE – Converging lines of piled rocks, embedded with poles and hide flagging, built by hunters to help spook and funnel bison toward a bison jump.

EARTH LODGE – Substantially-sized square or circular shaped, semi-subterranean structures composed of timber framing, covered partly or completely with earth, built by Plains Indians.

ETHNIC GROUP (ETHNICITY) – A group of people who identify with each other based on similarities in ancestry, language, or cultural traditions.

ETHNOGRAPHY – The scientific description and study of the customs and lifeways of individual human cultures.

FEATURE – In archaeology, a term used to denote various kinds of usually non-portable human activity such as a house pit, fire hearth, or cache pit.

FLINTKNAPPING – Shaping of flint, chert, obsidian, and other fine-grained stone into serviceable tools. Conchoidal fracture is the basis of flintknapping.

FLOTATION – A laboratory method whereby excavated soil is "washed" in a tub of water allowing lighter plant remains to float to the top, enabling their recovery.

FORAGERS – Societies who subsist on wild plant and animal food collected by themselves across the landscape; synonymous with hunter-gatherers in this book.

FORESHAFT – A smaller, detachable secondary rod holding the projectile point that was inserted into a main spear or dart shaft.

GENOME – The complete set of genetic material, including DNA and all of its genes, in an organism.

GLACIAL LAKE MISSOULA – A 3,000 square mile glacial lake that periodically covered western Montana during the last Ice Age, between 15,000 and 13,000 years ago.

GRID – A three-dimensional coordinate system that allows archaeologists to accurately plot artifacts and cultural features during excavations.

GROUND PENETRATING RADAR – A remote sensing tool that images the subsurface of the ground to detect archaeological features using pulses of electromagnetic radio waves.

HOLOCENE – The present geological epoch and interglacial period that began 11,700 years ago at the end of the last period of Pleistocene (Wisconsin) glaciation.

HOMINID – The primate family that includes humans and their fossil ancestors, including the Great Apes.

HOMININ – The taxonomic group that consists exclusively of modern humans, extinct human species, and our immediate ancestors, such as the archaic *Neanderthals*.

HOMO SAPIENS – Scientific nomenclature for the only existing, anatomically modern humans—all of us!

HUNTER-GATHERERS – Societies that obtain food exclusively by hunting, fishing, and foraging for wild plants rather than by agriculture (or horticulture) or raising domestic livestock.

ICE FREE CORRIDOR – A 900-mile long passageway in western Canada between the Cordilleran and Laurentide continental ice sheets. This is one of several possible Paleoindian routes into the Americas.

INDIAN RESERVATION – An area of land legally designated by treaty or other agreements with the U.S. Government and exclusively set aside for an Indian tribe or tribes.

INSOLATION – The amount of solar radiation reaching the earth. Variation in insolation is one cause of climate change, including the Ice Ages.

LAURENTIDE ICE SHEET – The massive continental ice sheet covering eastern Canada and a large part of the northern United States during Pleistocene glacial periods.

LITHIC REDUCTION – An archaeological term for flintknapping.

LITTLE ICE AGE – A cool climatic period dating between 1300 and 1850 A.D.

MAGNETOMETER – A remote sensing tool that identifies and measures the magnetic strength of metal items buried in the ground.

MANO – A hand-held stone cobble used to process or grind food on a stone metate or grinding slab.

MEDIEVAL CLIMATIC ANOMALY – A warm climatic period dating between 950 and 1300 A.D.

MEGAFAUNA – A collective term for large animals that lived during the Pleistocene epoch and became extinct by or during the Holocene such as wooly mammoths.

METATE - A large, flat stone on which organic materials such as dried seeds are ground with a *mano*.

METRIC SYSTEM – The international decimal system used for measurements by archaeologists worldwide, including in the United States.

MILANKOVITCH CYCLES – The regular changes in the Earth's orbit around the Sun, including its shape, axial tilt, and wobble, which affect solar insolation and result in glacial and interglacial periods.

MISSISSIPPIAN CULTURE – A major, sophisticated cultural pattern spread over the Southeast and mid-Continent involving agriculture, mound building, urban centers, and chiefdoms, dating from 800 to 1600 A.D.

MITOCHONDRIAL DNA – DNA in cell structures that is maternally inherited. Mutations in mtDNA enable geneticists to trace ancient lineages through the female line.

MONTANA STATE ANTIQUITIES ACT OF 1995 – The State law providing for the management and protection of archaeological and historical resources on state-owned lands.

NATIONAL HISTORIC LANDMARK – Nationally significant historic places designated by the Secretary of Interior (National Park Service) because they possess exceptional value or quality in illustrating or interpreting the heritage of the United States.

NATIONAL HISTORIC PRESERVATION ACT OF 1966 – The Federal law intended to preserve historical and archaeological sites. It is the cornerstone of historic preservation in the United States. It is commonly abbreviated as the NHPA.

NATIONAL REGISTER OF HISTORIC PLACES – The federal government's official list of districts, sites, buildings, structures, and objects deemed worthy of preservation. The National Park Service administers the National Register program.

NEANDERTHAL – An extinct hominin species that lived in Ice Age Eurasia between 200,000 and 35,000 years ago.

PALEOINDIAN – A collective term for American Indians living during the Late Pleistocene and early Holocene.

PALYNOLOGY – The study of plant pollen grains in archaeological sites.

PERISHABLES – In archaeology, artifacts made of organic materials that ordinarily decay but which are fortuitously preserved in whole or as fragments.

PETROGLYPH – Any carving made on a rock surface by ancient peoples.

PHYTOLITH – A fossilized particle of plant tissue made of silica that persists after the decay of the plant.

PICTOGRAPH – Any painting on a rock surface made by ancient peoples.

PITHOUSE – The archaeological remains of dwellings dug partly into the ground and covered by a roof of timbers, brush, hides, or earth.

PLEISTOCENE – The geological epoch that lasted from about 2.5 million to 11,700 years ago and included periodic episodes of continental-wide glaciation and retreat.

PREFORM – Unfinished tools, often triangular in shape, that are ready to be made into a knife blade or projectile point.

PREHISTORY – The time before written records.

PROJECTILE POINT – A catchall term for the fashioned stone tips mounted on the ends of spear, dart, and arrow shafts.

RADIOCARBON DATING – A widely used method of determining the age of organic materials by measuring the radioactive decay of the Carbon-14 isotope.

REPATRIATION – The legal return of human remains and objects to their geographic region and culture of origin, usually to comply with the Native American Graves Protection and Repatriation Act of 1990.

REPOSITORY – A facility in which artifacts and records are stored and managed, usually a museum, university, agency or tribal curation center.

ROCKSHELTER – Any alcove or overhang in cliffs and escarpments used by ancient peoples. Although a rockshelter is usually wider than it is deep, the term is often used interchangeably with caves.

SHAMAN – A person who acts as a medium between the physical and spiritual worlds and practices healing and divination, often while in trances and altered states of consciousness.

SHIELD-BEARING WARRIOR – A widespread rock art motif in the American West showing warriors with large painted shields, weapons, face paint, headdresses and other regalia.

SITE – In archaeology, a specific place that contains human evidence. Archaeological sites are given unique identifiers as part of the Smithsonian Institution's national trinomial numbering system.

SOVEREIGNTY – Under the U.S. constitution and federal treaties, the inherent authority of Indian tribes to govern themselves. The concept is based on the fact that Indian nations pre-existed the United States.

STRATIGRAPHY – The layering of natural sediments and cultural evidence in an archaeological site. The bottom layer is the oldest and the top layer is the youngest.

THRUSTING SPEAR – A long wood lance mounted with a stone, bone, or metal point used as a throwing (javelin) or stabbing weapon.

TIPI RING – A circular pattern of stone cobbles where Native peoples once resided in pole and hide tipis. Cobbles (and wood stakes) helped to hold down the base of hide covers.

TOOLSTONE – Any fine-grained stone (raw material) used by Native peoples to make tools.

TRADITIONAL CULTURAL PROPERTY – As part of the National Register of Historic Places program, cultural resources that are both rooted in a community's history and important for maintaining its continuing cultural identity and beliefs, customs, and practices.

TRAVOIS – A pole sled composed of two joined poles that is dragged behind a dog or horse and widely used by Plains Indians.

TRIBE – A social organization based on small groups or bands that has a temporary or permanent political organization defined by common ancestry, language, and culture.

VISION QUEST – A rite of passage among many North American Indian societies where young men and women seek guardian spirits and their assistance through seclusion, fasting, and prayers. Rock art and circular stone formations (fasting beds) often mark the spot where vision quests occurred.

WOODLAND – the period before the widespread Mississippian culture in the eastern United States, characterized by pottery and horticulture villages, beginning about 3,000 years ago.

WORKS PROGRESS ADMINISTRATION – A federal agency created as part of the New Deal during the Great Depression to employ people in public works projects. It became the Works Project Administration in 1939.

YOUNGER DRYAS – A temporary return to a colder climate and glacial conditions from 12,900 to 11,700 years ago.

BIBLIOGRAPHY

Aaberg, Stephen A. "Alder Complex Macrofossils," In "Paleoarchaic Foragers of the Middle Rockies: The Barton Gulch Occupations," ed. Leslie B. Davis, unpublished MS 2013, copy in author's collection.

"First Peoples Buffalo Jump, Ulm Pishkun (24CA1012) National Register of Historic Places Nomination." Nomination prepared for Montana Department of Fish, Wildlife and Parks, Helena. 2015. Report on file, Montana State Historic Preservation Office, Helena.

Aaberg, Stephen A., Chris Crofutt, Jayme Green, William Eckerle, Sasha Taddie, and Seven DeVore. "Absaroka Agency (24ST0089) Evaluation Investigations, Stillwater County, Montana." Aaberg Cultural Resource Consulting Service. 2008. Report on file, Montana Department of Transportation, Helena.

Adovasio, J. M., and Jake Page. *The First Americans: In Pursuit of Archaeology's Greatest Mystery*. New York: Random House Inc., 2002.

Adovasio, J. M. and David Peddler. *Strangers in a New Land: What Archaeology Reveals about the First Americans.* Buffalo, New York: Firefly Books, 2016.

Agonito, Rosemary and Joseph Agonito. *Buffalo Calf Road Woman: The Story of a Warrior of the Little Bighorn.* Helena, Montana: Twodot, 2006.

Ahler, Stanley A. and Marvin Kay. *Plains Village Archaeology: Bison-hunting Farmers in the Central and Northern Plains.* Salt Lake City, Utah: University of Utah Press, 2007.

Ahler, Stanley A., and Anthony W. Swenson, "KNRI and Upper Knife-Heart Region Pottery Analysis." In "The Phase I Archaeological Research Program for the Knife River Indian Village National Historic Site." Thomas D. Theissen, ed., *Occasional Studies in Anthropology* No. 27, 1-171, National Park Service Midwest Archaeological Center, Lincoln, Nebraska, 1993.

Alt, David D. *Glacial Lake Missoula and Its Humongous Floods.* Missoula, Mont.: Mountain Press Publishing Company, 2001.

Armstrong, Stephen. "Alder Complex Kitchens: Experimental Replication of Paleoindian Cooking Facilities." *Archaeology in Montana* 34, no. 2 (1993): 1-66.

Baker, Joseph Anthony. "Cultural Ecology and Paleoethnobotany at the Pictograph Cave Site." Master's thesis, University of Montana-Missoula, 1989.

Barsh, Russell Lawrence and Chantelle Marlor. "Driving Bison and Blackfoot Science." *Human Ecology* 31 (2003): 571-593.

Baumler, Mark. "Assault on Basalt: The Cashman Quarry Site." *Montana: The Magazine of Western History,* Vol. 56 (2008): 74-76.

Bird, Michael I., Damien O'Grady and Sean Ulm, "Humans, water and the colonization of Australia." *Proceedings of the National Academy of Sciences* 113, no. 41 (2016): 11477-11482.

Binnema, Theodore. *Common & Contested Ground: A Human and Environmental History of the Northwestern Plains.* Norman: University of Oklahoma Press, 2001.

Bouldurian, Anthony T. and John L. Cotter. *Clovis Revisited: New Perspectives on Paleoindian Adaptations from Blackwater Draw, New Mexico.* Philadelphia: University of Pennsylvania Museum of Archaeology and Anthropology, 1999.

Brink, Jack W. *Imagining Head-Smashed-In: Aboriginal Buffalo Hunting on the Northern Plains.* Edmonton, Alberta: Athabasca University Press, 2008.

Brownell, Joan L. "Absaroka Agency History: Second Crow Indian Agency 1875-1884." 2014. On file Montana Department of Transportation, Helena.

Brumley, John. "Medicine Wheels on the Northern Plains: A Summary and Appraisal." *Archaeological Survey of Alberta Manuscript Series* No. 12, Edmonton, Alberta, 1988.

Butler, B. Robert. "The Quest for the Historic Fremont and A Guide to the Prehistoric Pottery of Southern Idaho." *Occasional Papers of the Idaho Museum of Natural History, Number* 33, Pocatello, Idaho, 1983, page 18, Figure 9.

Callahan, Errett. *The Basics of Biface Knapping in the Eastern Fluted Point Tradition: A Manual for Flintknappers and Lithic Analysts.* 3rd Edition. Lynchburg: Piltdown Productions, 1996.

Callaway, Ewen. "Plant and animal DNA suggests first Americans took the coast route." *Nature* 536, no. 138 (11 August 2016) doi: 10.1038/536138a.

Canby, Thomas Y. "The Search for the First Americans." *National Geographic Magazine*: 156 (1979): 330-363.

Capace, Nancy. *Encyclopedia of Montana*. Santa Barbara, California: Someret Publishers, Inc., 2000.

Chaney, Rob. "US cancels drilling leases in the sacred Badger-Two Medicine area." *The Missoulian*, November 16, 2017.

Clark, Jorie, Jerry X. Mitrovica and Jay Alder. "Coastal Paleogeography of the California-Oregon-Washington and Bering Sea continental shelves during the latest Pleistocene and Holocene: implications for the archaeological record." *Journal of Archaeological Science* 52 (2014): 12-23.

COHMAP Members. "Climate Change of the Last 18,000 Years: Observations and Model Simulations." *Science* 241 (1988): 1043-1052.

Collins, Michael B. and Bruce A. Bradley, "Evidence for Pre-Clovis Occupation of the Gault Site (41BL323), Central Texas." *Current Research in the Pleistocene* 25 (2008): 70-72.

Conner, Stuart, "1982 Archaeology of the Crow Indian Vision Quest," *Archaeology in Montana* 23, no. 3 (1982): 85-128.

Crabtree, Don. *An introduction to flintknapping*. Occasional Papers of the Idaho State University Museum No. 28. Pocatello, Idaho, 1971.

Crowder, David L., *Tendoy Chief of the Lemhis*. Caldwell, Idaho: Caxton Printers, Ltd., 1969.

Cummings, Linda Scott, Kathryn Puseman, and Laura Ruggiero. "Pollen, Phytoliths, and Macrofossil Remains." In "Paleoarchaic Foragers of the Middle Rockies: The Barton Gulch Occupations." Leslie B. Davis, ed., unpublished 2013 MS, copy in author's collection.

Dalhberg, Frances, Ed. *Woman the Gatherer*. Revised edition, New Haven: Yale University Press, 1983.

Davis, Carl M. "Wickiup Cave." *Plains Anthropologist* 20, no. 70 (1975): 297-305.

"Not in warfare alone: Conical timber lodges in the Central Rocky Mountains and Northwestern Plains." *Plains Anthropologist* 60, no. 223 (2015): 40-71.

"Effects of Climate Change on Cultural Resources in the Northern Rockies." In *Climate Change and Rocky Mountain Ecosystems. Advances in Global Climate Change Research* 63, pp. 209-219, Jessica E. Halofsky and David L. Peterson, eds. Springer International Publishing, Cham, Switzerland, 2017.

Davis, Carl M. and Sara A. Scott. "The Pass Creek Wickiups: Northern Shoshone Hunting Lodges in Southwest Montana." *Plains Anthropologist* 32, no. 115 (1987): 87-92.

Davis, Carl M., James D. Keyser and Cynthia D. Craven. "Coyote House: Prehistoric Butte Top Occupation in the Pine Parklands." *Archaeology in Montana* 35, no. 2 (1994): 5-57.

Davis, Carl M., Leslie B. Davis and Ann M. Johnson. "The Late Precontact Intermountain Tradition and the Historic Sheep Eater Shoshone," unpublished 2009 MS, copy in author's collection.

Davis, Carl M. and Edrie Vinson, "The Kootenai Falls Portage Trail" *Archaeology in Montana* 21, no. 3 (1980): 129-148.

Davis, Leslie B. "Twentieth Century Commercial Mining of Northern Plains Bison Kills." In Bison Procurement and Utilization: A Symposium. *Plains Anthropologist Memoir* 14 Pt. 2 (1978): 254-286.

"Quarriers of Stone." *Montana Outdoors* (July/August 1987) Montana Fish, Wildlife and Parks, Helena.

Davis, Leslie B., ed. "From Microcosm to Macrocosm: Advances in Tipi Ring Investigation and Interpretation." *Plains Anthropologist* Memoir 19 (1983).

Davis, Leslie B., ed. "The Three Waters Quarries and Schmitt Chert Mine Investigations (1972-1989) A Work in Progress." Unpublished 2006 MS, copy in author's collection.

Davis, Leslie B., ed. "Paleoarchaic Foragers of the Middle Rockies: The Barton Gulch Occupations." Unpublished 2013 MS, copy in author's collection.

Davis, Leslie B., ed. "Maize Gardening on the High Plains: The Hagan Earthlodge Village Revisited." Unpublished 2014 MS, copy in author's collection.

Davis, Leslie B. and Michael Wilson, eds. "Bison Procurement and Utilization: A Symposium." *Plains Anthropologist* Memoir No. 3, Pt. 2 (1978).

Davis, Leslie B., Stephen A. Aaberg, William P. Eckerle, John W. Fisher, Jr., and Sally T. Greiser. "Montane Paleoindian Occupation of the Ruby Valley, Southwestern Montana." *Current Research in the Pleistocene* 6 (1989): 7-9.

Densmore, Frances. *How Indians Use Wild Plants for Food, Medicine & Crafts*. New York: Dover Publications, Inc., 1974.

Dillehay, Thomas D., C. Ramirez, M. Pino, M.B. Collins, J. Rossen, and J.D. Pino-Navarro, "Monte Verde: Seaweed, Food, Medicine, and the Peopling of South America." *Science* 320 (2008): 784-786.

Dumanoski, Dianne. *The End of the Long Summer: Why We Must Remake Our Civilization to Survive on a Volatile Earth*. New York: Crown Publishers, 2009.

Echo-Hawk, Roger C. "Ancient History in the New World: Integrating Oral Traditions and the Archaeological Record in Deep Time." *American Antiquity* 65, no. 1 (2000): 267-290.

Erlandson, Jon M., and Todd J. Braje. "From Asia to the Americans by boat? Paleogeography, paleoecology, and stemmed points of the northwest Pacific." *Quaternary International* 239, no. 1-2 (2011): 28-37.

Ewers, John C., *The Blackfeet: Raiders on the Northwest Plains*. 1958. Reprint, Norman: University of Oklahoma Press, 1983.

Fagan, Brian, ed. *The Little Ice Age: How Climate Made History 1300 – 1850*. New York: Basic Books, 2000.

Fagan, Brian M. *Ancient North America: The Archaeology of a Continent*. London: Thames and Hudson Ltd., 1991.

Fagan, Brian *The Complete Ice Age: How Climate Change Shaped the World*. London: Thames & Hudson Ltd., 2009.

The Great Warming: Climate Change and the Rise and Fall of Civilizations. New York: Bloomsbury Press, 2009.

Cro-Magnon: How the Ice Age Gave Birth to the First Modern Humans. New York: Bloomsbury Press, 2010.

Fahey, John. *The Flathead Indians*. Norman: University of Oklahoma Press, 1974.

Farr, William E. Going to buffalo: Indian hunting migrations across the rocky mountains: part 1, making meat and taking robes. *Montana: The Magazine of Western History* 53 (2003): 2-21.

Fenn, Elizabeth A. *Encounters at the Heart of the World: A History of the Mandan People*. New York: Hill and Wang, 2014.

Finley, Judson Byrd and Maureen P. Boyle. "The frequency and typology of ceramic sites in western Wyoming." *Plains Anthropologist* 59, no. 222 (2014): 38-55.

Fisher, John W. Jr. and Tom E. Roll. "Ecological Relationships Between Bison and Native Americans During Late Prehistory and the Early Historic Period." In *International Symposium on Bison Ecology and Management in North America*, pp. 283-302, Lynn R. Irby and James E. Knight, eds., Bozeman: Montana State University, 1998.

First Peoples Buffalo Jump: Research Results and Interpretation." In *Pisskan: Interpreting First Peoples Bison Kills at Heritage Parks*, p. 87-110. Salt Lake City: University of Utah Press, 2016.

Flenniken, J. Jeffrey. "The Lithic Technology of the East Lake Site, Newberry Crater, Oregon." Lithic Analysts. 1987. Deschutes National Forest, Bend, Oregon. Copy in author's collection.

Francis, Julie E., and Lawrence L. Loendorf. *Ancient Visions Petrogylphs and Pictographs of the Wind River and Bighorn Country, Wyoming and Montana*. Salt Lake City: University of Utah Press, 2002.

Fenneman, Nevin M. *Physiography of Western United States.* (New York: McGraw-Hill Book Company, 1931.

Fredlund, Glen G. "Alder Complex Pollen and Phytoliths". In "Paleoarchaic Foragers of the Middle Rockies: The Barton Gulch Occupations," Leslie B. Davis, ed., unpublished 2013 MS, copy in author's collection.

Fredlund, Lynn. "Distribution and Characteristics of Avonlea South of the Yellowstone River in Montana." In *Avonlea Yesterday and Today: Archaeology and Prehistory*, Saskatchewan Archaeological Society, Saskatoon. Leslie B. Davis, ed. (1988): 172-182.

Frison, George C. *Prehistoric Hunters of the High Plains*. 2nd Edition. San Diego: Academic Press, 1991.

The Mill Iron Site. Albuquerque: University of New Mexico Press, 1996.

Survival by Hunting: Prehistoric Human Predators and Animal Prey. Berkeley: University of California Press, 2004.

Frison, George C., and Larry C. Todd. *The Colby Mammoth Site: Taphonomy and Archaeology of a Clovis Kill in Northern Wyoming*. Albuquerque: University of New Mexico Press, 1986.

Gero, Joan M., and Margaret W. Conkey. *Engendering Archaeology: Women and Prehistory*. Hoboken, New Jersey: Wiley-Blackwell, 1991.

Gilbert, M. Thomas P., Dennis L. Jenkins, Anders Gotherstom, Nuria Naveran, Juan. J. Sanchez, Michael Hofreiter, Philip Francis Thomsen, Jonas Binladen, Thomas F. G. Higham, Robert M. Yohe II, Robert Parr, Linda Scott Cummings, and Eske Willerslev. "DNA from Pre-Clovis Human Coprolites in Oregon, North America." *Science* 320 (2008): 786-89.

Greer, Mavis A. Loscheider. "Archaeological Analysis of Rock Art Sites in the Smith River Drainage of Central Montana." Ph.D. dissertation, University of Missouri-Columbia, 1995.

Grinnell, George Bird. *The Cheyenne Indians: Their History and Ways of Life*, 2 volumes, New Haven: Yale University Press, 1924.

Harrell, Lynn L., Ted Hoefer II and Scott T. McKern. "Archaic House Pits in the Wyoming Basin." In *Changing Perspectives of the Archaic on the Northwestern Plains and Rocky Mountains*, pp. 334-365, Mary Lou Larson and Julie E. Francis, eds. Vermillion: University of South Dakota Press, 1997.

Hart, Jeff. *Montana Native Plants and Early Peoples*. Helena: Montana Historical Society Press, 1976.

Harris, Eugene E. *Ancestors in Our Genome: The New Science of Human Evolution*. New York: Oxford University Press, 2015.

Haynes, Gary. *The Early Settlement of North America, The Clovis Era*. Cambridge, United Kingdom: Cambridge University Press, 2002.

Hill, Christopher L. "Stratigraphic and geochronologic contexts of mammoths (*Mammuthus*) and other Pleistocene fauna, Upper Missouri River Basin (northern Great Plains and Rocky Mountains), U.S.A." *Quaternary International* 142-143 (2006): 87-106.

Hill, Christopher L. and Leslie B. Davis. "Stratigraphy, ams radiocarbon age, and stable isotope biogeochemistry of the Lindsay mammoth." *Current Research in the Pleistocene* 2 (1998): 109-112.

Holen, Steven R., Thomas A. Demere', Daniel C. Fisher, Richard Fullager, James B. Paces, George T. Jefferson, Jared M. Breton, Richard

A. Ceruti, Adam N. Rountrey, Lawrence Vescera, and Kathleen A. Holen, "A 130,000-year-old archaeological site in southern California, USA." *Nature* 544 (2017): 479-483.

Hoxie, Frederick E. *Parading through History: The Making of the Crow Nation in America, 1805-1935.* New York: Cambridge University Press, 1995.

Hughes, Richard E. "The sources of Hopewell obsidian: Forty years after Griffin." In *Recreating Hopewell*, pp. 361–375, Charles, D. K. and J. E. Buikstra, eds. Gainesville: University Press of Florida, 2006.

Husted, Wilfred M. and Robert Edgar. *The Archaeology of Mummy Cave, Wyoming: An Introduction to Shoshonean Prehistory.* Lincoln: Midwest Archaeological Center and Southeast Archaeological Center Special Report No. 4. National Park Service Technical Report Series No. 9., Lincoln, Nebraska, 2002.

Isenberg, Andrew C. *The Destruction of the Bison.* Cambridge: Cambridge University Press, 2000.

Johnson, Ann M., "Problem of Crow Pottery." *Archaeology in Montana* 20, no. 3 (1979): 17-29.

Jones, J. Scott. "The Anzick site: Analysis of a Clovis Assemblage." Master's thesis, Oregon State University, Corvallis, 1997.

Kahn, Brian. "We Just Breached the 410 PPM Threshold for CO2," *Scientific American*, April 21, 2017.

Kelly, Robert L. *The Lifeways of Hunter-Gatherers: The Foraging Spectrum.* 2nd Edition. Cambridge, United Kingdom: Cambridge University Press, 2013.

Keyser, James D. "The LaMarche Game Trap: An Early Historic Game Trap in Southwestern Montana." *Plains Anthropologist* 19, no. 65 (1974): 173-179.

Indian Rock Art of the Columbia Plateau. Seattle: University of Washington Press, 1992.

The Five Crows Ledger: Biographic Warrior Art of the Flathead Indians. Salt Lake City: University of Utah Press, 2000.

Keyser, James D. and Michael A. Klassen. *Plains Indian Rock Art.* Seattle: University of Washington Press, 2001.

Keyser, James D., David A. Kaiser, George Poetschat and Michael W. Taylor, ed. *Fraternity of War: Plains Indian Rock Art at Bear Gulch and Atherton Canyon, Montana*. Portland: Oregon Archaeological Society Press, 2012.

Keyser, James D., John Greer, Carl M. Davis, Mavis Greer, Marvin W. Rowe, Sara A. Scott, and George Poetschat, "Dating the Bear Gulch and Atherton Canyon Rock Art Sites, Central Montana." *Archaeology In Montana* 52, no. 1 (2011): 7-36.

Kinney, W. Jeff. "The Hagen Site, 24DW1: A Review of Historical Data and a Reassessment of Its Ceramic Assemblage and Position in Northern Plains Prehistory." Master's thesis, University of Montana-Missoula, 1996.

Koch, Paul L. and Anthony D. Barnosky, "Late Quaternary Extinctions: State of the Debate," *Annual Review of Ecology, Evolution and Systematics* 37 (2006): 215-250.

Kolbert, Elizabeth. *The Sixth Extinction: An Unnatural History*. New York: Picador Press, 2014.

Kornfeld, Marcel, George C. Frison and Mary Lou Larson. *Prehistoric Hunter-Gatherers of the High Plains and Rockies*. 3rd edition, Walnut Creek, California: Left Coast Press, 2010.

Knudson, Ruthann. "We are All One: Anzick Children Reburied." *Mammoth Trumpet* 3, no. 2 (2015): 11-14.

Krech, Shepard III. *The Ecological Indian Myth and History*, New York: W. W. Norton & Company, 1999.

Lahren, Larry A. "The Meyers-Hindman Site: An Exploratory Study of Human Occupation Patterns in the Upper Yellowstone Valley from 7000 B.C. to A.D. 1200." Anthropological Researches International, Livingston, Montana, 1976.

Lahren, L. A. and R. Bonnichsen. "Bone foreshafts from a Clovis burial in southwestern Montana." *Science* 186 (1974): 147-150.

Lange, Ian M. *Ice Age Mammals of North America: A Guide to the Big, the Hairy, and the Bizarre*. Missoula, Montana: Mountain Press Publishing Company, 2002.

Larson, Mary Lou and Julie E. Francis, eds. *Changing Perspectives of the Archaic on the Northwest Plains and Rocky Mountains*. Vermillion: University of South Dakota Press, 1997.

Laubin, Reginald and Gladys, *The Indian Tipi: it's history, construction and use*. 2nd Edition, Norman: University of Oklahoma, 1989.

Linderman, Frank B. *Plenty Coups: Chief of the Crows*. Lincoln: University of Nebraska Press, 1962.

Loendorf, Lawrence L., and Nancy Medaris Stone. *Mountain Spirit: The Sheep Eater Indians of Yellowstone*. Salt Lake City: University of Utah Press, 2006.

Lyman, R. Lee. "North American Paleoindian Eyed Bone Needles: Morphometrics, Sewing, and Site Structure." *American Antiquity* 80, no. 1 (2015): 146-160.

Lyman, R. Lee and Michael J. O'Brien. "A Mechanical and Functional Study of Bone Rods from the Richey-Roberts Clovis Cache, Washington, U.SA." *Journal of Archaeological Science* 25 (1998): 887-906.

MacDonald, Douglas H. *Montana Before History: 11,000 Years of Hunter-Gatherers in the Rockies and the Plains*. Missoula, Montana: Mountain Press Publishing Company, 2012.

Macdougall, Doug. *Frozen Earth: The Once and Future Study of Ice Ages*. Berkeley: University of California Press, 2000.

McLaren, Duncan, Daryl Fedje, Angela Dyck Quentin Mackie, Alisha Gauvreau and Jenny Cohen. "Terminal Pleistocene epoch human footprints from the Pacific coast of Canada." *PloS One* 13, no. 3 (2018): e0193522; doi: 10.1371/journal.pone.0193522.

Madsen, Brigham D. *The Lemhi: Sacajawea's People*. Caldwell, Idaho: The Caxton Printers, Ltd., 1979.

Madsen, David B. and David Rhode. ed. *Across the West: Human Population Movement and the Expansion of the Numa*. Salt Lake City: University of Utah Press, 1994.

Mangum, Neil C. *Battle of the Rosebud: Prelude to the Little Bighorn*. El Segundo, California: Upton and Sons, 1987.

Mann, Charles C. *1491 New Revelations of the Americas Before Columbus*. New York: Alfred A. Knopf, 2005.

Mann, John W. *The Lemhi Shoshone and the Salmon River Country*. Lincoln: University of Nebraska Press, 2004.

Marquis, Thomas B. *Wooden Leg: A Warrior Who Fought Custer*. 2nd revised edition, Lincoln: Bison Books, University of Nebraska Press, 2003.

McCleary, Timothy P. *Crow Indian Rock Art: Indigenous Perspectives and Interpretations*. New York: Routledge, 2016.

McCleary, Timothy, Thomas Carter and Edward Chappell. *Tipis and Square Houses: The Chief Plenty Coups Homestead and the Building of the Crow Reservation in Central Montana, 1884-1910*. Helena: Montana Fish, Wildlife and Parks, 2005.

McGeshick, Joseph R. *The History of the Assiniboine and Sioux Tribes of the Fort Peck Indian Reservation, Montana, 1800-2000*. Helena: Montana Historical Society Press, 2008.

McGinnis, Anthony. *Counting coup and cutting horses*. Lincoln: University of Nebraska Press, 1990.

Meadows, William C. "New Data on Kiowa Protohistoric Origins." *Ethnohistory* 63, no. 3 (2016): 541-570.

Meltzer, David J. *First Peoples In a New World Colonizing Ice Age America*. Berkeley: University of California Press, 2009.

Merritt, Christopher. "Rosebud Battlefield State Park: Summary Report of 2011 Archaeological Investigations", University of Montana-Missoula. 2011. Report on file, Montana Department of Fish, Wildlife & Parks, Helena.

Merritt, Christopher W., Thomas A. Milter and Kelly J. Dixon. "Archaeological Investigations of the Rosebud Battlefield (24BH2461), Southeastern Montana: 2012 Site Mapping and Boundary Delineation Project", University of Montana-Missoula. 2014, Report on file, Montana Department of Fish, Wildlife & Parks, Helena.

Milter, Thomas Andrew. "History and Archaeology of the Rosebud Battlefield, June 17, 1876." Master's thesis, University of Montana, 2013.

Mitchell, Mark D. *Crafting History in the Northern Plains: A Political Economy of the Heart River Region, 1400 – 1750*. Tucson: University of Arizona Press, 2013.

Montana Preservation Alliance. "A Historic Preservation Plain for the Rosebud Battlefield, located in Bighorn County, Montana." 2007. Report on file, Montana Department of Fish, Wildlife & Parks, Helena.

Montana State Parks, *Indian Tribes of Montana Yesterday and Today*, Helena, Montana, 2012.

Morrow, Juliet E. and Stuart J. Fiedel. "New Radiocarbon Dates for the Anzick Clovis Burial." In *Paleoindian Archaeology: a hemispheric per-*

spective, pp. 123-138, Juliet E. Morrow and Cristobal G. Gnecco, ed., Gainesville: University of Florida, 2006.

Moulton, Gary E., ed. *The Definitive Journals of the Lewis and Clark Expedition, Through the Rockies to the Cascades*, volume 5, Lincoln: University of Nebraska Press, 1988.

Mulloy, William T. *The Hagen Site: A Prehistoric Village on the Lower Yellowstone*. Missoula: University of Montana Publication in Social Sciences Number One, 1942.

A Preliminary Historical Outline for the Northwestern Plains. Laramie: University of Wyoming Publications No. 22, 1958. *The Native American Rights Fund Legal Review*, "Kootenai Religious site saved", Spring 1987, No.1-2.

Olson, Steve. *Mapping Human History Genes, Race, and Our Common Origins*. New York: Houghton Mifflin Company, 2002.

Otis, D. S. *The Dawes Act and the Allotment of Indian Lands*. Norman: University of Oklahoma Press, 1973.

Owsley Douglas W. and D. R. Hunt "Clovis and Early Archaic Period Crania from the Anzick Site (24PA506), Park County, Montana." *Plains Anthropologist* 46, no. 176 (2001): 115-124.

Patricia L. Parker and Thomas F. King, "Guidelines for Evaluating and Documenting Traditional Cultural Properties," *National Register Bulletin 38,* Washington, D.C.: U.S. Department of the Interior-National Park Service, 1998.

Pauketat, Tim R. *Cahokia: Ancient America's Great City on the Mississippi*. New York: Penguin Books, 2010.

Platt, Steve and Alan Woodmansey. "Unearthing Crow Tribal History." *Public Roads* July/August 2012: 16-19.

Potter, Ben A., Joel D. Irish, Joshua D. Reuther, and Holly J. McKinney. "New insights into Eastern Beringian mortuary behavior: A terminal Pleistocene double infant burial at Upward Sun River," *PNAS* 111 (2014): 17060-17065.

Potter, Ben A., Joshua D. Reuther, Vance T. Holliday, Charles E. Holmes, D. Shane Miller, and Nicholas Schmuck. "Early Colonization of Beringia and Northern North America: Chronology, routes, and adaptive strategies." *Quaternary International* (2017), http://dx.doi.org/10/1016/j.quaint.2017.02.034.

Puckett, Karl. "Two more leases in Badger-Two Medicine cancelled," *The Great Falls Tribune*, January 12, 2017.

Rasmussen, Morten, Sarah L. Anzick, Michael R. Waters, Pontus Skoglund, Michael DeGiorgio, Thomas W. Stafford Jr., Simon Rasmussen, Ida Moltke, Anders Albrechsten, Shane M. Doyle, G. David Poznik, Valborg Gudmundottir, Rachita Yadav, Ann-Sapfo Malaspinas, Samuel Stockton White V, Morten E. Allentoft, Omar E. Cornejo, Kristina Tambets, Anders Eriksson, Peter D. Heintzman, Monika Karmin, Thorfinn Sand Korneliussen, David J. Meltzer, Tracey L. Pierre, Jesper Stenderup, Lauri Saag, Vera M. Warmuth, Margarida C. Lopes, Ripan S. Malhi, Soren Brunak, Thomas Sicheritz-Ponten, Ian Barnes, Matthew Collins, Ludovic Orlando, Francois Balloux, Andrea Manica, Ramneek Gupta, Mait Metspalu, Carlos D. Bustamante, Mattias Jakobsson, Rasmus Nielson and Eske Willerslev. "The genome of a Late Pleistocene human from a Clovis burial site in western Montana." *Nature* Vol. 506, February 13, 2014.

Reeves, Brian O. K. "Cultural Change on the Northwestern Plains: 1000 B.C. – A.D. 1000." Edmonton: *Archaeological Survey of Alberta Occasional Paper* No. 29, 1983.

Reich, David. *Who We Are and How We Got Here: Ancient DNA and the New Science of the Human Past.* New York: Pantheon Books, 2018.

Rinella, Steven. *American Buffalo: In Search of a Lost Icon.* New York: Spiegel & Grau, 2008.

Roll, Tom E., ed. "Kootenai Canyon Archaeology: The 1979 LAURD Project Final Mitigation Report," Bozeman: Montana State University, 1982.

Rood, Ronald J. "Archaic communal jackrabbit hunting in central Wyoming: Faunal remains from the Dick Myal Housepit site, 48FR6256." *Plains Anthropologist* 63, no. 247 (2018): 260-278.

Ross, Alexander. *Fur Hunters of the Far West*, Kenneth A. Spaulding, ed. Norman: University of Oklahoma Press, 1956.

Rowe, Marvin W. "Dating by AMS Radiocarbon Analysis," in *Handbook of Rock Art Research*, pp. 139-166, David S. Whitley, ed., Walnut Creek: Altamira Press, 2001.

Russell, Osborne. *Journal of a Trapper (1834-1843).* Aubrey L. Haines, ed. Lincoln: Bison Books, University of Nebraska Press, 1955.

Schlesier, Karl H., ed. *Plains Indians, A.D. 500-1500 The Archaeological Past of Historic Groups*. Norman: University of Oklahoma Press, 1994.

Schwab, David Charles. "A Spatial Analysis of the Ghost Cave (24YL2) Archaeological Assemblage." Master's thesis, University of Montana-Missoula, 1981.

Schwab, David, Stuart W. Conner and Ann M. Johnson. "Depression Era Archaeology in Montana." *Archaeology in Montana* 37, no. 2 (1966): 1-42.

Scott, Douglas D. "Analysis of Ammunition Components from the Rosebud Battlefield and Battle Butte Sites." Connor Consulting, Grand Junction, Colorado. 2013. On file Montana Department of Fish, Wildlife & Parks, Helena.

Scott, Sara A. "The Ties That Bind on the Northwestern Plains: Contexts for Prehistoric Trade and Travel." PhD. dissertation, University of Montana-Missoula, 2014.

"Indian Forts and Religious Icons: The Buffalo Road (Qoq'aalx 'Iskit) Trail Before and After the Lewis and Clark Expedition." *International Journal of Historic Archaeology* 19 (2015): 384-415.

Scott, Sara A., Carl M. Davis, Karen L. Steelman, Marvin W. Rowe and Tom Guilderson. "Direct AMS Dates from Four Late Prehistoric Period Rock Art Sites in West-Central Montana." *Plains Anthropologist* 50, no. 3 (2005): 57-71.

Scott, Sara A., Carl M. Davis, and J.M. Adovasio. Radiocarbon analyses of four perishable artifacts from Ghost and Pictograph caves, Montana." *Plains Anthropologist* 59, no. 229 (2014): 70-95.

Secoy, Frank Raymond. *Changing Military Patterns of the Great Plains Indians*. Lincoln: University of Nebraska Press, 1992.

Schackley, M. Steven. "Introduction to X-Ray Florescence Analysis in Archaeology." In *X-Ray Florescence Spectrometry (XRF) in Geoarchaeology*, pp. 7-44. M. Steven Schackley, ed., New York: Springer-Verlag, 2011.

Shumate, Maynard. "The Taft Hill bison jump." *Archaeology in Montana* 8 (1967): 12-34.

Skoglund, Pontus, Erik Ersmark, Eleftheria Palkopoulou, and Love Dalen. "Ancient Wolf Genome Reveals an Early Divergence of Domestic Dog Ancestors and Admixture into High-Latitude Breeds." *Current Biology* 24 (2015): 1515-1519.

Snodgrass, Richard. The Human Skeletal Remains" In *The Hagen Site: A Prehistoric Village of the Lower Yellowstone,"* Appendix: pp. 92-98, Missoula: University of Montana Publication in Social Sciences Number One, 1942.

Stafford, Thomas W. J. "Accelerator C-14 dating of human fossil skeletons: Assessing accuracy and results on New World specimens," p. 45-55, In *Method and Theory for Investigating the Peopling of the Americas.* R. Bonnichsen R and D.G. Steele, eds. Corvallis: Oregon State University, 1994.

Stanford, Dennis J. and Bruce A. Bradley. *Across the Atlantic Ice: The Origin of America's Clovis Culture.* Berkeley: University of California Press, 2012.

Steward, Julian H. "Basin-Plateau Aboriginal Sociopolitical Groups." *Bureau of American Ethnology Bulletin* No. 120. Washington, D.C.: Smithsonian Institution, 1938.

"Culture Element Distributions: XXII Northern and Gosiute Shoshone." *Anthropological Records* 8:3, Berkeley: University of California Press, 1943.

Sunstrom, Linea. "Archaic Hunting Practices Depicted in a Northwestern Plains Rock Art Style." *Plains Anthropologist* 34, no. 124 (1989): 149-169.

Swanson, Earl H. Jr. *Birch Creek: Human Ecology of the Cool Desert of the Northern Rocky Mountains 9,000 B.C. – A.D. 1850.* Pocatello: Idaho State University Press, 1972.

Sykes, Brian. *The Seven Daughters of Eve: The Science That Reveals Our Genetic Ancestry.* New York: W. W. Norton & Company, 2002.

Taylor, Dee C. "The Wilsall excavations: An exercise in frustration." *Montana Academy of Science Proceedings* 29 (1969): 147-150.

Taylor, R.E., and Martin J. Aitken, ed. "Chronometric Dating in Archaeology." In *Advances In Archaeological and Museum Science* Volume 2, pp. 65-95, New York: Plenum Press, 1997.

Thomas, David Hurst. *Archaeology.* 2nd Edition, New York: Holt, Rinehart and Winston, 1971.

Thoms, Alston V. "Rock of ages: propagation of hot-rock cookery in western North America." *Journal of Anthropological Archaeology* 36 (2009): 573-591.

Thoms, Alston V. and Greg C. Burtchard, eds., *Prehistoric Land Use in the Northern Rocky Mountains: A Perspective from the Middle Kootenai River*. Pullman: Washington State University Center for Northwest Archaeology, 1987.

Thompson, Sally, Kootenai Culture Committee & Pikunni Traditional Association *People Before the Park: The Kootenai and Blackfeet Before Glacier National Park.* Helena: Montana Historical Society Press, 2015.

Turney-High, Harry Holbert. *Ethnography of the Kutenai*. Menasha, Wis.: American Anthropological Association, 1941.

Vanaman, Walter T. "The Diggers at Pictograph Cave." *Archaeology in Montana* 32, no. 1 (1991): 67-74.

Vaughn, J. W. *With Crook at Rosebud*. Mechanicsburg, Pennsylvania: Stackpole Books, 1956.

Verbicky-Todd, Eleanor. *Communal Bison Hunting Among the Plains Indians*. Occasional Paper No. 24. Edmonton: Archaeological Survey of Alberta, 1984.

Vrooman, Nicholas C. P. "*The Whole Country was…'One Robe": The Little Shell Tribe's America.* Helena: Drumlummon Institute and Little Shell Tribe of Chippewa Indians of Montana, 2013.

Walker-Kuntz, Sunday A, E. R. Hajic, and L. A. Peterson. "The Spiro Site (24CB1332): A Middle Plains Archaic Housepit Site." *Archaeology in Montana* 47, no. 2 (2006): 1-56.

Waters, Michael R., and Thomas W. Stafford, Jr. "Redating the Mill Iron Site, Montana: A Reexamination of Goshen Complex Chronology." *American Antiquity* 79, no. 3 (2014): 541-548.

White, Sam. *A Cold Welcome: The Little Ice Age and Europe's Encounter with North America*. Cambridge: Harvard University Press, 2017.

Whittaker, John C. *Flintknapping: Making and Understanding Stone Tools*. Austin: University of Texas Press, 1994.

Wiley, Gordon R., and Jeremy Sabloff. *A History of American Archaeology*. 3rd Ed. New York: W. H. Freeman Co., 1993.

Wilke, Philip J., J. J. Flenniken, and T.L. Ozbun. "Clovis Technology at the Anzick Site, Montana." *Journal of California and Great Basin Anthropology* 13, no. 2 (1991): 242-272.

Lewis-Williams, David J. "Brainstorming Images: Neuropsychology and Rock Art Research. In *Handbook of Rock Art Research*, pp. 332-357, David S. Whitley, ed., Walnut Creek: AltaMira Press, 2001.

Yong, Ed. "A New Origin Story for Dogs." *The Atlantic*, June 2, 2016.

Zedeño, Maria Nieves, Jesse A. M. Ballenger, and John R. Murray. "Landscape Engineering and Organizational Complexity among Late Prehistoric Bison Hunters of the Northwestern Plains." *Current Anthropology* 55, no. 11 (2013): 23-58.

INDEX

Italicized page numbers indicate illustrations.

ACKNOWLEDGEMENTS

The book is inspired by the innumerable questions I've been asked about prehistory, human evolution, and American Indian cultures over the course of my archaeology career. It is informed by countless discussions with fellow archaeologists, historic preservationists, and tribal friends. I cannot possibly list everyone who was part of those conversations, but this does not alter the fact that I am tremendously grateful to all.

I owe a strong debit of gratitude to Drs. Floyd Sharrock and James Adovasio for spurring me on to a professional archaeology career. Colleague Jim Keyser provided immeasurable guidance, encouragement and humor every step of the way—this book is no exception.

The following people generously shared advice, site information, photographs, permissions and critiques of the manuscript in part or whole: Steve Aaberg, Leo Ariwite, Steve Armstrong, Francis Auld, Jon Axline, Beta Analytic, Joan Brownell, Eric Carlson, Jorie Clark, Peter Clark, William Big Day, the late Les Davis, Kelly Dixon, Bill Eckerle, Jack Fisher, Mavis and John Greer, Shannon Gilbert, Fred Haefele, Chris Hill, Ann Johnson, Jim Keyser, the late Ruthann Knudson, Halcyon LaPoint, Craig Lee, Larry Loendorf, Nancy Mahoney, Tim McCleary, Doug Melton, Chris Merritt, Tom Milter, David Minick, Damon Murdo, John Murray, Lynelle Peterson, Steve Platt, Ryan Powell, Arian Randall, Penny Redli, Patrick Rennie, Sara Scott, Gary Smith, Teana Limpy, Rick Thompson, Tim Urbaniak, David Wade, David Whitley, Bruce Whittenberg, Stan Wilmoth, Phil Wilke, Pei-lin Yu, and Maria Zedeño. My sincere thanks to all—naturally, I accept full responsibility for any errors or misinterpretations.

Lynn Baca graciously edited the draft manuscript according to the wise axiom that just because it's data doesn't mean it is interesting. My very special thanks goes to Chris Cauble, Sarah Cauble, and the staff of Riverbend Publishing for taking on this manuscript and turning it into a readable public archaeology work about Montana.

Last but not least, I thank my parents Carl and Martha Davis for their generosity, perspectives, and passing along good books. My gratitude to Sara Scott knows no bounds for her insights, critiques, and forbearance as I struggled to bring this writing project to a useful conclusion, and to Madeline and Spencer for allowing us to take them, time and again, to just one more archaeological site.

ABOUT THE AUTHOR

Raised in Dillon, Montana, Carl M. Davis received a bachelor's degree in anthropology from the University of Montana and a master's degree in anthropology from the University of Pittsburgh. He worked for 35 years as an archaeologist on national forests in Montana and Oregon, and in 2015 retired as the Regional Archaeologist for the U.S. Forest Service Northern Region in Missoula, Montana. For his dedication to preserving and promoting Montana history, Davis received the 2018 Montana Heritage Keeper Award, presented by the Montana Historical Society Board of Trustees. He resides in Missoula with his partner, Sara Scott.

SOC003000 SOCIAL SCIENCE/Archaeology
HIS028000 HISTORY/Native American
HIS036140 HISTORY/United States/State & Local/West
SOC021000 SOCIAL SCIENCE/Ethnic Studies/Native American Stu

"A masterful job....If you have an interest in Montana archaeology, this is the book for you."
LAWRENCE LOENDORF, SACRED SITES RESEARCH, INC.

"An excellent account of Montana's human past.... Non-archaeologists and archaeologists alike will enjoy and learn from the authoritative information and insights that pack this book."
JACK FISHER, DEPARTMENT OF SOCIOLOGY & ANTHROPOLOGY, MONTANA STATE UNIVERSITY

Six Hundred Generations is a stunning look at the archaeological evidence of Montana's long Indigenous human history. Focusing on 12 unique archaeological sites, the book takes readers on an extraordinary journey through time, technologies, and cultures. Beginning with the First Americans who followed mammoths into this landscape, peer-awarded Montana archaeologist Carl Davis describes how Native Americans lived, evolved, and flourished here for thousands of years. The engaging writing is accompanied by a rich array of photographs and numerous illustrations by noted artist-archaeologist Eric Carlson.

"Sweeping, highly readable, and beautifully illustrated."
MARÍA NIEVES ZEDEÑO, SCHOOL OF ANTHROPOLOGY, THE UNIVERSITY OF ARIZONA

"An important new book.... I recommend it to anyone with an interest in Montana archaeology and history."
GARY P. SMITH, DEPUTY PRESERVATION OFFICER, MONTANA STATE OFFICE, BUREAU OF LAND MANAGEMENT

"Readers of all kinds will enjoy the clear, conversational tone, the satisfying explanations of scientific methods and inquiry, and the beautiful illustrations by Eric Carlson."
PEI-LIN YU, DEPARTMENT OF ANTHROPOLOGY, BOISE STATE UNIVERSITY

RIVERBEND
PUBLISHING

ISBN: 978-1-60639-111-2 $24.95
52495
9 781606 391112